Superterrorism: Policy Responses

Blackwell
Publishing

Superterrorism:
Policy Responses

Edited by

Lawrence Freedman

Blackwell Publishing

© 2002 by The Political Quarterly Publishing Co. Ltd

First published 2002 by Blackwell Publishing as a special issue of *The Political Quarterly*

Blackwell Publishing, Inc., 350 Main Street, Malden, Massachusetts 02148–5018, USA
Blackwell Publishing Ltd, Osney Mead, Oxford OX2 0EL, UK
Blackwell Publishing Asia Pty Ltd, 550 Swanston Street, Carlton, Victoria 3053, Australia
Blackwell Verlag GmbH, Kurfürstendamm 57, 10707 Berlin, Germany

First published 2002 by Blackwell Publishing Ltd

Library of Congress Cataloging-in-Publication Data has been applied for

ISBN 1–4051–0593–3

A catalogue record for this title is available from the British Library

Set in 9.5/11pt Palatino by Joshua Associates, Oxford
Printed and bound in the United Kingdom by Cambrian Printers Ltd, Aberystwyth
For further information on Blackwell Publishing, visit our website:
www.blackwellpublishers.co.uk/

CONTENTS

Notes on Contributors   vi

Introduction   1
LAWRENCE FREEDMAN

The Nature of Modern Terrorism   7
JOHN GEARSON

The Roots of Terrorism: Probing the Myths   25
KARIN VON HIPPEL

The Coming War on Terrorism   40
LAWRENCE FREEDMAN

Finance Warfare as a Response to International Terrorism   57
MARTIN S. NAVIAS

Responding to 11 September: Detention without Trial under the
Anti-Terrorism, Crime and Security Act 2001   80
HELEN FENWICK

American Hegemony: European Dilemmas   105
WILLIAM WALLACE

The Eleventh of September and beyond: NATO   119
ANNE DEIGHTON

The Eleventh of September and beyond: The Impact on the European
Union   135
CHARLES GRANT

Russian–Western Relations after 11 September: Selective Cooperation
versus Partnership (a Russian View)   154
NADIA ALEXANDROVA ARBATOVA

Index   173

Notes on Contributors

Nadia Alexandrova Arbatova is Head of the Department of European Political Studies, Center for European Integration, Institute for World Economy and International Relations (IMEMO), Russian Academy of Sciences; Director of the Center on International Relations, Institute of Europe, Russian Academy of Sciences; and Director of Policy Studies and Editor at the Committee for Russia in a United Europe.

Anne Deighton is the University of Oxford Lecturer in European International Politics, and a fellow of Wolfson College.

Helen Fenwick is Professor of Law at the University of Durham.

Lawrence Freedman is Professor of War Studies at King's College London and Head of the School of Social Sciences and Public Policy.

John Gearson is Senior Lecturer in Defence Studies, King's College, London. He acted as a consultant to the City of London on the terrorist threat to the City following the Bishopsgate bombing and lectures on terrorism at the UK Joint Services Command and Staff College.

Charles Grant is Director of the Centre for European Reform.

Karin von Hippel is a Senior Research Fellow at the Centre for Defence Studies, King's College London. She is currently directing a project on European responses to terrorism funded by the MacArthur Foundation. She has also worked for the United Nations in Somalia and Kosovo.

Martin Navias is a finance lawyer and also a Senior Research Associate in the Department of Mediterranean Studies at King's College London.

William Wallace is Professor of International Relations at the London School of Economics.

Introduction

LAWRENCE FREEDMAN

PRIOR to 11 September 2001 most acts of terrorism had depended on conventional explosives and, at their most deadly, had managed to cause casualties in the low hundreds, usually by destroying an aircraft in mid-flight. Yet it was also evident that a number of groups had been looking for ways to achieve far worse effects, and a number of incidents indicated that new terrorists were going for mass attacks. Of these, one of the most unnerving was the March 1995 nerve-gas attack on the Tokyo subway by the Japanese cult Aum Shinrikyo, killing twelve but also affecting thousands of others. The first attack on New York's World Trade Center by activists linked to Osama bin Laden in February 1993, which left six dead and 5,000 injured, had been intended to collapse the towers. It was known that Algerian radicals had intended to blow up a hijacked Air France jet over Paris. All this fed long-standing fears of the possibility that terrorist groups might gain access to real weapons of mass destruction and use them without the restraint thus far exhibited by states which held these weapons. This line of thought led to the identification of 'superterrorism' as a great danger that deserved special attention by all those concerned with national security. Because of the technical and production requirements the culprit was likely to be a state, or at least a group sponsored by a state.

Yet what made 11 September 'super' was the terrorists' organisation, the ability to mount simultaneous attacks, commitment (in the acceptance of certain death) and choice of targets, picking in the World Trade Center and the Pentagon the economic and military faces of the world's only superpower. Turning hijacked aircraft into guided missiles allowed terrorists to cause mass casualties with much simpler methods than the most destructive weaponry. The total casualty list, covering four aircraft (one of which crashed without hitting its intended target) and the buildings, is now put at over 3,000; but to understand the impact of the attacks it is important to recall that initial estimates assumed the numbers would be well into five figures and for some time the figure used was over 6,000. The iconic status of the targets successfully attacked, and the startling and shocking nature of the images broadcast worldwide, added to the immediate and global impact.

Like 7 December 1941, when Japanese forces bombed Pearl Harbor, 11 September 2001 became at once a day in the American calendar for ever to be associated with 'infamy', and the moment was described internationally as transformative. The world, we were told, would never be the same again. A new seriousness was introduced into our lives, a sense of danger and a sense of purpose at the same time. It was ordinary people who had suffered and, given the cosmopolitan setting of the attacks, they came from many countries.

© The Political Quarterly Publishing Co. Ltd. 2002
Published by Blackwell Publishing, 108 Cowley Road, Oxford OX4 1JF, UK and 350 Main Street, Malden, MA 02148, USA

Such a jolt had been provided to the international political system that there was every reason to expect new attitudes and patterns of behaviour to emerge among even the great powers. A set of new and troubling vulnerabilities within the socio-economic systems of the West had been illuminated with a demonstration of exactly how they might be exploited by a sufficiently ruthless group. The perpetrators were confidently identified at once as al-Qaeda, established by the Saudi Osama bin Laden and, at this time, based in Afghanistan. They could operate on a global scale. This was true both of this particular operation, set in motion in Afghanistan, developed in Germany and executed in the United States, but also of numerous other individual operations and campaigns in which al-Qaeda, as a rather loose network of like-minded groups, was in some way engaged.

Since 11 September there have been indications that al-Qaeda and its associates and sympathisers are still active, particularly in Pakistan, where a church has been attacked, Frenchmen killed on a bus, and an American journalist kidnapped and brutally murdered. In Tunisia, German tourists visiting an old synagogue were caught in an explosion. Moroccan police thwarted a plot to mount attacks against British and American warships in the Straits of Gibraltar. The possibilities of suicide attacks have been reinforced almost daily by news of attacks against Israel and the development of a martyrdom cult among Palestinians. As yet there has been no more superterrorism, although the inclination of the Bush administration has been to worry most about a state-sponsored chemical, biological or even nuclear attack rather than another attempt by non-state groups to employ everyday civilian technologies in the service of mass terror. Publicity was given to Richard Reid, a British petty criminal who converted to Islam, and who failed to ignite explosives being carried in his shoe on American Airlines Flight 63 on 22 December 2001, and to the American Jose Padilla, also a convert to Islam from petty crime, who was arrested on 8 May 2002 and later rather dramatically proclaimed by the US authorities to be part of an advanced plot to detonate a so-called 'dirty' bomb—that is, a weapon designed to release radioactive materials into the atmosphere—in Washington DC. It appears that this effort was both amateurish and aspirational. Officials on both sides of the Atlantic have spoken of a new attack in terms of 'when and not if', but as yet we can, fortunately, talk of neither a trend nor an established phenomenon. It may be that 11 September will remain a 'one-off', although it is also the case that if this is so it will only be as a result of a lot of hard work by the intelligence community.

Tightening up on security to prevent further attacks was one unavoidable policy response. By the end of June 2002, 1,600 individuals with alleged links to the al-Qaeda group or its affiliates were being detained in ninety-five countries, with about 180 held in Europe, including twenty-six in Britain.[1] The other unavoidable response was to take action to root out the terrorists, and this soon turned out to mean overturning the Taleban regime in Afghanistan, which had become fused at the top with al-Qaeda and had become dependent upon it for financial and physical support.

This was the first stage of the 'war on terrorism'. It did not have a particularly auspicious start; the Americans hoped that a combination of strategic bombing and special force operations would demoralise the Taleban, but there were few targets worthy of sustained air attack and the inevitable mis-hits were gaining sympathy for the enemy. At the end of October the air campaign was switched to support land operations, albeit those of the Northern Alliance, the local opposition to the Taleban, rather than the US army. This showed quick results and by 8 November the first major Taleban stronghold of Mazar-e-Sharif had fallen, soon to be followed by the capital city of Kabul. After the cities had fallen the new strategy worked less well, not so much because it allowed Taleban/al-Qaeda fighters to regroup and counterattack, which they never managed to do, but because it allowed them to escape: into the remoter areas of Afghanistan and eventually over the border into the more ungovernable parts of Pakistan. For much of the spring of 2002 coalition forces, including Royal Marines, were engaged in sweeps into these areas, coming occasionally across caches of ammunition but little else, so that precious few of the enemy leadership were captured. The United States and its allies could content themselves with the thought that this leadership had been effectively neutralised, but that was not quite the same as bringing them to justice. Moreover, as predicted, not all the warlords that made up the Northern Alliance were quite as ready to usher in a new age of democracy and good government in Afghanistan as the Western allies wished. The economic and political reconstruction of this ravaged country was set to be a long-term project.

The military lessons of this campaign were fewer than initially thought, as it became apparent that many of the key breakthroughs on the ground had come through a tried and tested Afghan way of warfare, involving hard bargaining, as much as a new Western way. The Americans had been understandably more ready to work with local allies, who knew the terrain and local culture, than with their old allies, who brought little to the campaign that the Americans could not provide themselves and, if the experience of Kosovo was anything to go by, would want a considerable say in the direction of a campaign. Even the British, who were involved far more than any others, were initially rebuffed when they argued for the rapid introduction of international forces following the fall of Kabul. Eventually the logic of this proposal was understood, indicating that at times alternative insights provided by old allies had their value, while the local allies were using the campaign to pursue their own agendas, which did not always conform to that of the United States. During the course of 2002 the Afghan operation gradually became far more international. An International Security Assistance Force was established in Kabul, initially with a British command, while the effort in the south of the country to prevent a Taleban revival and to search for al-Qaeda activists became increasingly multinational. Nonetheless the early

American approach confirmed an impression of unilateralism that continued to linger.

This volume explores these issues: has the new form of terrorism been accurately characterised? Is the enemy terrorism, or people who happen to use terrorism as their preferred means of obtaining their political objectives? What changes, if any, need to be made in the area of financial regulation or criminal law to cope with this phenomenon? Have the challenges posed brought the international community closer together or aggravated divisions?

In the opening chapter John Gearson explains the origins of the concern over superterrorism, and the comparison with older-style terrorism. The newer versions are assumed to be much readier to inflict massive loss of life and move to ever more horrific methods in their efforts to do so. He warns against overstating the novelty of the 'new' terrorism and points to an essential continuity with the old in that, in most cases, it remains purposive. The quality of the political response to such groups as al-Qaeda is therefore critical, and this in turn depends on an adequate understanding of their character and objectives. This theme is picked up by Karin von Hippel who demonstrates, largely through an analysis of the situation in Somalia, that the simple views that poverty in itself is responsible for terrorism, or that terrorists emerge naturally out of weakened or collapsed states, are not supported by evidence, although these factors are relevant to the development of a full view of the problem. The perpetrators of the 11 September attacks, for example, came from the stronger Arab states. More disturbingly, extremist views do not necessarily evaporate on contact with the Western world but can at times be aggravated as a sense of alienation deepens.

Her conclusion, that 'the international community, and the United States in particular, ignores unpleasant parts of the world at its peril', is similar to that reached in my own chapter. This considers the various characterisations of the 'war on terror'. By noting the comparisons with the debate on humanitarian intervention, which was to the fore prior to 11 September, I suggest that there is an effort under way to establish the principle that the use of violent means against non-combatants for political objectives is always unacceptable. Exactly how and when this principle can be applied may require some tests, but even here it remains necessary to consider the political character of the 'enemy', which should open up the range of means available to frustrate and thwart them.

Meanwhile, cutting off financial support is a major objective of the anti-terrorist coalition. Martin Navias's chapter describes the extensive and sophisticated operation behind al-Qaeda's activities, linking the less regulated banking and financial frameworks in the developing world with the more orderly and sophisticated complexes in the developed. Dealing with this challenge requires not so much new measures as the refinement and application of those that began to be put together during the 1990s to deal with money laundering. Given the discouraging results thus far, it has to be hoped that the high stakes in this particular endeavour will lead to improved political, technical and bureaucratic coordination across the various countries and authorities involved. Helen Fenwick addresses another controversial aspect of the counterterrorist campaign, namely the suspension of normal civil liberties because of the special danger posed by activists. While accepting that forms of detention may be necessary, she argues that because such measures are inherently anti-democratic they must also be strictly limited. She applies this test to the UK's Anti-Terrorism, Crime and Security Act 2001 and finds that it fails.

The final four chapters address the large questions of the transformative nature of recent events and in particular their impact on transatlantic relations. Initially it was assumed that a sense of solidarity and common purpose would bind countries together in the anti-terrorist coalition; in the event the apparent readiness—and ability—of the United States to go it alone and pay scant attention to the sensitivities of its allies has increased a sense of divergence. This was reinforced by a range of other issues, from steel tariffs to the environment. To the extent that Washington was really interested in a coalition, it would be not so much of the willing as of the compliant. In practice, the rhetorical side of this approach may be more significant than the practical, although, as William Wallace notes in his chapter, the transatlantic rhetoric of the past, however disingenuous, did help European governments to accept American leadership. He points out that US hegemony still relies on consent rather than raw power, and that as allies still have important roles to play it will be necessary to develop a new political understanding that will allow European leaders some possibility of demonstrating to their publics that they are working within a shared framework of values and institutions with the United States.

In their chapters, Anne Deighton and Charles Grant look at the two key institutions for Europeans, NATO and the European Union. Anne Deighton shows how fundamental questions about what the organisation is for and how it should operate have been forced on to the NATO agenda. Yet these questions are not new, having already been raised by the changing shape of the post-Cold War world, the demands of enlargement and the growing ambition of the EU in the area of security policy—pressures which will not abate. Charles Grant notes that the criticisms that cross the Atlantic in both directions may have some validity. The Europeans have not done enough to be taken seriously as contributors to international action and leave too much to the Americans. He sees signs that they may be starting to do more, and to the extent that they do so then there will be a restraint on the American inclination to unilateralism.

In the final chapter Nadia Arbatova provides a distinctive Russian perspective, describing how President Putin used the crisis to align his country with the United States, in part because of the problems Russia has also faced with Islamist extremists, not least in Chechnya. She also notes the difficulties this poses for a Russian political elite that has grown increasingly wary of Western intentions, and the extent to which Putin may be gambling that a new alignment can be based on foreign policy when democratisation and economic reform remain so high on the Western agenda. Her chapter, like those that precede it, demonstrates that while 11 September did recast international politics and pose new policy questions for all governments, the effect was not so transformative that all that had gone before became irrelevant. Established debates and evolving issues were given a new context by these dramatic events, but not necessarily a wholly new content.

Note

1 *Sunday Times*, 30 June 2002.

The Nature of Modern Terrorism

JOHN GEARSON

IN March 1995, six years before the terrible events of 11 September, another shocking event occurred. In an attack on the Tokyo underground using sarin gas, the Japanese cult Aum Shinrikyo killed 12 people and affected 5,000,[1] and the way in which terrorism was understood changed for ever. For the first time, an independent substate group, acting without state patronage or protection, had managed to produce and deploy biochemical weapons on a significant scale. A crucial technological threshold appeared to have been crossed.

Terrorists had achieved the unthinkable and were now able to pose threats to states that previously only other states had. The result was a period of unprecedented interest in 'superterrorism' as it came to be called, notably in the United States, with the focus on the means and technology at the disposal of terror groups, rather than on the organisations themselves and their objectives. A new fanaticism represented by cults and religiously motivated groups, equipped with weapons of mass destruction and prepared to use them, now presented the world with a 'New Age of Terrorism', it was argued. Meanwhile, the old terrorism appeared to be on the wane, although significantly a number of its characteristics appeared surprisingly resilient, finding expression in the new terrorism and the new terrorists themselves. The debate which ensued pitched analysts of 'old terrorism' against the new exponents of 'superterrorism' in a circular debate over the likely path of terrorist development.

However, when it finally arrived, the superterrorism that was revealed on 11 September 2001 was not at all the sort that had been predicted by most of the analysts on both sides of the debate, although indications of it had been emerging throughout the 1990s. Instead of technologically sophisticated weapons of mass destruction, the superterrorists of 11 September utilised the long-established terrorist approach of careful planning, simple tactics and operational surprise to effect the most stunning terrorist 'spectacular' in history. In the aftermath of 11 September, the anthrax mail attacks in the United States complicated the picture. On the one hand they appeared to confirm the worst fears of the New Age of Terrorism theorists, highlighting the vulnerability of modern societies to unconventional attacks, the lack of resilience in the official response and the ease with which a nation might be brought to its knees by a tiny number of people; on the other, the indications were that the anthrax concerned was probably domestically produced in an American weapons laboratory and probably well beyond the abilities of substate groups to manufacture. Furthermore, the attacks, although of significant psychological impact, did not result in mass casualties and

© The Political Quarterly Publishing Co. Ltd. 2002
Published by Blackwell Publishing, 108 Cowley Road, Oxford OX4 1JF, UK and 350 Main Street, Malden, MA 02148, USA

rather indicated the extent to which mass *effect* was inherent in such weapons. Revealing more about ourselves than the terrorists, the super-terrorism debate of the 1990s was shown to have diverted counterterrorist thinking to some extent away from the core tasks of understanding the motives and likely objectives of terror organisations towards a preoccupation with technology, weapons systems and high end risks. This tendency has often been displayed by terrorism analysts, and as the world contemplates the likely evolution of terrorism after 11 September, the focus is on technology, weapons of mass destruction and mass casualties. Once again, the dangers of being diverted from other core tasks of counterterrorism are acute.

This chapter will consider the nature of terrorism, how it has come to be understood over the last two centuries, why there remains no agreed definition for it, and how the last decade of the twentieth century appeared to herald a new age of superterrorism. It will consider why the attacks of 11 September did not fit the model that had emerged in the preceding decade, how the future of terrorism has been altered and why the concept of the 'New Age of Terrorism' had led many to focus on the 'novel' idea of terrorism as asymmetric warfare. In doing so, the chapter will consider some of the enduring questions surrounding terrorism. It is defined by most target states as a crime—which, though understandable for police forces and justice ministries trying to bring prosecutions, tends to obscure the political context of most if not all terrorism. The idea of terrorism as a weapon of the weak and as a justified response to superior force will be contrasted with the fact that much terrorism has been perpetrated by states against their own people. It will also consider how new actors, new technologies and new tactics are undoubtedly changing the nature of terrorism; but it will emphasise that its enduring feature is its capacity as a force multiplier through the exploitation of fear. As the Chinese strategist Sun Tzu said, 'To fight and conquer in all your battles is not the supreme excellence; supreme excellence consists in breaking the enemy's resistance without fighting.' This is the essence of terrorism: the breaking of an enemy's will through the exploitation of fear. This fear can lead some states to terrorise themselves far better than the terrorists themselves, and this remains one of the most tricky challenges after 11 September in developing a counterterrorist strategy at home and abroad. Finally, the chapter will consider the extent to which terrorism has evolved from a tactic into a strategy, and how the challenge today has become one of containing terrorists' capacity for affecting strategic change.

Defining terrorism

The question of what is (and what is not) terrorism has, for many, disappeared down an academic dead end, never to return in a meaningfully useful way for policy-makers or the public. Indeed, it has been suggested that the attempt to find an agreed definition is doomed to failure and in any event has not advanced the study of the subject. That does not mean, as some have suggested, that the question is simply answered by reference to the target, such that, if it is unarmed and civilian, then an assault on it is terrorism.[2] Such reductionism could place all armies that cause 'collateral damage' into the category of terrorist. Furthermore, it would include as terrorist acts the strategic bombing of German cities in the Second World War, and also the dropping of the atomic bombs in 1945—designed to 'shock' the Japanese into submission. However, to resist such reductionism is not to deny that 'terrorism' as a state policy (usually one of internal repression) has killed more people than substate groups ever have. At times, the tendency has been too far in the other direction—to ascribe all non-state violence to terrorism. There has also been a tendency to confer the title on any form of disruptive or undesirable phenomenon, leading to neologisms such as 'bioterrorism', 'cultural terrorism' and even 'fashion terrorism'!

The confusion even occurs within individual governments. While the US State Department defines terrorism as 'premeditated, politically motivated violence perpetrated against non-combatant targets by sub-national groups or clandestine agents, usually intended to influence an audience',[3] the Federal Bureau of Investigation prefers a different form of words: 'the use of serious violence against persons or property, or the threat to use such violence, to intimidate or coerce a government, the public, or any section of the public in order to promote political, social or ideological objectives'. Such differences can in part be explained by the differing objectives of the departments concerned. Differences exist also between countries and allies. The formulation adopted for many years by the British government, which has tended to use a single definition, was 'the use of violence for political ends including any use of violence for the purpose of putting the public or any section of the public in fear'.

In the late 1990s, established terrorism legislation was reviewed by the British government as it considered the new requirements of international terrorism. Coming as the review did at the *end* of the worst terrorist violence that the UK has ever experienced and during the Provisional Irish Republican Army's most significant ceasefire, there was some irony in this. The previous legislation had been temporary and subject to regular renewal by Parliament; now, with the threat level apparently much reduced, the government, citing the increasing threat from transnational and often religiously motivated terrorism, presciently proposed bringing terrorism legislation into permanent statute. The Terrorism Act 2000, which finally came into force in the UK before 11 September in February 2001, adopted a definition close to the FBI's: 'the use or threat of serious violence against persons or serious damage to property, designed to influence the government or intimidate the public or a section of the public . . . for the purpose of advancing a political, religious or ideological cause'. Civil libertarians were dismayed at what was perceived as a widening of the state's powers, and particular concern was expressed at the definition of 'serious violence' as including actions 'designed seriously to interfere with or seriously to disrupt an electronic system'. Hacking, it seemed, now came under the definition of terrorism. The new Act also sought to remove any false separation between domestic and international terrorism, including within the scope of the legislation actions in support of terrorist activities in third countries.

A question raised by the definition debate and the anti-terrorism legislation introduced by various governments is what, if anything, is legitimate dissent using violent means? When is being a freedom fighter acceptable? The parallel debate on the definition of terrorism has been whether the groups are themselves freedom fighters or terrorists. The weak argue that the strong always condemn them as terrorists, and such freedom fighters condemn the states they are fighting as terroristic in their suppression of the innocent and the defence of the status quo—one of the main claims of bin Laden, who described the United States as fundamentally a status quo power.

The whole subject of terrorism has connotations of danger about it, and while it can in certain circumstances still be descriptive, the term has actually become pejorative—an insult, derived of meaning in many instances. This also has political consequences, since labelling a group or enemy as terrorist usually leads to an increase in the state's powers. Once the state's enemies have been labelled as terrorists, the public accepts more in 'defence' against terrorism: illegal arrests, torture and even state-sanctioned murder have been seen in some states as acceptable (or rather, reluctantly accepted as necessary) when one 'takes off the gloves' in fighting a ruthless terrorist enemy. More problematically, using the language of terrorism can in many ways blind one to what it is one is facing, to such an extent that the terminology actually hampers the state in its defence from violent threats. As one writer has put it: 'To call an act of violence a terrorist act is not so much to describe it as to condemn it, subjugating all questions of context and circumstance to the reality of its immorality.'[4]

Characteristics of terrorism

Historically, terrorism has been seen as a tactical phenomenon which fluctuates according to geography and culture and so cannot be strictly defined. It has sometimes been a tool for revolutionaries and nationalists, but has been used just as often by governments to maintain state power. Defining a person or group as terrorist implies a moral judgement, and it is this which has led to the greatest problems of definition. In answer to the hackneyed question: 'Is one man's freedom fighter another man's terrorist?' the answer perhaps should be that it is a non-question, or rather a false juxtaposition—one can be both. Freedom fighters have adopted terrorist tactics at times, but it did not stop them being freedom fighters (although it probably did not help their legitimacy). On the other hand, many have used terrorism and claimed to be fighting in the name of freedom when other, more financial and worldly goals have very obviously been a significant motivation. In the most modern representation of terrorism, bin Laden is in many ways actually defined by his terrorism—he is struggling, claims to be defending Muslims everywhere, but clearly does not and has added one group after another to his enemies. Now it is unclear where his campaign goes from here; perhaps nowhere, since it is unlikely that he or his movement can transcend the struggle itself.

In the past, general wars have been accompanied by systematic terror, as have civil wars, revolutionary wars, wars of national liberation, labour disputes and other broadly defined resistance movements. Terrorists would characterise themselves as serving a goal or a cause, having been driven to use force to attain their goals in the face of the overwhelming power of the state. However hard it is to understand the manifestations of terrorism in the modern world, cloaked as it so often is in the rhetoric of religion and even mysticism, it remains axiomatic that terrorism is and always has been purposeful and planned; political in its aims and motives; violent or threatening of violence; indiscriminate in its targeting, accepting no restraint in this area; and, crucially, designed to have psychological repercussions beyond the immediate target or victim.

To separate this violence from that of organised states, which have taken upon themselves the monopolistic right of legitimate use of organised violence, terrorism is also generally defined as perpetrated by subnational groups or non-state entities. It has traditionally been believed that terrorists seek maximum publicity and that their campaigns are carried out by organisations with a chain of command or cell structure. Publicity has become a difficult question in recent years, given the rise of the unclaimed attack, and this has formed part of the argument in favour of the New Age of Terrorism concept. In the past, terrorist outrages were either followed with long and turgid communiqués from the 'military' command of the terror group, explaining why the particular target was struck, or heralded by a warning that a device had been planted and would explode at a particular time. As Brian Jenkins of Rand Corporation famously put it, 'Terrorists want a lot of people watching not a lot of people dead.' Given the increasing number of attacks which have been neither claimed nor announced, it has been argued that publicity is no longer a main priority of the perpetrators and that the objectives have changed from achieving ends to simply punishment—terrorists now seem to want people dead. However, terrorists act to influence not only their enemy but also their supporters. Communication between the supporters and potential supporters of a group can be just as important as that between the attackers and the attacked, and the psychological impact can be both on victims and on supporters. The need to claim 'credit' for an attack is not as important if, in the minds of the terrorists, the act speaks for itself. Terrorist violence has at times been seen as primarily symbolic, and the question arises whether this has changed.

Our understanding of modern terrorism can be traced back to the anarchists of the late nineteenth century and their adoption of a policy of 'propaganda by deed'. Their violence was designed to gain publicity, provoke repression and, as a consequence, undermine the government. The violence was symbolic, and, while expressive, its main purpose was to have consequences beyond the immediate victims. Contrary to much of the analysis that has emerged since 11 September, the campaign of bin Laden and al-Qaeda can be seen in this light, with few differences other than (albeit importantly) the scale of effect that a small number of individuals can achieve. It is this scale of effect and the potential for even greater destruction that preoccupied the superterrorism theorists of the 1990s and of which 11 September appeared to provide a demonstration—although, in some ways, the opposite conclusion can also be drawn: for the events of 11 September and its aftermath have shown why terrorists will not necessarily evolve to their maximum destructive potential in the future.

In assessing the implications of the potential for achieving strategic effect (as opposed to change) that the attacks of 11 September revealed, many have concluded that terrorism has transcended its past to become a strategic activity designed to achieve strategic ends. While the point is debatable, it seems clear from events since 11 September that strategically, the al-Qaeda campaign has been stalled, if not derailed. This is because to be strategically successful terrorism must appear irresistible, with groups trading their weakness for time—time in which to undermine the morale of the target state and time in which to increase support for the cause. By sustaining a campaign that frustrates and humiliates the state, terrorists can increase a feeling of vulnerability and eventually lead the population to question the purpose of the counterterrorist campaign. However, crucial to such a strategy is never to become a strategic threat to such an apparent extent that the state has no option but to make the group's destruction a central goal of national security policy. In the UK the enduring campaigns of Irish republicans in Northern Ireland and the mainland, plus the revenge attacks by loyalist terror groups, were characterised by an appalling slaughter that took well over 3,000 lives over a period of more than thirty years in the modern era; but the death toll from an individual attack never exceeded twenty-nine. Furthermore, the 'spectaculars' perpetrated by the Provisional IRA on the mainland achieved strategic effect (and possibly even strategic change) once the focus was directed at economic targets rather than more traditional symbols of state power, or indeed at civilians themselves. At the culmination of their mainland campaigns in Britain, the Provisional IRA exploded two of the largest explosive devices ever seen in peacetime in Britain in the City of London, which together cost the British state more than all the preceding bombs had done collectively.

While it seems clear that bin Laden understood the economic implications of the attacks on the World Trade Center, the expressive violence that took thousands of lives represented such a strategic challenge to the United States that it became inconceivable that thereafter the destruction of al-Qaeda could be anything other than the central goal of US policy. The previous ten years of attacks against US interests—including, of course, an earlier attack on the World Trade Center, as well as plots to destroy the tunnels and bridges linking Manhattan Island with the rest of New York, and attacks on US military and diplomatic interests around the world—had created in bin Laden an enemy against whom the United States found it difficult to mobilise, despite the potential for disaster that he represented. A similar pattern was seen in Japan, where the activities of the Aum Shinrikyo sect, including repeated (botched) attempts to release chemical and possibly even biological weapons, went largely unpunished, even uninhibited, for many years, before the 1995 attack on the Tokyo underground resulted in the complete suppression of the organisation. To defeat the strong, the weak terrorists must survive to mount repeated and damaging campaigns against their enemies while garnering support that over time cannot be defeated through coercive military or paramilitary action.

Today, people rarely accept they are terrorists; rather, they identify the systems they oppose as terrorist and argue that to condemn what states call 'terrorism' is to endorse the power of the strong over the weak. However, bin Laden himself came close to acknowledging the attacks of 11 September as terrorist in nature in his video discussion with a supporter. The definition debate also gets bogged down in the question of whether the problem is terrorist violence or its underlying causes. Unlike the anarchists, who did not deny their purpose, modern groups use names to associate themselves with armies and military organisations, images of freedom and liberation, righteous vengeance or neutral positions. The emphasis is on how they have been forced to take up arms and have been driven to violence. The judgement on what is morally the more reprehensible depends on whether you associate with the group or individual perpetrating acts of terrorism, or with the victims of terrorism. Commentators from the developing world have often noted that for much of the modern era of terrorism, all liberation movements, bona fide or not, have been called 'terrorist' by their opponents, as indeed was the French resistance movement during the Second World War (by the German targets).

To the apologists and political representatives of terror organisations, the opponents of terrorism defend the status quo and the terrorists are forced to operate clandestinely because of their weakness, carrying out dramatic acts of violence to attract attention. Most of terrorism's targets state that the defining characteristic of terrorism is the act of violence, not the motivation or justification, but this interpretation remains open to criticism on the grounds that it defends the rights of state entities (which claim legitimacy whatever the effect of their use of organised violence) rather than individuals and groups. Perhaps more powerfully, critics of terrorism point to the failure of substate groups to observe the norms and rules of war, which, although not always followed by states, have granted civilians non-combatant immunity from attack, prohibit the taking of civilian hostages and regulate the treatment of prisoners of war. (Interestingly, the United States has avoided granting the

Taleban and al-Qaeda detainees the status of prisoner of war.) Terrorists, it is said, violate all these rules, and while states' armed forces have also done so at various times, terrorists refuse to be bound by *any* rules.

Antecedents

Rather than an Age of Terrorism emerging in the twentieth century, it can reasonably be asked whether there has ever been a time without what we now, in attempting to categorise all non-state political violence, all-embracingly call terrorism. The original use of the term 'terrorist' in English can be traced back to the French Revolution: it entered the language in 1795 in the writings of Edmund Burke commenting on the regime of terror of Maximilien Robespierre and the Committee of Public Safety in France. Terror emerged as an instrument of state power exercised by a revolutionary state and, like today, was neither random nor indiscriminate (as it is often portrayed) but organised, deliberate and systematic. The Jacobins spoke positively of themselves as terrorist, Robespierre lauding 'virtue, without which terror is evil; terror, without which virtue is helpless'.[5] But they do not represent the first example of terrorism that has been plucked out of history. The Sicarii, an offshoot of the religious sect of Zealots in Palestine in AD 66–73, was arguably a social movement, but also a radical anti-Roman religious movement that attacked Jewish 'collaborators'. Using short swords, they often attacked in daylight in crowded public places to demonstrate the state's impotence and to strike fear beyond their immediate targets, provoking conflict. More terrifyingly, the selection of targets appeared random—though it actually was not. Like a number of modern-day terror organisations they eventually attracted too much attention from their enemies, and their rebellion in AD 6 was crushed by the Romans, who crucified 2,000 people.

A thousand years later, the Assassins, a Shia sect of Ismailis and Nizari, operated from 1090 to 1275. This group used only the dagger at close range, by this mode of attack both accentuating the terror inflicted and revealing a willingness to die in pursuit of their mission echoed by today's suicide bombers. While they are particularly remembered for attacking the Crusaders, most of their targets were other Muslims: they killed governors and prefects, and even tried to murder Saladin twice. Historically their struggle was a fruitless attempt to defend religious autonomy, but they have been remembered. The Thugs, an Indian secret society, rarely killed Europeans but otherwise were indiscriminate in killing as a sacrifice (they had no discernible political ambitions); they operated for 600 years, possibly killing as many as 500,000 before being suppressed by the British. Some have even suggested that following the American Civil War the Ku Klux Klan, which fought Reconstruction and terrorised the coloured population, can be included in this panoply of terrorist groups.

However, for all the historical examples of political violence one can identify, it is the anarchists of the late nineteenth century, with their 'propaganda by deed', who have most shaped modern thinking and the fear of terrorism. The experience crucially detached terrorism from its historically accurate linkage with state, rather than non-state, policy. The anarchists sought to invoke fear and repression as a means to revolutionary change, and were very successful in assassinating heads of state—one head of state per year was killed in the 1890s, including US President William McKinley. One of the best-known of these groups was the Russian revolutionary Narodnaya Volya (People's Will), which adopted selective targeting and political assassination, killing Tsar Alexander II in 1881. While the attack was in itself apparently successful, once again the result was vigorous repression by the state and the group's destruction; when revolution came to Russia it was the Bolsheviks, not People's Will, who claimed power.

The anarchists also inspired fear in a rather modern way through the Anarchist International, a shadowy network of anarchists acting in various countries. It proved to be largely a myth, but one which stimulated exaggerated fears disproportionate to the impact or political significance of the groups themselves; anarchism and terrorism were hereafter often linked. The anarchists also introduced the idea of cell organisation and distributed manuals on how to be anarchists—notably the *Anarchist's Cookbook*, a forebear of today's focus on the internet as a source of terrorist information-sharing and the fear of the internationalisation of terrorism by bin Laden. Indeed, the *Anarchist's Cookbook* has for some time itself been available on the internet.

Irish terrorism had emerged with the Dynamiters in the 1870s and the Phoenix Park murders by Irish National Invincibles of Lord Cavendish, the Chief Secretary for Ireland, and his under-secretary, who were killed in daylight with twelve-inch surgical knives, although whether political assassination should be classified as terrorism continues to test our understanding of the terminology. The most famous member of the Young Bosnians (Mlada Bosna) was Gavrilo Princip, the assassin of Archduke Franz Ferdinand in 1914—the event which reputedly sparked the First World War.

Terrorism became a state monopoly in a number of countries in the 1930s and 1940s, reminding observers that enforcement terrorism has historically been far more destructive than agitational terrorism. Following the Second World War, terrorism seemed to be the preserve of indigenous nationalist groups which emerged out of various anticolonial campaigns in, among other countries, Israel, Cyprus, Kenya and Algeria. The idea of 'freedom fighters' emerged at this time, along with the debate over the terminology and definition of terrorism. A number of movements saw independence arrive supported in part by terrorism. Thus, political legitimacy attached to a number of 'wars of national liberation', which many developing countries saw not as terrorist campaigns, but as wholly legitimate armed struggles.

In the radical 1960s and 1970s, terrorism broadened to include ideologically motivated groups such as Germany's Red Army Faction, Italy's Red Brigades, France's Direct Action and America's Weathermen; today there are still a few fringe groups keeping the ideological terrorist flame alive.[6] This modern period also saw the emergence of various ethnoseparatists operating outside the traditional colonial context, including the Palestine Liberation Organisation and various groups connected with the Arab–Israeli dispute; ETA, the Basque separatists in northern Spain; the FLQ in Quebec; and, most bizarrely the South Moluccans, who hijacked a train in Holland to publicise their cause.

Modern trends

The 1970s and 1980s saw revolutionary terrorist groups defeated one after another around the world. International terrorism came to be identified through the activities of various groups associated with the struggle against Israel, and a spate of aircraft hijackings and hostage-takings and the alleged use of terrorist organisations by certain state sponsors as tools of foreign policy. The 1986 bombing of a disco in Berlin frequented by US forces was attributed to Libya, and the United States responded by bombing Tripoli. Libya became quiet, but the bombing of Pam Am flight 103 over Lockerbie followed in 1988, as did an increase in arms supplies to the IRA by Colonel Qadhafi's regime. Meanwhile, the Soviet occupation of Afghanistan in 1979 led to a US-backed insurgent movement, including a number of international volunteers, defeating the Red Army. The Iranian Revolution of 1978–9 had led to a revival in Shiite terrorism, now backed by Iran, and the emergence of suicide terrorism in Lebanon following the Israeli invasion of 1982. This campaign, which eventually led to the withdrawal of foreign peacekeeping forces from Lebanon after the suicide bombing of a US Marine Corps base in Beirut and the simultaneous attack on a French paratroop base in the city, appeared to validate the tactic. It was thereafter emulated and taken to new and unprecedented lengths by the Liberation Tigers of Tamil Eelam (LTTE) in Sri Lanka. This separatist movement adopted the tactic of martyrdom to devastating effect to revive its campaign, eventually assassinating the former Indian Prime Minister Rajiv Gandhi in 1991, and used it more often than any group before.

Suicide terrorism has been seen in many contexts, including Chechnya, Sri Lanka, Yemen, Lebanon and Israel. The LTTE's Black Tigers, who launched their first attack in July 1987, offer significant evidence that suicide terrorism is not merely a religious phenomenon and that, under certain extreme political and psychological circumstances, secular volunteers are fully capable of martyrdom.[7] But whether the individual perpetrators of such attacks were lone zealots or simply pawns in psychological operations often remained unclear. Is suicide terrorism a tactic of opportunity or an institutionalised strategy? Out of over 270 suicide attacks between 1980 and 2000, the LTTE carried out 168, Hizbollah 52, Hamas 22 and the PKK 15, according to one study. It also suggested three main types of suicide terrorism: groups that neither practise suicide terrorism on a regular basis nor approve of its use as a tactic, but which may initiate it on occasion for specific reasons; groups that formally adopt suicide terrorism as a temporary tactic, the leadership obtaining (or granting) ideological or theological legitimation for its use, recruiting and training volunteers, and then sending them into action with a specific objective in mind; and finally groups that use suicide terrorism as a permanent strategy.

The events of 11 September suggested that al-Qaeda might fit into this final category of terrorism as a permanent strategy, but the argument for inclusion in the second category of suicide terrorism with specific objectives in mind appears more compelling. Bin Laden may have drawn various false conclusions about US national resolve during the 1990s as a result of a number of attacks on US forces engaged in wars of choice, and underestimated the US willingness to accept causalties in defeating distant enemies as a result of episodes such as the withdrawal from Beirut in 1985.

An increased willingness to engage in suicide terrorism was not the only change in this period; the traditional structures of the groups concerned also evolved. Flatter, less hierarchical organisations began to emerge that were to find ultimate expression in the description of al-Qaeda as a loose network, analogous in some ways to a modern business school model of a responsive business organisation.[8] In the United States, the return of domestic terrorism and the unprecedented attack of 1995 in Oklahoma, resulting in mass casualties, by a reportedly right-wing conspiracy of just two people brought to prominence the concept of 'leaderless resistance'—the idea that individuals with little or no institutional affiliation or relationship with any command element might 'buy into' the doctrine and objectives of other more traditional groupings, but would undertake operations individually and independently.

If such people proved capable of sophisticated planning and execution and gained access to advanced technology, the implications for counterterrorism and law enforcement were grim. The Oklahoma bomber, Timothy McVeigh, proved that an individual using 'old terrorist' techniques, but determined to kill hundreds of people, found few barriers to entry into the terrorist profession. His capture and subsequent prosecution demonstrated the inability of such individuals to pose a strategic threat, but his descendant in terrorist terms, Richard Colvin Reid, who was caught trying to ignite his shoes on a flight from Paris to Miami after 11 September, revealed just how dangerous such leaderless terrorists could be and how the technique had spread. Indeed, al-Qaeda has proven particularly difficult to assess since the fall of the Taleban regime (and before it, for that matter) due to its amorphous structure. It may in fact embrace various types of terrorist operative, from the cell-structured trained professionals down to the leaderless opportunist, further complicating effective penetration and analysis.

John Gearson

Superterrorism

As the Cold War ended, America's conventional military dominance had been underlined by victory in the Gulf War. Thereafter, the United States only reluctantly allowed itself to become entangled in post-Cold War conflicts, and during the 1990s there occurred a rediscovery of asymmetric conflict in American military thinking. Connected to this process, the concept of super-terrorism emerged, closely linked to the other product of the upheavals of the Iranian Revolution, the end of the Cold War and the Gulf War—the phenomenon of the 'rogue state'. That concept evolved through various iterations including rogues, outlaw states, pariah states and, more recently, 'states of concern'. Members have variously included Cuba, Iran, Iraq, Libya, North Korea, Serbia, Syria, Burma and Sudan. Deemed to have little stake in international order, such states were said to be commonly engaged in what was perceived as unacceptable behaviour, involving military aggression and other forms of violence, both internal and external. The concept of 'rogue states' was the subject of great debate and controversy, coming as it did to function as a post-Cold War lightning rod of US foreign and defence policy, and was dismissed by many as no more than an umbrella term for states that disagreed with America. More problematically, it was used to describe a diverse array of states with varying histories, governments, technical capabilities and military ambitions. The states included on the list were also perceived differently by various allies, most significantly in the differing attitudes towards Iran of Europe and the United States.

The United States consistently charged many if not all of the rogue states of supporting or sponsoring terrorism, which, even if they did not engage in aggressive war against their neighbours, did make them a threat to international order. Indeed, the whole threat of international terrorism appeared to be viewed by some observers through the prism of the sponsors, rather than the context of the individual groups. Long believed to be engaged in the development of weapons of mass destruction, rogue states that also sponsored terrorists were of particular concern. Aum Shinrikyo's sarin attack on the Tokyo underground led to an outpouring of assessments on the likely use of WMD by terrorist organisations supported by the weapons programmes of rogue states. While it was accepted that virtually all terrorist organisations would face severe barriers in any attempt to procure, produce and, crucially, deploy effectively a mass casualty weapon (which Aum had only partially overcome after enormous expense and effort), if such a group were allied with a sponsor, the threat could prove greater than had previously been thought. This fitted in with the emerging rediscovery of asymmetric challenges in US military thinking and supported the discovery of superterrorism.

In the 1990s, analysts suggested that developing states and non-state groups would select 'asymmetric means' to undermine or attack Western interests. In the military field, the performance of the coalition during the Gulf War demonstrated the technological superiority of US and allied conventional forces, and the much-vaunted 'revolution in military affairs' (RMA) promised to widen further the gap between first-world and third-world conventional military forces. As a result, potential adversaries were believed likely to be forced to adopt alternative weapons and unconventional or 'asymmetric' strategies, homing in on first-world military weaknesses and avoiding their strengths, possibly by attacking them through vulnerabilities in their open civil societies. Asymmetric strategies included information warfare, the use of WMD and terrorism. As modern Western societies became more dependent on critical infrastructures, so adversaries, especially terrorists, were thought likely to see the opportunities in such new targets.

Perhaps, it was mooted, as well as a 'revolution in military affairs', one could now begin to speak of a 'revolution in terrorist affairs'.[9] Information warfare might soon be embraced by terrorists; just as the United States and numerous other countries were investing substantial resources in information warfare capabilities, with the aim of achieving 'information dominance', so terrorists could do the same. While the ultimate objective of an offensive information warfare attack would be to eliminate an adversary's information-gathering, filtering, processing and delivery system before a conflict actually began, developed societies' dependence on such advanced information systems and computers made them particularly vulnerable. Information warfare offered 'dangerous regimes' or terrorists that lacked resources a relatively cheap option for inflicting, or threatening to inflict, significant damage on technologically advanced countries like the United States and Britain. This debate broadened into a concern for critical civilian information infrastructures, including computer-based information for financial networks, telephone exchanges, electricity grids and air traffic control networks. In this connection, it was argued that of great concern were the large numbers of foreign students studying computer science and the physical sciences in American universities. Thus, 'third wave' thinking of the sort presented by the Tofflers permeated counterterrorism assessments, always with the caveat that, though there was no evidence for such capabilities as yet, it was inevitable that they would be utilised eventually. The number of foreign students seeking flying training, or indeed travelling to the United States to receive weapons training (a facility offered by certain British Muslim organisations on the internet in the months leading up to 11 September) was not commented upon.

At the strategic level, an asymmetric strategy meant seeking to avoid direct military confrontation; at the operational and tactical levels, it meant seeking ways to 'level the playing field' if forced into engaging the West militarily. As the British Strategic Defence Review of 1998 stated in its (brief) discussion of the phenomenon: 'Potential adversaries may choose to adopt alternative weapons and unconventional (or asymmetric) strategies, perhaps attacking us through vulnerabilities in our open civil society.' However, it was noted by thoughtful observers that merely identifying theoretical vulnerabilities did not mean that adversaries would necessarily attack them. Indeed, the focus on

Western societal vulnerabilities had something of the Western perspective about it and failed to consider adequately how such societies might look to their adversaries. Furthermore, the Western advantage derived from the RMA digitisation of battlefield systems might also turn out to be an 'asymmetric revolution'. Thus the concept of asymmetric warfare began to be deprived of any useful meaning, as terrorism had been before it. However, the thinking behind the asymmetric conflict debate of the 1990s crucially informed the debate on the 'new terrorism' and appeared to offer proof that the threat of asymmetric warfare from substate groups was a real one.

The superterrorism debate was rooted in the assumption of the worst case asymmetric theories for the use of chemical and biological terrorism. By the 1990s, terrorism analysts had begun to discern a trend away from an ever-increasing number of terrorist incidents, with the data suggesting the opposite: the State Department's annual survey of international terrorism identified 348 terrorist attacks in 2001, down from the 666 recorded in 1987.[10] Instead, observers identified a new threat from religiously motivated, mass casualty terrorism in which the need for a 'body count' transcended any constraints which had held back earlier terrorist campaigns—fewer but increasingly deadly incidents was the prediction. Traditional terrorism had relied on the bomb and the bullet as the weapons of choice for over a century, and had managed to cause casualties in the low hundreds, but now the New Age of Terrorism heralded by the attack by Aum Shinrikyo had arrived. Drawing together the strands of religion as a motivation, the propensity to use suicide attack as a tactic and the proliferation of WMD as a potential means, superterrorism now posed, it was claimed, a high-consequence, if still low-probability, threat. Such superterrorists could employ chemical, biological or even nuclear (radiological) weapons, would probably be supported by state sponsors and could potentially threaten casualties in the thousands and upwards.

However, proof of the increased willingness to cause mass casualties was based on a small sample of attacks or attempted attacks during the 1990s, including the first attack on the World Trade Center in 1993, the attack on the Tokyo underground in 1995, the bombing of the Murrah federal office building in Oklahoma City, also in 1995 (killing 169), a series of 13 simultaneous car bombings in Bombay, the attack on US military facilities in Saudi Arabia at Khobar Towers (killing 19 and injuring 500), the bombing of two American embassies in East Africa in 1998 (killing 224 and injuring over 5,000), and the attack on the USS Cole in 2000 (killing 17 and costing the US navy $170 million). Sceptics pointed out that most of these attacks still employed bombs and conventional explosives to achieve their effects, and that the incidents identified included an act of domestic terrorism in the United States by a Gulf War veteran and an attack by a Japanese cult in Japan, as well as religiously motivated Islamic extremism, and that the data were too limited to allow significant conclusions to be drawn.

Contrary to the fears of the superterrorism lobby, it was also argued that state sponsors might be reluctant, given the unstable nature of virtually all terrorist organisations in history, to entrust their most precious military research output to those elements over which they had the least direct control. The emphasis fell on the state sponsors simply because they were the most easily identified elements in a terrorist plot and fitted in with the focus of existing Western national security structures. Furthermore, the claimed religious motivation could be said to be masking political objectives in most, if not all, of the attacks. The willingness to commit suicide and to take significant numbers of lives did not necessarily make the terrorism different from what had preceded it; rather, it represented a change of tactic in pursuit of the same ends. The use of WMD by superterrorists was such a low-probability event, it was argued, that it would be better to focus on high-probability risks. Indeed, a tendency to exaggerate and distort the real threat was revealed in the wilder reports of the capabilities of the Aum Shinrikyo cult and its alleged crossing of the technological threshold by acquiring biological weapons capability in the 1990s—a claim that was shown to be false. Terrible though the death of twelve people from the use of sarin gas (a chemical not a biological weapon) was, it did not represent quite the technological watershed as which it has sometimes been presented.[11]

Nonetheless, the superterrorism idea began to take hold, and in a notorious interview on prime-time television in 1997, the US Secretary of Defense William Cohen held up a five-pound bag of sugar to demonstrate how much anthrax it would take to kill the population of Washington DC. The result was to focus attention on the low-probability end of the spectrum of threat—not least as the mass casualty terrorism that had been predicted failed to materialise before 11 September—and also to blur two complementary, but actually distinct, strands in American threat assessments: how to deal with rogue states and what were the future challenges of terrorism. The national security apparatus of the United States and its allies was culturally and administratively structured to deal with state-based threats when thinking about international challenges. The superterrorism debate allowed the focus to turn increasingly to the most dangerous scenarios for state-assisted mass casualty events. Terrorism, when it was thought about outside of this context, was regarded primarily as a criminal activity at the national level, which occasionally spilled over into attacks against Western interests. It was rarely seen as a strategic threat outside of the state-sponsored realm. In fact, it was in this period that the ability of the 'new' terrorists to organise, communicate and travel globally, effortlessly moving through Western societies, using many of the information age's advances to plan 'old' terrorist attacks, grew and was practised.

Postmodern terrorism

Overall, the distinction between old and new terrorism was perhaps over-done; most significantly, the focus on rogue state support for superterrorism appeared to be disproved by the al-Qaeda example when the assault on the United States began. As the editor of this volume has pointed out, Afghanistan was an example not so much of state-sponsored terrorism as of a terrorist-sponsored state.[12] Adopting the methodology of old terrorism, al-Qaeda used surprise, planning and training, coupled with a willingness to commit suicide, to cause thousands of casualties, eschewing the complexities of developing technologically demanding chemical and biological substances and the proven difficulties of effective dissemination. Its interest in mass casualties had been demonstrated in earlier attacks and plots, including the 1996 plan to hijack a number of US aircraft over the Pacific; but the attacks remained resolutely symbolic, if also demonstrative, perhaps even representing expressive violence. The capacity of global reach terrorism to cause thousands of casualties had been proven, but the inevitability of the use of non-conventional weapons had not. The example of 11 September may just as easily push terrorism in the opposite direction, towards a strategically more effective series of painful and repeated humiliations of American and Western presences around the world. The 'white powder' episode in America which followed 11 September was all the more perplexing as a consequence, and appeared to prove nothing other than the potential for Western societies to be dislocated by psychological challenges and the relatively limited physical effect such attacks could have compared with, say, a thousand-pound truck bomb of home-made explosives.

That the residual threat of mass effect and mass casualty terrorism, by whatever means, is available to the groups concerned, however, has been demonstrated by the events of 2001, and the need for appropriate preparedness on the part of target states is clear. 'Traditional terrorism' has been revealed to remain a likely weapon of choice for most terrorists and an enduring long-term danger. Terrorists still need certain sanctuaries, and while there may indeed be al-Qaeda elements in as many as forty or fifty countries, the chances of their having laboratories producing unconventional weapons is slim. The greatest dangers have been revealed to be the existence of lawless grey areas and regions around the world where literally thousands of activists can be trained unhindered over a number of years; the inability of intelligence agencies to cooperate effectively in the sharing of already acquired intelligence material; and the extent to which Western states can become transfixed by high-consequence, low-probability threats to the detriment of prudent action against high-probability, lower-consequence threats. Instead of terrorism, we should perhaps think in terms of 'terrorisms' and free ourselves from the tyranny of the search for an all-embracing and universally acceptable definition.

Modern states are actually not particularly well equipped to fight, or even capable of fighting, transnational and stateless terrorism. If convenient state sponsors cannot be identified, how will the fight be taken to the enemy if it chooses not to reveal itself? The majority of the world's advanced militaries are still configured for interstate conflict and, inasmuch as they consider other challenges, these have been labelled as support to civil authorities in the UK (where terrorism is perceived as a crime), or operations other than war in the United States. Strategic terrorism may require a rethink of many of these approaches well beyond what has been undertaken to date. What is clear is that states acting independently (even ones as powerful as the United States) are incapable of fighting such threats alone, however much they would like to believe otherwise. The challenges of modern terrorism require unprecedented cooperation between civil and military agencies, intelligence-sharing by competing providers and allies, and careful consideration of which civil liberties need to be sacrificed and which do not. They also require a move away from a focus on the type of conflict that the West is most comfortable concentrating on, simply because it fits existing models for understanding conflict and a preoccupation with mass casualty terrorism, and instead a continuous and careful analysis of the groups concerned, their contexts, and the range of tactics and techniques open to them. While certain individual terrorists may indeed see the need to match or even exceed the threshold of violence and destruction presented on 11 September, as the arrest of a suspect allegedly plotting to attack the United States using a radiological explosive device of some sort suggested, many others will seek again to surprise their target by the tactics and methodologies they adopt. Terrorists have over the past thirty years proven themselves generally operationally conservative, but also highly adaptable and able to innovate.

Terrorism in all its forms is, by its very nature, an asymmetrical response to superior force, and terrorists have always used their capabilities as force multipliers—usually through the exploitation of terror. The generation of fear, in effect the use of purposeful violence as a form of psychological warfare, can now be carried much further, enhanced by the modern media and the proliferation of mass media as much as by the proliferation of weapons. The old terrorist tactics of creating psychological effect in the target societies beyond the direct victims, communicating with supporters and encouraging a repressive response by the targeted remain central to their campaigns. The use of suicide terrorism does not necessarily mean this has changed and, while new technologies have improved significantly the capacity of substate groups to cause mass casualties and therefore cannot be ignored, it is more likely that weapons of mass effect, coupled with traditional tactics and weapons, will continue to be used, even by those terrorists on the 'super' end of the spectrum. Crucially, however, the capacity for strategic change remains debatable, since the strategic objectives sought by al-Qaeda and bin Laden have not, as yet, been advanced by the events of 11 September— indeed, so far the opposite is the case. Difficult though it is to accept, the vast majority of all terrorist violence, even suicide attacks, remain totally purposeful and, although rarely successful, are undertaken with ends in mind. The potential of terrorists to achieve strategic effect in the future may to a large extent, then, depend on how America and its allies react to these challenges, rather than on what the terrorists themselves do.

Notes

1 Although fewer than 1,000 people required medical treatment.
2 Michael Radu, 'Terrorism after the Cold War: Trends and Challenges', *Orbis*, Spring 2002, pp. 275–87.
3 It is significant to note that the State Department includes in the definition of non-combatants 'military personnel who at the time of the incident are unarmed and/or not on duty', and that it regards as acts of terrorism 'attacks on military installations or on armed military personnel when a state of military hostilities does not exist at the site'. *Patterns of Global Terrorism 2001*, Washington DC, US State Department, May 2002, p. xvi.
4 Conor Gearty, *The Future of Terrorism*, London, Phoenix, 1997, p. 11.
5 Maximilien Robespierre, quoted in Bruce Hoffman, *Inside Terrorism*, London, Gollancz, 1998, p. 16.
6 What claim to be remnants of the Red Brigades recently assassinated an economics professor who was advising the right-wing government in Italy on labour market reform.
7 Rohan Gunaratna, 'Suicide Terrorism: A Global Threat', *Jane's Intelligence Review*, 20 Oct. 2000.
8 These ideas have been developed by, among others, Bruce Hoffman of Rand Corporation.
9 Stephen Sloan, 'Terrorism and Asymmetry', in Lloyd J. Matthews, ed., *Challenging the United States Symmetrically and Asymmetrically*, Carlisle Barracks, PA, US Army War College Strategic Studies Institute, 1998, p. 180.
10 *Patterns of Global Terrorism 2001*, p. 171.
11 See Milton Leitenberg, 'The Experience of the Japanese Aum Shinrikyo Group and Biological Agents', in Brad Roberts, ed., *Hype or Reality? The 'New Terrorism' and Mass Casualty Attacks*, Alexandria, VA, Chemical and Biological Arms Control Institute, 2000, pp. 159–72.
12 Lawrence Freedman, 'The Third World War?', *Survival*, vol. 43, no. 4, Winter 2001–2), pp. 61–88.

The Roots of Terrorism: Probing the Myths

KARIN VON HIPPEL

AN effective counter- and anti-terrorist campaign must be holistic, and incorporate a spectrum of activities that attack both symptoms and causes. Dealing with symptoms involves military, intelligence, financial, legal and police activities to 'root out terrorists'. These may be extremely challenging, but they are still relatively straightforward. Terrorists will be pursued through a mixture of 'high-tech' and 'low-tech' means, removed from society, and their operations blocked, whether they are in Kandahar, Paris or Minneapolis. The US government has acknowledged that all this might take years, without necessarily succeeding in eradicating all members of al-Qaeda and affiliated organisations, or preventing all future acts of terror. But there is a steely determination—by the US government and dedicated members of the coalition—that these 'rooting out' activities will be *the* priority in the years to come.

These same determined actors are categorically less decisive, however, concerning the other end of the spectrum, that is, how to attack the 'roots' of 'new terrorism'.[1] Whereas in the aftermath of 11 September governments focused on immediate responses, by the time nearly a year had passed more energy was being dedicated to trying to understand why al-Qaeda and related groups hate the 'American way' so much that they desire to destroy thousands of innocent civilians, cause immense economic damage and kill themselves in the process. If we can determine what drives people to commit such heinous crimes, it is suggested, perhaps we can change their behaviour. Or, if their grievances really are just, perhaps we can change ours.

Beyond the more radical elements of the al-Qaeda platform, which are considered non-negotiable and fanatical, other alleged underlying causes can be tackled if true, or debunked if myths. One such argument—pertaining to America ignoring the plight of Palestinians in the Middle East—though still heard in certain circles, has been mostly discredited. As Simon and Benjamin explained, the terrorists would not be mollified by

a change in US policies toward the Muslim world . . . The 11 September attacks . . . were being planned when Ehud Barak had been elected in Israel on a peace platform. Previous attacks were planned and carried out in periods when the peace process was advancing. Rather, al-Qaeda is bent on Israel's elimination and humbling the United States into insignificance as a global military, economic and cultural power.[2]

That said, a resolution to the crisis in the Middle East would go some way towards removing an obstacle and perceptions of inequity by many Arabs

© The Political Quarterly Publishing Co. Ltd. 2002
Published by Blackwell Publishing, 108 Cowley Road, Oxford OX4 1JF, UK and 350 Main Street, Malden, MA 02148, USA

and Muslims, keeping in mind that other radical groups, such as Hamas, object to Israel's existence entirely.

Two other theories circulate as received wisdom. The first is that poverty is at the root of terrorism; and the second is that 'failed' or collapsed states are breeding grounds and safe havens, where terrorists establish training camps and trade illicit goods with ease. These arguments contain partial truths, and thus require closer consideration. Only when we have a more precise understanding of causality can an effective campaign be developed to address root causes.

The poor

Since 11 September a number of politicians, including President Bush, have linked poverty with terrorism. At the March 2002 World Development Summit in Monterey, Mexico, leaders declared that the fight against poverty was intrinsically linked to the fight against terrorism. Earlier, on 6 February 2002, in criticising US policy, the then French foreign minister Hubert Vedrine remarked:

We are today threatened by a new simplism [sic] which consists in reducing all the world's problems to the battle against terrorism. That's not a responsible approach . . . We must tackle the situations of poverty, injustice, humiliation, etc. Today there is clearly a radical difference between our approach and that of the US administration.[3]

Common sense would dictate that there is a direct correlation between poverty and terrorism; yet the evidence gathered thus far does not lend credence to this proposition, and if anything, supports the opposite.

The nineteen hijackers who committed the 11 September atrocities, and their spiritual father bin Laden, were neither poor nor uneducated. Others noted that a large percentage of the Egyptians who belonged to one of the groups affiliated to al-Qaeda came from 'stable middle-class homes and were university educated'.[4] If poverty really were the root cause of terrorism, more terrorists would come from the poorest part of the world, sub-Saharan Africa; and this, so far, is not the case.

Alan B. Krueger and Jitka Maleckova studied Israeli and Arab terrorism in the Middle East, and their results demonstrated that these terrorists not only enjoyed a living standard above the poverty line, but normally had at least a secondary education. The authors report that 'Any connection between poverty, education and terrorism is indirect, complicated and probably quite weak . . . it is more accurately viewed as a response to political conditions and long-standing feelings (either perceived or real) of indignity and frustration that have little to do with economics.' Indeed, their study showed that *unemployed* Palestinians were *less* likely to support violent attacks against the Israeli military and civilians.[5] One sobering finding, that the majority of Palestinians believed that violence has proved to be more effective than negotiation in achieving their goals,[6] is consistent with other conflicts.

The Kosovo Liberation Army managed to secure NATO military intervention after engaging in a relatively short-term violent struggle, while Rugova's longer campaign of passive resistance achieved very little.

The authors explain their findings by noting that people normally become politicised through education, which enables them to articulate their beliefs and to surround themselves with others with the same proclivities. In contrast, those who are destitute must spend the majority of their time merely trying to subsist. Moreover, the researchers explain that 'educated, middle or upper class individuals are better suited to carry out acts of international terrorism than are impoverished illiterates because the terrorists must fit into a foreign environment to be successful.'[7] While the Krueger and Maleckova study is concerned only with the Middle East, information gathered thus far about the al-Qaeda network is consistent with their findings, including the point about successfully adapting to foreign environments. In alien cities, members of al-Qaeda have had no trouble finding employment, renting apartments, attending graduate schools and enrolling for flying lessons, all of which would have been much more difficult had they been uneducated and indigent.

International development organisations, especially the European Commission, the UN and the OECD, along with bilateral donors, understand that counterterrorism will consume a growing percentage of budgets and time in the years to come. To the extent that poverty eradication does discourage terrorism, re-allocating funds from development to counterterrorism within foreign aid budgets would be counterproductive. Thus, donors have correctly recognised the importance of uncovering and articulating the connection between the two in order to ensure the optimal use of scarce resources.

Potential links

While it appears that a higher socio-economic status may be positively associated with participation in and support for acts of terror, the research is mixed as to whether this also extends to volunteers for suicide bombing assignments. Because the families of these 'martyrs' are compensated generously by a number of charitable organisations, it could be argued that the financial reward could be an incentive for a poor family. In the case of the Palestinians, the sponsors even include the Iraqi government; one journalist noted an increase in payments by Iraq to families of suicide bombers in the West Bank and the Gaza Strip in March 2002 from $10,000 to $25,000.[8]

While Nasra Hassan discovered in her study of Palestinian suicide bombers that they were mostly educated, middle-class men, Jessica Stern found from her interviews with those involved in the Kashmir dispute that 'wealthy Pakistanis would rather donate their money than their sons to the cause, [and] families in poor, rural areas are likely to send their sons to "jihad" under the belief that doing so is the only way to fulfill this spiritual duty.'[9] Typically, terrorist campaigns are funded through charitable organisations, or directly through 'taxes' on the population at home and in the diaspora, as well as from the sale and barter of arms and, often, drugs. Similar fundraising mechanisms have been used in many conflicts, for example by the Eritreans in their war against Ethiopia in 1998–9, or by the Kosovar Albanians in the 1990s. Stern explains that families of suicide bombers are often elevated to a higher status in their community, receiving financial help to start businesses or build new homes.

More research needs to be conducted on 'new terrorist' movements to determine how relevant wealth and education are as factors. We also need to have a better understanding of the psychological profile of these terrorists, to understand who they are and what motivates them. The thousands of foreign fighters in Afghanistan included the upper-middle-class northern Californian John Walker and law students and web-page designers from the United Kingdom, as well as volunteers from parts of the developing world. Presumably the US government has gathered interesting data from the hundreds of detainees in Guantanamo and Afghanistan, though whether any of that information will be released to the public is unclear. It certainly would help; currently many international organisations are trying to formulate development policy responses to terrorism based on an insufficient empirical database.

Once a more consistent picture emerges, targeted responses can be developed. Nevertheless, any response has to be carefully sold so as not to appear patronising, as Krueger and Maleckova note: 'connecting foreign aid with terrorism risks the possibility of humiliating many in less developed countries, who are implicitly told they only receive aid to prevent them from committing acts of terror.'[10] Humiliation can in itself cause increased levels of commitment and recruitment to 'the cause'. Moreover, others in developing states may exaggerate the risks of terrorism as a way to legitimise their authority, and in turn, possibly receive more development aid, or even military assistance. In Somalia, for example, the Somali Transitional National Government (TNG), opposition figures such as Hussein Aidid, and even the Ethiopian government have each made accusations of terrorist connections, primarily for self-serving motives. The report submitted by the Somali TNG to the UN Security Council noted the following: 'There are two options before the Counterterrorism Committee in dealing with the situation in Somalia: to watch the country slide back into anarchy and chaos or to fully support the struggling Somali state by providing the necessary resources to enable it to play a meaningful role in the fight against terrorism.'[11]

One response: education

As more evidence is gathered about al-Qaeda and what inspires men to join its ranks, there is one area where development assistance could already be used to target root causes, and that is in support of quality public education for all children in developing countries. UNICEF notes that more than 100 million children do not have access to basic education. In many developing states, education is not publicly funded, and is normally fee-based, which many parents simply cannot afford (though a few countries like Cuba are notable exceptions). In some Muslim countries, poor parents send their children to Qur'anic schools because they are subsidised or free, and the children also receive food, clothing and books, at no cost to the family.

The more hard-line Muslim theological schools are known as Deobandi *madrasas*, named after the original *madrasa* established in 1867 in Deoband, an Indian town near Delhi. The schools were constructed because some Indian Muslims feared that British colonial secular education, which was supported by the Hindus, would destroy Muslim culture, and that only a deep under-standing of the Qur'an would protect Indian Muslims from these corrupting influences. The movement eventually reached Pakistan, and *madrasas* were established in areas near the Afghan border. Of the several million Afghan refugees who were 'temporarily' displaced in Pakistan for most of the 1980s and 1990s, children from the poorest refugee families attended these *madrasas*, including those who later became the Taleban.

Jessica Stern noted that whereas in the past the Islamic schools in Pakistan received some funding from the state, today most are privately funded by wealthy individuals, charitable organisations from many Arab and Muslim states, and some governments, including Iran. She explains, 'Without state supervision, these madrasahs are free to preach a narrow and violent version of Islam.'[12] She also noted that they provide their students with few practical skills that would equip them for work in modern society—many children do not learn any maths or science, for example—and students instead aim to join the *jihad*. Foreign students also attend the *madrasas*, though whether these students are on scholarships and from poor families is not known.

In other poor Muslim societies, such as Somalia, where the UNDP estimates that only 14 per cent of children attend primary school, and a mere 17 per cent are literate, Qur'anic schools have also been established. Some consist of little more than a dozen children sitting under a thorn tree reading the Qur'an for a few hours in the morning, while others are more sophisticated, and funded or subsidised by wealthy Somalis and Arabs. These schools compete with internationally funded and fee-based secular schools (except in Somaliland, where public schools are subsidised by the government). The fee-based schools cost parents approximately $1 a day per child, and this is too costly for the majority of Somalis; thus the temptation to send their children to some form of school may be too great to resist, even if the family does not believe in the extreme form of Islam that may be espoused in the Qur'anic school. As reported in a recent International Crisis Group report on Somalia, these schools 'are vulnerable to penetration by those with more radical Islamist agendas'.[13]

Thus, while the links between poverty and terrorism may not be so clear, what can be determined is that children who attend *madrasas* and other Qur'anic schools not only learn to despise 'corrupting Western influences' from an early age, but also gain few practical skills. In those parts of the world where families have no other option, support for quality public education for all children (including the provision of books, uniforms and school meals), could counter the radical influences espoused by these schools, and teach children practical skills that can be used in the global marketplace. Since fears of Western corrupting influences on education date back to the nineteenth century, if not before, all such interventions must be conducted with extreme care, and developed together with appropriate authorities in developing countries, otherwise they may be counterproductive. While many members of the Taleban were educated in the *madrasas*, others who were involved in the 11 September attacks were not, and it is important to seek a better understanding of the types of education they did have, in order to develop appropriate interventions for those populations.

State collapse and terrorism

The second partially misguided theory brought to bear when discussing the root causes of terrorism links it with 'failed' states. Although reference to *failed states* has become routine in recent years, this author endorses the terms *collapsed* or *imploded*. The term 'failed' implies that there are standards of success to which all states aspire, which is not the case. No state has a complete monopoly on organised violence—and perhaps the variations can tell us about when and how a state will implode. Likewise, many of today's more 'successful' states have similar characteristics to collapsed states, for example, when residents take the law in their own hands and pay 'taxes' to non-state authorities (as, for example, in parts of Sicily). The term 'failed' also suggests that if an unruly dictator had maintained control over the mechanisms of the state—as in Haiti, which before the 1994 US intervention was ruled by tight networks of terror—it would therefore not have failed. Lastly, it ignores the reality that many of these states, especially in Africa, were probably doomed anyway, since Africa's illogical borders and state institutions were imposed by Europeans, without regard to ethnic groups, religion or physical territorial markers.[14]

Interestingly, this is the second time in the last decade that the topic of state collapse has exercised policy-makers. In the early to mid-1990s, state collapse was a subject of serious concern, with Somalia and Afghanistan at the epicentre. Even the CIA commissioned a study in 1994, from a group called the State Failure Task Force, to look at correlates since the 1950s. Our misunderstanding of the concept and inability to respond appropriately contributed to the failure of the US and UN interventions in Somalia in 1993–5, which in turn interfered with an appropriate response to the genocide in Rwanda.

Breeding grounds

The 11 September attacks once again propelled the subject of state 'failure' or collapse on to the international agenda, with Afghanistan and Somalia still the focus, though the link with terrorism is not as strong as it may appear. The factors that could make these places attractive to terrorist organisations include weak or non-existent government structures, and the inability of the international community to oversee and regulate trade or movements of people and goods through landing strips and unguarded coastlines, though such activity may be followed or even taxed by local actors. A few international organisations might monitor particular activities—for example, the International Civil Aviation Organisation manages Somali airspace—but the lack of a permanent international presence throughout these territories severely impedes the gathering of reliable intelligence. International organisations must instead depend on sporadic visits (rarely to insecure areas), the local media and other sources of information, much of which is difficult to verify. Thus terrorists could operate with relative impunity, and without fear of either a government crackdown on operations or international intervention.

These attractions may be countered by the difficulties facing terrorists when operating in an insecure and foreign environment, where security is itself highly fragmented and infrastructure unreliable. Indeed, it is not clear that collapsed states, or parts of states that are no longer controlled by the government, are used as havens, where terrorists live, 'breed' and train. When bin Laden took refuge in Sudan, it was not in the southern parts of the territory that are considered 'lawless', but rather in Khartoum in the north, where the government is firmly in control. Similarly, when he established his base in Afghanistan in 1996, it was no longer a collapsed state, but controlled by the Taleban, which eventually succeeded in ruling most of the territory.

Such places may in fact be more at risk when they are embroiled in wars that are perceived as threatening Islam, as evidenced by the participation of bin Laden and other al-Qaeda members in the fight against the Soviet occupation of Afghanistan, or more recently in conflicts in Kashmir, Chechnya, Bosnia and allegedly Kosovo. In collapsed and weak states that are not in the midst of full-scale wars, such as Somalia, power is diffuse; there is no superpower or infidel to fight against, nor obvious local candidates with whom a reliable partnership can be developed. These territories are thus potentially less attractive to terrorists.

Since it has been without an effective central authority since 1991, Somalia has a claim to be considered the most egregious and protracted case of state collapse—beyond even Afghanistan—though many other states have hovered between collapse and extreme fragility for years (e.g. Sierra Leone). It is for this reason that such great interest, most of it seriously exaggerated, has been generated in potential al-Qaeda links with Somalia after 11 September.

At the end of September 2001 the *Daily Telegraph* reported that 'between 3,000 and 5,000 members of the al Qa'eda and al-Itihad partnership are operating [in Somalia], with 50,000 to 60,000 supporters and reservists.'[15] On 10 December Paul Wolfowitz, the US Deputy Secretary of Defense, remarked: 'People mention Somalia for obvious reasons. It's a country virtually without a government, a country that has a certain Al Qaeda presence already.' Several days earlier, Walter Kansteiner, Assistant Secretary of State for African Affairs, said: 'The United States is concerned that Somalia's lack of central authority makes it an attractive base for terrorists.'

Bin Laden also boasted of al-Qaeda involvement in the incident in Mogadishu on 3–4 October 1993, in which eighteen US army Rangers were killed in a fierce night battle, though he more than likely overstated his role. The indictment by the US government against bin Laden and his cohorts over the 1998 US embassy bombings noted only that 'persons who had been trained by al Qaeda (and by trainers trained by al Qaeda) participated in an attack on United States military personnel serving in Somalia as part of Operation Restore Hope.'[16] There is also speculation that Somalia was used as a transit place for materials and people who participated in the bombings.

It is not known how many Somalis have been trained by al-Qaeda, or, of those, how many participated in the attacks that night. We may never know these facts, and thus need to use caution when making such inferences, as they can deflect attention and resources from the places where the al-Qaeda threat may be more immediate. A US official recently admitted to the ICG, as cited in its May 2002 report, that 'We're still at a very early stage of gathering intelligence. We still don't know who is operating there. There is no sound target and no evidence yet of al-Qaeda members operating in Somalia in any concerted way.'[17]

There may have been some al-Qaeda presence in Somalia in the past decade, through links with Somalia's own relatively small fundamentalist group, the al-Itihaad al-Islam, whose power peaked in the late 1990s after suffering military defeat by Ethiopian troops and Ethiopian-backed Somali forces. This is not to say that al-Itihaad is a spent force, but rather that estimates of its power in Somalia, and links with al-Qaeda, have been vastly exaggerated. As Ken Menkhaus explained,

For the past five years, Al Itihaad's strategy has been to integrate into local communities and clans, and work within legitimate sectors—as teachers, health workers, journalists, merchants, and in judicial structures—toward a long-term goal of preparing Somalia for eventual Islamic rule. As a result, there are no local administrations in Somalia controlled by Al Itihaad, and the handful of small, remote bases that radical Islamists once held are abandoned. Bombing those outposts would be an expensive and pointless exercise in rearranging rocks.[18]

Moreover, given the small number of foreigners inside Somalia, any al-Qaeda presence today would be noticeable. And since Somali society is highly fragmented, with sub-sub-clans competing for control of neighbourhoods in some instances, it is unlikely that such a presence would be kept secret for long. For these reasons, since early 2002 the US government has been less worried about Somalia being used as a base or a haven for escaping al-Qaeda fighters. As a senior member of the US military remarked, 'We know that a member of al-Qaeda would stick out like a sore thumb in any Somali village.'[19] Nevertheless, the US, UK, German, Spanish, Italian and other governments have mounted a serious surveillance operation, using naval vessels and satellites to monitor the Somali coastline and territory, while US and European government officials have visited parts of Somalia.

Economic activity

If cases of state collapse or partial collapse were considered serious breeding grounds for terrorism, then numerous other parts of Africa should be on the list, such as Congo. The only other countries in Africa, besides Sudan and Somalia, that have been mentioned as having alleged links to al-Qaeda are Sierra Leone and Angola—because of the diamond trade, not because they have provided safe havens to terrorists (although this should not be ruled out as a possibility). Further, in these two cases, the allegations are that al-Qaeda acted merely as broker, exchanging arms for diamonds. There is increasing international attention to the issue of brokers, and this could be helpful in closing down terrorist access to certain goods. It is exactly the economic dimension that should be of greater concern to the counterterrorist coalition, much more than the 'breeding ground' issue. As already mentioned, in places where government controls are lax, corrupt, inept or incapable, international crime and terrorism can be abetted through increases in trafficking and the expansion of pipelines used to move humans, drugs, small arms, natural resources, black money and potentially nuclear materials. Raw materials such as diamonds, oil and timber are exploited without regard to domestic sustainability and are used to finance wars and illegal activity.

Because of the lack of regulatory oversight, it is impossible to compile reliable data for smuggling or trade in goods, mostly through trans-shipment activity, and movements of people. It may also be the case that, with the international community closing the economic loopholes in the more regulated economies, weak and collapsed states will become more attractive. In late November 2001 the US government froze the funds of the main Somali remittance bank, al-Barakaat, because of suspected links with al-Qaeda, in an attempt to crack down on what economic activity it is possible to regulate.

In the case of Somalia, deductive reasoning would again lead one to assume that al-Qaeda is operating there at least economically, but so far there is little evidence to support this case, beyond what the US government claims to have concerning al-Barakaat. On the whole, Somalis are more interested in economic activity than dedicated to extremes in religion. They are very aware of the harsh penalties threatened by the counterterrorist coalition for any collaboration with al-Qaeda, which explains the offers by Somalis to assist the US government in searching for any al-Qaeda presence in Somalia. In December 2001, for example, the interim Prime Minister, Hassan Abshir

Farah, said that US military teams would be welcome to come to Somalia to investigate any al-Qaeda presence, though this offer does not mean as much as it might appear to: the government controls only part of the capital, so could not assist US military teams in other parts of the country. Whether or not al-Qaeda are taking advantage of the situation in Somalia or in other weak states to move goods and people, the likelihood is stronger for the lack of oversight and accountability. This should be a cause of concern for the counterterrorist coalition.

A final reason to worry about weak and collapsed states is that the inherent insecurity can be exploited by religious fundamentalists. Because religion can unify people, above and beyond clan, tribe or wealth, it often provides a sense of community and security where this is lacking. In some cases, Islam can reach extreme levels, as for example in the re-application of harsh Sharia law in parts of Somalia in the mid-1990s. Most Somalis would say they prefer not to live by such a strict interpretation of Islam, but they were willing to accept it because it provided security. (Harsh Sharia law is less evident today in Somalia, though it was used in several places from the mid-1990s to 2000.) Similarly, the rise and acceptance of the Taleban in Afghanistan in the mid-1990s was partly due to the increase in warlordism and lawlessness.

State collapse: the response

It is imperative that a serious effort is made to re-establish effective government and the rule of law in places where these are absent or weak, in order to counter the centrifugal forces that cause states to collapse, the by-products of which could lead them to become attractive territories for terrorist activity. Since the evidence linking Somalia to al-Qaeda is inconclusive, the motivation for supporting reconstruction in Somalia (and other fragile or collapsed states) is preventative. A more accountable state would also allow improved access, as well as better communication and economic links, and thus enhance intelligence-gathering.

Holistic reconstruction plans that encompass reform of governance, security sector and economy would certainly go some way to prevent these places from becoming potential breeding grounds for terrorism. While it may not be realistic to assume that Western donors will embark on an enormous programme of state-building in these states throughout the developing world, more serious effort, attention and financial assistance would make an enormous difference. Many donors support a policy of conditionality, where 'good performers' receive more international assistance, and 'poor performers' become even more marginalised and receive significantly less aid in comparison. As recognised by the Swiss Agency for Development and Cooperation,[20] and as is evident from the 11 September attacks, this approach can be counterproductive. Targeted reforms for 'poor performers' need to be developed and applied in more creative ways. Reforms should include formal methods of accessing credit (which in turn can be monitored), including the establishment of financial institutions, and support for greater trade and appropriate investment.

In Somalia, the dynamic emergence of strong patterns of local sovereignty, and the appearance of functioning and legitimate patterns of local administration, constitute a political and social adaptation of Somali society to the prolonged collapse of the Somali government. Somalis have thus forced the international community to consider substate political formations as entities that merit being accorded political legitimacy and some form of international recognition and support. This is another reason why the term 'failed' is inappropriate, since parts of Somalia may be more accountable than many so-called 'intact' states. At the same time, in the areas of Somalia that remain relatively chaotic, especially parts of the south, the duration of state collapse and the negative ramifications of almost complete infrastructural damage will also complicate reconstruction. The longer this situation of lawlessness endures in these parts, the harder it will be to convince those in control of strategic resources to relinquish them, and subsequently, to help rebuild the state.

Strong authoritarian states

It is becoming apparent that poverty and a lack of education do not necessarily propel people to become terrorists, though support for quality public education could be one way of attacking root causes in some parts of the world. It is also evident that while collapsed states may not be the serious breeding ground alleged, they could allow terrorists to conduct economic activity and trade in illicit goods unhindered. Wars involving Muslim populations can also be hijacked and exacerbated by terrorist participation. These themes require further research and more creative policy responses.

The real breeding grounds, however, may be the strong, authoritarian Arab and Muslim states, such as Egypt, Algeria and Saudi Arabia. As Walter Laqueur noted in 1999, 'It is difficult to think of a single Middle Eastern country that has not experienced terrorism in recent times, except perhaps under the most severe dictatorships, such as Iran and Iraq, where the only kind of terrorism exercised is terrorism from above.'[21] The al-Qaeda terrorists who participated in the 11 September attacks, and those who have been arrested for other acts, come from these states. They oppose the authoritarian rule in their own countries, and view their leaders as corrupted by western influences. Moreover, the United States in particular, but also European governments, are viewed as hypocritical by al-Qaeda—and indeed others—because they espouse democracy and human rights worldwide, yet support elitist and non-democratic governments in these states.

If this is indeed a serious problem, and one of the root causes of anti-Western terrorism, then it is not clear what industrialised states can do. It is not realistic to assume that the US government should overthrow these governments; and anyway, al-Qaeda supporters would not wish a democratic, secular 'infidel' state to replace the current regimes. Western states could usefully promote education and employment opportunities, particularly for women, who have significant influence within the family, provided this is done with extreme caution, careful consideration of methodology and respect for the local culture, keeping in mind the lesson of the original *madrasas*. Support needs to be channelled as much as possible to indigenous civil society organisations, which have a better understanding of how to operate success- fully in difficult and often oppressive environments.

The US government claims that sixty countries are home to or are linked with al-Qaeda members, yet does not publish the list of those countries. It would be interesting to ascertain how many of them are industrialised, impoverished, authoritarian Muslim states, extremely fragile, or collapsed.

Fundamentalist charities

Financial support that promotes terrorism comes from a variety of sources, including the diaspora. For the first time, the counterterrorist coalition has attempted to crack down on some of this financing, the case of al-Barakaat in Somalia being one example. Also, we are only beginning to understand the impact of and role played by fundamentalist charities. A distinction needs to be made here between Islamic charities that provide critical health services and education in neglected rural areas, others that promote a more radical agenda, and some that do both. Indeed, one of the basic tenets of Islam is charity, and charity given in a way that does not humiliate the receiver. This discreet method of delivery, however, complicates matters, because some Islamic charities, along with several governments (such as that of Iran), espouse a more radical agenda through their aid. The United States has added nine Islamic charities to its list of organisations that fund terrorism, though many more operate with either tacit or overt government approval in countries such as Saudi Arabia.

In Somalia, the ICG report noted that the Gulf and Arab states, notably Saudi Arabia, Yemen, Qatar and the United Arab Emirates (UAE), 'provided funds to Islamic NGOs for humanitarian and social welfare programs throughout the Somali crisis. Libya has also had sporadic involvement in Somali affairs, mainly because of Gaddafi's personal familiarity with numer- ous Somali leaders since the 1970s and his apparent desire to recast his country as a regional power broker.'[22] These states have also provided the Somali TNG with grants, uniforms for police officers and other aid, as they did for the failed Benadir administration in 1998. While some of the aid has provided vital humanitarian and development assistance, other funds have been channelled into promoting a radical Islamic agenda.

Because Western international assistance to Somalia is not significant in scale, totalling $60 million in 2001, the influence of these Islamist movements has increased on the quiet. The ICG report noted that the fundamentalist movements inside Somalia 'owe their rapid growth since 1990 less to genuine popularity than access to substantial external funding'.[23] Islamic charitable assistance is rarely noted in UN appeals for Somalia, and few of these countries actively participate in the Somalia Aid Coordination Body, established to serve as the permanent coordination body for donors, UN agencies, NGOs and other international organisations. As Mark Bradbury noted,

It is clear, however, that significant relief and development assistance is being channelled to Somalia from Muslim countries . . . the success of Al Ittihaad has, in part, been based on investing in a social and economic welfare programme that the West will not fund. Rebuilding a Somali state will require vast resources. It is not at all clear that the West is prepared to provide these.[24]

Enhancing the dialogue with Islamic and Arab governments would open the way to better information sharing, but accessing financial information for extremist organisations will be difficult. The best option would be for OECD donors to provide sufficient aid so that these other organisations cannot gain a foothold; or, if they already have a presence, Western aid could be used to help build local capacity that in itself can counter radical influences.

Other responses

In developing appropriate responses to the terrorist threat, Western donors should involve diasporas as much as possible. The Somali diaspora is active, and provides much-needed financial support. Religious leaders throughout the Muslim world could also be engaged in community discussions, along with other civic leaders, over the role of Islam in society, and potentially could sway marginal supporters not to endorse radical interpretations that distort the Qur'an through calls to kill Americans, for example. The killing of innocent civilians is contrary to Islamic law, as is suicide, and these messages need to be disseminated by local leaders. The counterterrorist coalition must develop creative ways of working with these leaders.

Reducing humiliation will be a long-term project, but can be achieved through spreading the benefits of globalisation as widely as possible, especially by enhancing international assistance programmes, opening markets, and making greater diplomatic efforts to achieve peace in conflict zones, whether they be in eastern Congo or the Middle East. President Bush can demonstrate goodwill and positive intentions by fulfilling promises made in Mexico in March to increase the US foreign aid budget by 50 per cent from 2004, which would contribute to overcoming perceptions of inequity.

Beyond improving and increasing international assistance, reform must also take place at home. It is often argued that the hijackers became radicalised in European and American cities precisely because they felt marginalised and excluded, and experienced prejudice. Western states need to understand how this transpires, particularly with asylum-seekers.

The lesson of Afghanistan is that the international community, and the United States in particular, ignores unpleasant parts of the world at its peril.

The limited research undertaken thus far to discover the root causes of international terrorism has perhaps provoked more questions and challenges than answers. Sharpening the focus on root causes can lead to politically awkward situations and policy choices. Nevertheless, they need to be addressed if the counterterrorist campaign is to succeed.

When referring to al-Qaeda, one of the dangers often highlighted is the 'sleeper' element, whereby members can be activated in any part of the world on command, while at all other times they successfully blend in with the local environment. The challenge for the international counterterrorist coalition is how to ensure that these sleepers never wake up.

Notes

1 As opposed to 'old terrorism', where the motives are more tangible, and can often be resolved through negotiation, even if the struggles are seemingly intractable; see John Gearson's chapter in this volume on 'The Nature of Modern Terrorism'.
2 Steven Simon and Daniel Benjamin, 'The Terror', *Survival*, vol. 43, no. 4, Winter 2001, p. 12.
3 Interview given by M. Hubert Vedrine, minister of foreign affairs, to France-Inter's *Question Directe* programme (excerpts), Paris, 6 Feb. 2002.
4 Saad Eddin Ibrahim, who interviewed these men in prison, as cited in Simon and Benjamin, 'The Terror', p. 7.
5 Alan B. Krueger and Jitka Maleckova, 'Education, Poverty, Political Violence and Terrorism: Is There a Causal Connection?' Charles University, Working Papers, Research Program in Development Studies, Woodrow Wilson School, Princeton University, May 2002, pp. 1, 16.
6 Ibid., p. 14.
7 Ibid., p. 31.
8 See 'Washington Accuses Syria of Terror Role', BBC News, 1 April 2002, http://news.bbc.co.uk/hi/english/world/middle_east/newsid_1906000/1906018.stm; Bill Keller, 'Springtime for Saddam', *New York Times*, 6 April 2002, p. A15, as cited in Krueger and Maleckova, 'Education, Poverty, Political Violence and Terrorism'.
9 Nasra Hassan, 'An Arsenal of Believers', *New Yorker*, 19 Nov. 2001, pp. 36–41; Jessica Stern, 'Pakistan's Jihad Culture', *Foreign Affairs*, Nov./Dec. 2000.
10 Krueger and Maleckova, 'Education, Poverty, Political Violence and Terrorism', p. 2.
11 See Somalia submission on the UN web page: http://www.un.org/docs/sc/committees/1373/.
12 Stern, 'Pakistan's Jihad Culture'.
13 *Somalia: Countering Terrorism in a Failed State*, ICG Africa Report no. 45, 23 May 2002, p. 4.
14 For more information, see Karin von Hippel, 'The Proliferation of Collapsed States in the Post-Cold War World', in Michael Clarke, ed., *Brassey's Defence Yearbook 1997*, London, Brassey's, 1997.
15 'Banks-to-terror Conglomerate Faces US Wrath', *Daily Telegraph*, 28 Sept. 2001.
16 US District Court, Southern District of New York, indictment, p. 18, para. w, 16 June 1999.

17 As cited in *Somalia: Countering Terrorism in a Failed State*, p. 14.
18 Ken Menkhaus, 'Somalia: Next Up in the War on Terrorism?' *CSIS Africa Notes*, no. 6, Jan. 2002, p. 1.
19 Interview with the author at Central Command, Tampa, Florida, 4 March 2002.
20 See '11 September, Terrorist Violence and its Significance for Development Cooperation', Swiss Agency for Development and Cooperation SDC working paper, May 2002, p. 12.
21 Walter Laqueur, *The New Terrorism: Fanaticism and the Arms of Mass Destruction*, Oxford, Oxford University Press, 1999, p. 145.
22 *Somalia: Countering Terrorism in a Failed State*, p. 9.
23 Ibid., p. 13.
24 Mark Bradbury, *Somalia: The Aftermath of September 11th and the War on Terrorism*, Oxfam Great Britain report, Feb. 2002, p. 25.

The Coming War on Terrorism*

LAWRENCE FREEDMAN

AT the start of June 2002 President George W. Bush described for the graduates of the US Military Academy, West Point, how they would have to fight the developing war on terror. They would confront an enemy that, unlike those of the past, lacked 'great armies and great industrial capabilities'. Not pausing to query whether this might undermine the rationale for the great army of the United States, he continued:

The gravest danger to freedom lies at the perilous crossroads of radicalism and technology. When the spread of chemical and biological and nuclear weapons, along with ballistic missile technology—when that occurs, even weak states and small groups could attain a catastrophic power to strike great nations. Our enemies have declared this very intention, and have been caught seeking these terrible weapons. They want the capability to blackmail us, or to harm us, or to harm our friends—and we will oppose them with all our power.

Such enemies could be beyond deterrence or containment, the mainstay doctrines of the Cold War, because they have no 'nation or citizens to defend'. Then, indicating perhaps that nations might be involved, Bush complained that this threat could not be mitigated by putting 'faith in the word of tyrants, who solemnly sign non-proliferation treaties, and then systemically break them'. His conclusion: waiting was dangerous. 'We must take the battle to the enemy, disrupt his plans, and confront the worst threats before they emerge. In the world we have entered, the only path to safety is the path of action. And this nation will act.' The enemy, however would be difficult to find—'hidden in caves and growing in laboratories'. There were terror cells in sixty countries. Every instrument of power, including diplomacy, would be needed to deal with it. Nonetheless, the US military must therefore be 'ready to strike at a moment's notice in any dark corner of the world'.[1]

So, almost nine months after the most audacious and costly terrorist attack ever, which had led to the President first declaring his war on terror, and after what he considered to be a successful first stage of that war in Afghanistan, he set out the core themes for the war's future development. The most important feature of this speech as far as commentators were concerned was its pre-emptive quality, the readiness to go out and deal with enemies before they could do damage. This fitted in with the expectation, created by the State of the Union speech the previous January, that the United States was gearing up

---

* An early version of this chapter was delivered as the Ramsay Murray Lecture, Selwyn College, Cambridge, on 26 April 2001.

 Published by Blackwell Publishing, 108 Cowley Road, Oxford OX4 1JF, UK and 350 Main Street, Malden, MA 02148, USA

for an attack against Iraq, as a key member of the 'axis of evil', a drive stalled for the moment precisely because this was an enemy with a 'great army', or at least one large enough to cause the United States serious difficulty when defending its homeland.[2]

Another theme, which fitted in with a raft of alarming warnings from senior administration officials, was that the attacks on 11 September could well be repeated. Director of Homeland Security Tom Ridge observed that this was a matter of when and not if. Defense Secretary Donald Rumsfeld asserted that 'inevitably' terrorists would acquire and use chemical, biological or nuclear weapons. The timing of these warnings in late May 2002 could be seen as a response to revelations about the poor work of intelligence agencies, which had had evidence of the preparations being made by the suicidal hijackers but had failed to 'join the dots'. While ensuring that next time there could be no accusations of complacency, the imprecise and all-encompassing nature of these warnings meant that they were useless in terms of defensive planning.[3] It should be noted that it was not only in the United States that the assumption of 'when but not if' was made. Europeans assumed that their major cities and nationals abroad were as likely to be targeted as those of the United States.

The conclusion that in critical respects the United States could not yet concentrate solely on the offensive but was still on the defensive was confirmed by the major reorganisation of government proposed to improve the flow of critical intelligence and bring together a number of agencies under a new Office of Homeland Security. The other clear message was that the greatest danger lay in terrorists getting access to weapons of mass destruction. Yet the attacks of 11 September, as Bush himself had observed, had been mounted by a few dozen men, acting on behalf of a movement rather than a state, with low technology and at minimal cost. Al-Qaeda could claim some involvement in practically all conflicts, large and small, in which there was an Islamic element, which is why this war had such a wide geographical spread. Their tactics in all these conflicts derived from those long used in guerrilla warfare and its more terroristic variants. Nor was there real novelty in organising a number of simultaneous attacks and persuading the most accomplished militants to base their plans on suicide. All this came together to produce attacks that commanded attention because of their location and scale. There was evidence of an interest in chemical or biological weapons, and a reasonable assumption that if these weapons were acquired they would be used, but there was no reason to suppose that this was a high-probability threat. Even when a scare was raised over a suspected plot to explode a radiation bomb, something which had clearly interested al-Qaeda from 1993,[4] reports suggested that this was at an elementary stage and that, even if some device were constructed, the effects would be modest, becoming severe only if panic ensued. The management of the anthrax attacks that followed 11 September, probably from an indigenous US source, indicates that when anxiety levels have been raised it can become even more difficult for governments to manage effectively the communication of risk. The responses to the spate of warnings in May and June 2002 suggested that if, once anxiety levels have been raised, little happens, then the credibility of warnings declines.

Although Iraq may have tested a radiological device at some time, reportedly with poor results, like the other states which constituted the 'axis of evil' it had not, as far as could be ascertained, played any direct role in the 11 September attacks. Yet Iraq, undoubtedly guilty of developing the most noxious technologies, seemed to have become the target for the coming stage of the war on terror. This could be justified only on a pre-emptive basis: not because the 'perilous crossroads of radicalism and techno-logy' had been reached, but because we dare not let it be reached. Al-Qaeda's diffuse, non-state radicalism and Iraq's state-generated technology were on separate paths. They did not have to meet for either to cause trouble, but it was their potential combination that was deemed to be most frightening.

The two were not natural allies, despite their shared loathing of the United States and Israel, with the secular/religious divide of considerable import-ance. Iraq, as a country, could expect to enjoy international rehabilitation once Saddam Hussein was no longer in power. Al-Qaeda has no *raison d'être* other than denying unbelievers and apostates any influence in the affairs of the Islamic world and working towards the creation of a series of mighty theocratic states. Since the fall of the Taleban in Afghanistan, the only regime Osama bin Laden considered truly Islamic, it is bound to follow a subversive, radical route to power, as part of a network of like-minded but more nationally based groups. In this it is not unlike the leftist groups of the 1970s, which were also sustained through a loose, ideologically based and at times truly global network.

It would, therefore, have been possible to specify the enemy in terms of its ideology and objectives. Instead the enemy was defined in terms of terrorism rather than just one group of terrorists. If that is the case, then it is the tactic rather than the objective that is most at fault, and the purpose of the current war would be to establish a new anti-terrorist norm in international politics. Though terrorism covers a wide range of activities adopted by many diverse actors, on this view all these activities would be judged illegitimate and deserving of special attention by an international anti-terrorist coalition. We can note, for example, that of the 346 international terrorist attacks in 2001 (other than those of 11 September) as counted by the US State Department, 178 were bombings against a multinational oil pipeline in Colombia—constituting 51 per cent of the year's total number of attacks.[5] Once it becomes necessary to distinguish between forms of terror, on the grounds that some acts are more iniquitous than others, by what criteria should they be evaluated? This chapter attempts to establish a framework for thinking about the future of the war on terror.

Humanitarian intervention

Prior to 11 September 2001, it seemed to be the case that whereas the security problems of the past could be blamed on strong states which wished to get stronger through conquest and hegemony, the sources of most contemporary problems were weak states, unable to manage their own affairs and thus descending into the old apocalyptic scourges of persecution, war, famine and disease. Even famine and disease, on close inspection, often turned out to be the result of 'political' as much as 'natural' disasters. To mitigate the effects of these disasters and to eliminate their causes would require a considerable effort. It meant acting to stop large-scale abuses of human or minority rights by repressive states, calm civil wars or other forms of intercommunal violence, and help reconstruct shattered societies.

This could be presented as a matter of obligation as well as interest. If these situations are left to fester and intensify, the scourges not only rebuke the international conscience but also spread and begin to impinge directly on our own societies. The instability they generate is rarely localised or readily contained, with refugees, drugs, small arms, every imaginable form of criminal activity and also terrorism soon flowing to the rest of the world. This developing agenda posed a direct challenge to the traditional assumptions of international affairs, and in particular the privileged position of the state. The doctrine of non-interference in internal affairs was undermined by the evident problems many new states had in managing their internal affairs and the steady elevation of minority and human rights above state rights.

At the same time, the strong incentives to deal with these political disasters have always been balanced by the high costs and military risks of intervention, and the lack of means of addressing their root causes, short of taking over these weak states in a quasi-imperial role. The multiplication of cases meant that there was little to be done but to pick and choose about where and how to intervene, and a certain amount of effort has gone into setting tests for where available resources might best be applied. Prime Minister Tony Blair notably set out in Chicago in 1999, at the height of the war in Kosovo, five tests, relating to confidence in the analysis, exhaustion of diplomatic efforts, availability of military options, a readiness for the long haul and some connection with national interests.[6]

By and large, the leading European countries had the will to intervene in these conflicts, but only limited means with which to do so. The Americans were far better endowed with means, but lacked the will. Even before the second Bush presidency, the ascendant view in the United States was that only the most extreme cases should be addressed, and then with great caution.[7] Western countries could do little to solve such deep-seated social cleavages and economic mismanagement, and to the extent that they tried they probably made things worse. The fear was of a succession of 'quagmires', so that even before entrance into distant quarrels was contemplated, an 'exit strategy' had to be designed. The American preference, in line with the classical realist preoccupation with power balances, and reinforced by the sensitivity of its role as the lone superpower, was to focus foreign policy on the challenges to Western hegemony that might be posed by strong states. This meant not just rising great powers, such as China (very much the preoccupation of the first months of the Bush term), but those that were acquiring an artificial strength, notably by acquiring weapons of mass destruction. In the first months of the Bush administration these were already identified as the rogue states of Iraq, Iran and North Korea.

Is this a war?

Both sides to this debate viewed the attacks of 11 September as confirming the validity of their approaches. Liberal internationalists could claim that the limits of classical realism had been brutally demonstrated. Out of Afghanistan, one of the most miserable, factionalised and conflict-prone of third world countries, serially abused by neighbours and outsiders alike, came a precision attack directed against the greatest symbols of American economic and military power, the World Trade Center and the Pentagon. To deal with this challenge the United States had to become a player in Afghan politics, exactly the sort of place the Pentagon planners expected to be able to disregard. Lesson one: great powers ignored the poor and the wretched at their peril. No country can be dismissed as irrelevant to security. Indeed, the more forbidding and the more chaotic the society, the more (it seemed) it is able to provide safe havens for terrorists as well as criminals. Lesson two: it is vital to work closely with other states—in this case, those that shared borders with Afghanistan or appeared also to have been infected by al-Qaeda or could offer specialist intelligence or military resources in support.

Yet could liberal internationalism reassert itself on the basis of a 'war on terrorism'? The very language focused on the role of force and violence in political affairs. War is the ultimate realist experience. It sharpens divisions and ensures that multilateralism is at best only partial, in the form of an alliance. Beyond the alliance is the enemy. The purpose of war is to eliminate the enemy, or at least to render it incapable of exercising its malign influence. The possibility of attempting to accommodate its political agenda so that it no longer needs to be deemed hostile has been precluded. Such accommodation can easily be represented as 'appeasement', thereby encouraging rather than buying off threatening behaviour. Other significant or potentially significant actors may be reluctant to accept a role as allies; but once war has been declared, neutrality invites charges of appeasement and consorting with the enemy. At war, the United States expects its allies to be 'with us or against us' but nowhere in between.[8]

Because of the implications of such thinking, some have queried whether it is useful to think of the current conflict as a war at all. A number of arguments have been made here. First, redefining obnoxious criminal acts as warlike dignifies them and gives the perpetrators an unnecessarily heroic status.

Second, instead of objectives being framed in terms of law enforcement and the successful prosecution of the perpetrators, they are framed in terms of military victory.[9] Third, in a war the gloves are off and governments can do things that they cannot do when problems are described in more civilian terms, for example in finding ways to bypass the civil rights of anyone, including foreign nationals, suspected of being implicated in terrorism. This leads in exactly the opposite direction to a judicial approach. Fourth and finally, power within government shifts to the military and the Pentagon civilians, leading to a harsh foreign policy with scant scope for diplomatic initiatives, let alone attention to the conditions which breed terrorism.

There is something to all these arguments; but, after an attack on such a scale, mounted by a political entity based in a distant country, war was not a matter of choice but a strategic imperative. It was Osama bin Laden who had declared war, some years earlier; he had just not been taken seriously until he reached new levels of terrorist achievement. When the United States suffered a surprise attack, with severe casualties, there was no holding back. This was more than just a large crime or an affront to common decency. The US government could also point to the limits of an alternative approach. It had dealt with the 1993 attack on the World Trade Center through the courts, but this successful prosecution had palpably failed to stop a second attack. In 2001 it was hard to take seriously calls for hard evidence before any action was taken when the whole operation stank of al-Qaeda, or to begin to imagine how a broad-based militant movement, with many activist cells dispersed around the globe, could be put in the dock. In the event an attempt was made, although without great conviction, to ask the Taleban regime in Afghanistan to hand over the prime suspect. This was rebuffed in a disingenuous manner. In practice the Taleban and al-Qaeda had fused over the previous few years. It was impossible to deal with the terrorists without first overthrowing the regime.

By invoking Article 5 of the Atlantic Charter—that an attack on one should be considered an attack on all—the established allies of the United States signalled their understanding of this position. There was a general wish to show solidarity with the United States, and certainly a sense that at least it was prudent to do so. 'We are all Americans,' declared Le Monde, in a famous and unlikely headline of 12 September. Many governments were all too aware of how they might become victims of similar attacks, possibly also from al-Qaeda. Yet through these declarations of sympathy and sorrow for the Americans, made by many people of many countries, often despite themselves, there ran an undercurrent that the United States must not jeopardise this solidarity by moving too quickly or ruthlessly—'lashing out' was the phrase used. While the Americans did not rush to action, the declaration of war sent a signal that there was no intention of playing the victim.

A more substantial criticism was that it was a mistake to declare war on a tactic.[10] There is a tendency to declare war on problems, as a means of focusing attention and mobilising resources—hence the war on drugs, or cancer, or poverty. The war on terrorism was never quite understood in those terms, because the prominence of intelligent opponents capable of fighting back provides an essential feature of any war. Nor is it unusual for wars conducted against specific political entities to be assigned much wider and grander objectives—encouraging the hope that victory will ensure that some basic values will have been upheld. Positively, wars are fought for democracy, liberation, civilisation (at one point a contender in this case), and negatively they are fought against aggression, colonialism and now terrorism.

Defining terror

If declaring a war against terrorism is comparable to, say, a war against aggression, then that might mean not so much constant conflict as that a marker is in place. When the norm is violated, as was the norm of aggression when Iraq invaded Kuwait in August 1990, then there would be an expectation of collective action. We shall return to this issue of establishing an anti-terrorist norm later, but for the moment we can note one important difference. Cases of pure aggression, when one state invades another, are extremely rare, and becoming more rare. Terrorism, on the other hand, in some shape or form, is ubiquitous, because it can refer to small acts of violence as well as the catastrophic sort. It is one thing to fight al-Qaeda as a particularly noxious form of terrorism. It is another then to feel obliged to take on all forms of terrorism, especially given the notorious problem of deciding what is to be included in this category.

The question of how to define terrorism has become familiar to the point of tedium. The term is both descriptive and pejorative, hence the regular observation about how terrorists from one perspective are freedom fighters from another. Because 'terrorist' is such a natural insult it is used extremely loosely, covering all types of violent activity, or even just potentially violent activity. Its use is certainly not confined to groups who mainly target civilians. Those who concentrate on members of the security services or known agents of the state are regularly denounced for their terrorism. Even groups who have adopted unambiguously terrorist strategies can barely resist resorting to the abusive use themselves, as when governments are castigated as terrorists for repressive measures or for refusing to bow to secessionist movements or for not redressing economic or political inequities.

Nor is terrorism confined to those with overtly political agendas. It can be applied by those who expect their actions to be eloquent in themselves, without any accompanying manifesto or demands. Their motives may not be straightforward but rather intensely personal, perhaps reflecting a desire for vengeance on a cruel world, the peculiar attractions of a clandestine life, social alienation, the fantasies of millennial movements or the machinations of organised crime. Methods suitable for sniping at soldiers and bombing government buildings can serve racketeers (as impoverished 'freedom fighters' have often discovered).

A final problem is that much terrorist activity is barely terrifying while most regular combat is. Some individuals or groups may aspire to cause panic and chaos but they simply fail to generate enough notice or interest. To the extent that the IRA campaign in mainland Britain succeeded, it was because they attacked economic targets. Obviously they were responsible for much loss of life, and risked much more, so this should not be played down; yet for most of us living through this campaign it became another hazard of modern life, along with strikes on the railways, extremes of weather and flu epidemics, with its own familiar routines of alerts and evacuations. It was known that the IRA, and on occasion other groups, would mount 'spectaculars', but these events were so unexpected and infrequent that there were few adjustments to normal life that could be made to accommodate them, other than to tolerate the inconveniences of bag searches at department stores and intrusive airport security.

When terrorism is used effectively as a strategy it serves as a coercive means of obtaining political effects by using threats of violence against civil society. It is only when occasional outrages turn into sustained campaigns, and a recognisable pattern of activity emerges, that the effects on public life become palpable. This is evident in Israel as unnecessary trips to city centres are avoided, tourism drops off, uniformed men with guns suddenly appear at street corners and, on occasion, political initiatives are set in motion in order to isolate the terrorists or take the edge off their hostility. So, for the coercion to work, an irresistible and ruthless reputation must be generated. Occasional outrages do not have the same political effects. Without a substantial measure of support in the community on whose behalf it is perpetrated, a campaign may well succumb to improved security and weariness. Even then, the track record of terrorist methods serving the ambitious political goals with which they are usually associated is poor.

So while it may be the case that terrorism is a strategy adopted by the desperate and the marginalised to fight against the strong, it is not necessarily a good strategy. Alternatives are to appease, persuade, appeal to a better nature, embarrass or frustrate, as well as cause havoc and economic dislocation through non-violent action. A sophisticated strategy, especially in these days of complex interdependence and instant communications, will be as mindful of the effects of measures and countermeasures on the governments of allies and spectators, and the mood within international organisations, as of those on the notional 'enemy'.

What does this mean for attempts to develop criteria to indicate when a particular group should become a target of the 'war on terrorism'? President Bush initially attempted to focus on 'international' terrorism, or 'terrorism with a global reach', and this has the advantage of addressing those groups that wish to use terrorism to internationalise otherwise localised conflicts by taking advantage of modern forms of transportation and communication. Yet Bush had to walk back from the implication that terrorism mattered only when the United States was vulnerable. In addition, it was apparent that not all of those associated with al-Qaeda were interested in mounting attacks on the other side of the world; many, on the contrary, were content to engage in geographically restricted campaigns. This has led the Americans to be drawn into quite specific campaigns in the Yemen, Philippines and Georgia.

If one objective of the current campaign is to establish a new norm of international politics, to the effect that terrorist methods are illegitimate in all circumstances, then almost any cause might be invalidated by their adoption. If this is the way we want to move, then some way has to be found of limiting the concept and the imperatives for action. This is to some extent what has been going on with the attempt to create a norm of humanitarian intervention during the 1990s. Indeed, there are important links between the acts which prompt humanitarian intervention and those that prompt a war on terrorism. In both cases the victims are most likely to be defenceless civilians. The moral objection lies in the use of violent means against non-combatants for political objectives. In both cases taking action will probably mean ignoring inhibitions against interfering in the internal affairs of other states.

In another sense, however, there is an important difference. Vicious domestic persecution or ethnic cleansing are weapons used by the strong against the weak, so that the weak can find redress only if those who are attacking them are in turn attacked by even stronger powers, which is why this becomes a test for a contemporary form of internationalism. Victim status is becoming a prized commodity in international politics, because it is a means by which a group with no capacity of its own can acquire powerful external allies.

Terrorism, by contrast, is a weapon habitually used by the weak against the strong. It is a form of response that does not rely on taking on the enemy at its strongest point but instead looks for vulnerabilities in its social structure. So, while the victims of ethnic cleansing and other human rights abuses have by definition already been marginalised, the victims of terrorism are more likely to be found in the cities of the strong. This is why it is more likely to prompt a response by the strong, and why a war to ease humanitarian distress may well be against an established regime yet a war against terrorism may well be in its support.

I observed earlier that tests have had to be developed as to when humanitarian intervention is warranted, and they might also serve as a starting point for consideration of how to take forward a war on terrorism. I am suggesting that there is a shared norm that organised violence should not be used against civilians. There is much to be said for seeking to establish such a general norm, given that over the past century we moved from a situation where 90 per cent of the casualties of war were combatants to one where 90 per cent are civilians. It is also the case that the trend in Western military thinking is to emphasise capabilities to deal with enemy armed forces, and to stress the importance of restraint in situations where innocent civilians may get harmed. Leaving aside the fact that the strong would always prefer to confine conflict to open battle between regular forces, there are still

difficulties in upholding this approach, even allowing for the greater precision of modern military technology. The distinction between hurting civilians
by aiming for them and hurting them through aiming for something else, and
then missing, which invariably happens in air campaigns, is not always
appreciated, and there are also many dual-purpose targets, connected with
energy supplies and communications, that can cause harm to the civilian and
military sectors at the same time. In addition, terrorists hide within civil
society as well as targeting it, and invite attacks upon civilians so as to
radicalise the victims. So further tests are still needed. What might these be?
Some guidance might be found by following Blair's Chicago criteria for
humanitarian intervention.

On this basis, the first test suggests that if battle is to be joined against a
particular group then there must be confidence that the violence it employs is
truly illegitimate, so that we have not simply been beguiled by an authoritarian regime that is rhetorically accomplished. Will a cry of terrorism be
used as a cry of communism was in the past by inadequate and repressive
governments to suppress any inconvenient dissent? Second, we will want to
know if opportunities for political dialogue have been rejected. If the cause is
serious enough, and has a head of steam behind it, then at the very least
alternative and credible means of political resolution must be explored. Third,
are there useful forms of forceful action available that will not simply make
things worse, by generating more recruits for the terrorists and gaining them
political sympathy?

Fourth, there will also be a need to hang in for the long term, if for no
other reason than that terrorism, by its nature, rarely succumbs to a decisive
battle. These are not battles fought between organised armies whose troops
are sufficiently disciplined that they can be ordered to surrender or
sufficiently unmotivated that they may simply skulk home after a defeat.
Terrorist campaigns tend to depend on small numbers of highly motivated
people operating in cells. Demotivation takes time as cells are captured or
killed. The campaign is most likely to end by petering out. Thus the IRA has
agreed to a ceasefire and political negotiations, and is now putting arms
beyond use, but some of its members still do not want a ceasefire. Only over
time can they be neutralised. Arguably, this is what has happened in
Afghanistan. American, British and other Western troops have been engaged
in large-scale sweeps along the border with Pakistan to finish off al-Qaeda,
but they have found little. On the other hand, remaining al-Qaeda and
Taleban activists have not deemed it prudent to attempt any serious actions
of their own.

With regard to humanitarian intervention Blair's final test, that of relevance
to national interests, was to some extent always easy to pass because in
another part of his speech he had argued how national and international
interests could coincide. More realistically, the test remains significant
because the campaigns of terror that bother us most are apt to be those that
are directed against our own societies, or those of our closest allies and

partners, or those that threaten to upset a country which is important to us in economic, security or resource terms.

When we apply these tests we soon find that the easiest cases are those in which violence is used against the stable liberal democracies of the West, which contain ample non-violent mechanisms through which to promote causes and redress grievances. Not only does the violence lack legitimacy, but it is also likely to be manageable without calling upon the assistance of an international coalition, except in such areas as intelligence, extradition and frustrating fundraising (where the assistance has not always been forth-coming). By and large this is how the 'red' activists of the 1970s and 1980s, or the more durable IRA and ETA, were handled. These groups were never able wholly to destabilise the political and social structures they were attacking, even though they could on occasion inflict some harsh blows.

The hardest cases are those in which activities that might be warranted by resistance to oppression or self-defence have become so unacceptable that they move beyond justification. It is therefore not surprising to find that contemporary conflicts can involve a sort of competitive victimology, whereby the strong claim to be victims of terrorism, while the weak claim to be victims of inhuman persecution. Thus in early 1998 the United States was prepared to describe the Kosovo Liberation Army as terroristic,[11] yet not much more than a year later it was in effect in alliance with them as it responded with the rest of NATO to the disproportionate campaign waged against the Kosovan people by Serbia in the name of rooting out the KLA terrorists. In the two most testing international issues of the first half of 2002, the issue of whether the resort to terror deprives a cause of its legitimacy has been central. Israelis point to a society traumatised by suicide bombings, while the Palestinians point to the daily humiliations and harsh measures taken by the Israelis in the West Bank, territory that they are not supposed to occupy. Indians point to outrages perpetrated by Islamic militants, including an attack on their parliament, while Pakistanis point to the rigidity of the Indian hold on the disputed Kashmir.

The similarities do not stop there, and indicate the wider difficulties of the war on terrorism. Certainly the ascendance of the anti-terrorist norm has helped the Israelis and Indians gain sympathy from the United States, and to a lesser extent from its allies. Yet the extent to which the leaders of the Palestinians and Pakistanis, Yasser Arafat and General Musharraf respect-ively, could be held responsible for all acts of militancy became itself a matter of dispute. These leaders had to balance the risks to their regimes from hard-liners if they appeared to sell out a sacred cause with the risks of losing vital international support if they failed to crack down on terrorists. Even then, for the United States a tough stance against the Palestinians undermined the wider Middle Eastern backing required if the influence of extremists was to be weakened and Iraq challenged, while in the first stage of the war on terror Musharraf had played a central role by disassociating Pakistan from the Taleban in Afghanistan and allowing the United States to use his country's facilities. In his West Point speech Bush spoke of the importance of moral purpose. 'There can be no neutrality', he insisted, 'between justice and cruelty, between the innocent and the guilty. We are in a conflict between good and evil, and America will call evil by its name.' Yet conflicts involve power as well as morality, and so while Bush's assertion that 'targeting innocent civilians for murder is always and everywhere wrong' stresses the normative element, the power element still requires compromises and occasional concessions to regimes whose own moral record is, to say the least, imperfect.

The war on terrorism: past and future

While it is useful, then, to have some tests because they might at some point be needed to distinguish deserving from not so deserving cases, it is important not to lose sight of the wider political context in which they will have to be applied. Terrorism is a tactic that often comes naturally to radical political movements. It is most likely to be defeated when these movements have run their course and begun to fade away through constant rebuffs and frustration. It is arguable that on this basis two past wars on terrorism have already been largely won since the phenomenon reasserted itself as a direct threat to Western societies (rather than their colonial administrations) in the late 1960s.

At that time the ideological shift to the left in the youth movements of the West, prompted largely by the war in Vietnam, combined with a new assertiveness by a variety of deprived racial and other minority groups. The theorists of the anti-globalisation movement, in many ways the ideological inheritors of the anti-capitalist left, do not argue in favour of a violent insurrection, and to the extent that these movements have become associated with violence it is because of the rioting that, until 11 September, appeared to be the natural accompaniment to any international summit.

A more difficult question concerns secular Arab terrorism, linked to the Palestinian cause. Following the 1967 war and the Israeli occupation of the West Bank, the Palestine Liberation Organisation was unable to mount much of a guerrilla campaign. Twenty years passed before the first *intifada*, and that was largely a spontaneous uprising rather than an organised campaign. Nor were neighbouring states anxious to allow the PLO to use their territory as a base for mounting operations against the Israelis, as they were the ones that suffered retaliation. After almost unseating King Hussein in Jordan in 1970, before he got the upper hand, the PLO moved into Lebanon, where it proceeded to unsettle the country's delicate political balance, an event from which Lebanon has yet to recover fully. Even before then, Palestinian groups and their supporters had attempted to attack Israelis wherever they could be found, a campaign of which the Munich Olympic Games massacre of 1972 was the most conspicuous example. As Israeli security was generally tight, internationalising the conflict generally meant hijacking aircraft and making a nuisance. The result was generally to leave the PLO outlawed and discredited.

Israel's offensive into Lebanon in 1982, leading to the massacres and the Sabra and Chatila refugee camps, and the radicalisation of the country, raised the temperature further, with suicide bombers much in evidence, directed against the US presence in Beirut. In addition, the old radicals, Syria and Libya, still toyed with terrorism, partly as revenge for real and imagined slights against themselves as much as the Palestinians. In June 1985 flight TWA 847, carrying 153 passengers and crew, largely American, was seized by two Hizbollah extremists taking off from Athens en route to Rome. After a tortuous journey, during which some hostages were released and one was murdered, the aircraft ended up in Beirut. The hostages were removed into the city and then bargaining began, effectively for prisoners held by Israel who were at any rate due for release. Interviews were regularly given to the media.

It was at this point that the United States almost declared war on terrorism. Caspar Weinberger, then the US Secretary of Defense, remarked that 'it is a war and it is the beginning of a war.' When the crisis was effectively resolved, President Reagan made a nationwide broadcast, demonstrating to would-be hijackers the influence this tactic could bring. This was followed by the seizure of the US cruise ship *Achille Lauro*, and the killing of an invalid American. When the hijackers managed to get a deal to fly to Egypt, the Americans intercepted the aircraft and forced it to land in Italy, much to the dismay of the Italian government. Reagan went on TV with a message to terrorists: 'You can run but you can't hide.'[12] Sounds familiar?

By now the United States was focused on Libya as the most voluble pro-terrorist state. Secretary of State George Shultz said: 'My opinion is that we need to raise the cost to those who perpetrate terrorist acts . . . so they will have to think more carefully about it.' After an attack on a Berlin nightclub that left a US soldier dead, the United States bombed Tripoli. This move was immensely popular and judged a success, in that little was heard from Colonel Qadhafi for some time thereafter; but it was also followed by the bringing down of a transatlantic flight, Pan Am 103, over the Scottish town of Lockerbie in 1988, killing 259 passengers and 11 local people, as well as by arms shipments to the IRA. Even so, the diplomatic isolation of Libya as Britain and the United States demonstrated its complicity in Lockerbie led to Qadhafi working hard to demonstrate that his regime had changed its ways. Whatever Israel may have thought, even Arafat managed to present himself as a suitable interlocutor in the Middle East peace process by demonstrating that the PLO had put terrorism behind it. Moreover, in relation to its past lists of state sponsors of terrorism, by early 2002 the United States was prepared to acknowledge that, in addition to Libya, Sudan also understood the need to get out of the terrorism business. Syria was deemed to be making some limited moves in the right direction, and in fact has been reported to have made some significant contributions to the US intelligence effort;

nevertheless, as with Iran, the problem was not so much a readiness to support international terrorism as support for radical groups apt to attack Israel, such as Hizbollah and Hamas. So, while Israeli society has been under a sustained terrorist bombardment, neither the PLO nor secular radical Arab states now see terrorism as a sensible way of internationalising the conflict. This is more likely to be achieved by drawing attention to the illegitimacy of Israel's position in the West Bank and Gaza, leaving the question for Palestinian strategists as to whether this is put at risk by the ferocity of the suicide bomber campaign against Israeli civilians. Saddam Hussein is, of course, another product of 1960s secular Arab radicalism, and he tries to use the Palestinian campaign to boost his standing (including by giving subventions to the families of suicide bombers); yet he got into conflict with the West only because of some old-fashioned aggression against another Arab state, Kuwait, and thereafter the issue became the survival of the regime and the elimination of its capacity to inflict mass destruction rather than any ideological argument.

The current campaign concerns a different ideological tradition, originating in but not confined to the Middle East. It is further confused by representing one strand of Islamic militancy, distinct, for example, from the Iranian version which first made an international impact and got into arguments with the United States in the late 1970s. This strand was, if anything, in a form of alliance with the United States during the 1980s during the campaign to undermine the Russian position in Afghanistan. The fight against the Soviets was the training ground for committed young Arabs, such as Osama bin Laden, and the source of their Islamic zealotry. Its political importance initially seemed to rest more in the challenge posed to regimes in Muslim countries that were deemed to be failing in their promotion of Islamic law. It was certainly anti-Israel but elsewhere, for example in the Balkans, if anything it was again working with the United States to back the Muslim cause. Its anti-American character derived first from abhorrence of the way of life the United States represented and more particularly from objections to the strong American presence in Saudi Arabia, seen as a desecration of Islam's holiest places, after the Iraqi invasion of Kuwait. Its future depends on a series of ideological and political battles being fought within Muslim countries, as well as the evolution of the conflicts that animate it—in Central Asia as well as the Middle East.

In its war against the United States, this strand of Islamic militancy may not see many options other than terrorism. Since the end of the Cold War the United States has been confident of defeating all-comers in regular war, and now looks forward to spending as much as the rest of the world combined on its armed forces. Other than Saddam Hussein, who in 1991 allowed himself to be misled about the quality and combat proficiency of American forces, opponents have generally preferred to avoid open battle with the United States. Instead they have adopted guerrilla tactics. The objective in all cases has been to persuade the United States to take itself out of a particular fight, and this has generally been successful. This was the purpose of communist tactics in Vietnam. The same tactics can also be said to have worked in Beirut in October 1983, when a suicide bomber drove a truck into the US marine barracks, and then a decade later in Somalia when US Rangers were caught and eighteen were killed. In both cases these incidents were followed by US withdrawal.

What conclusions might be drawn from this? The United States has demonstrated in the past that when it comes to wars of choice it is vulnerable to guerrilla tactics, elements of which may be characterised as terrorism. These have the effect of making casualties suffered disproportionate to the stakes involved. The mistake made by al-Qaeda, therefore, was to go for a spectacular attack that turned a war of choice into a war of necessity, so that instead of being encouraged to leave the Middle East and Central Asia, as would have been hoped, the United States became drawn into those regions more deeply than before. This was the opposite of what had been intended.

This leaves open the question, which clearly perturbs the Bush administration, as to whether 11 September has set new standards for terrorists, obliging all those who follow to raise their game, which means looking at chemical, biological and radiological weapons. This is the spectre of the combination of radicalism with technology, as described by President Bush, with which this chapter opened. While it is the case that the Bush administration had Saddam Hussein in its sights before 11 September, the attacks led to the case that the logical next step in any escalation would be the ultimate in superterrorism, and Iraq was the most likely source of the wherewithal for such an attack. It is simply too dangerous, runs the argument, to wait until that happens; the self-defence has to be anticipatory. Dealing with this risk is also conceptually undemanding, even if militarily possibly extremely demanding. The demands of regime change in Iraq are substantial, but in its military aspects at least this is a problem of a type that the United States understands. While the solution may be expensive and complex, and risk great loss of life, taking on Iraqi armed forces will involve operations the US knows how to conduct and with which, unlike guerrilla warfare, it is comfortable.

There is, however, another possibility, and that is that the lesson to be learned from the fate of al-Qaeda is not to raise the level of violence excessively high, so as to create a retaliatory imperative for the victims, but to keep it focused and carefully targeted, for example on American (and other Western) personnel and assets in places where they might be convinced that they are not at all welcome and would rather not stick around. Although this has yet to happen, a similar conclusion might be drawn by Palestinian militants (and should have been drawn from the Lebanon) that it is sustained guerrilla operations against exposed positions, rather than city-centre spectaculars, that eat away at public resolve to sustain these positions.

This is not to deny that these groups would be delighted to acquire weapons of mass effect, or that the retributive urges could overcome strategic sophistication when contemplating their use, or that there are other grounds for fearing the success of Iraqi effort to acquire such weapons. Rather, it is to warn that that the war on terrorism may well continue to take the United States into the sort of operation it dislikes, without an enemy in the field to be annihilated or obliged to surrender, into remote and inhospitable areas where struggles for local political power provide radical groups with the opportunity to define their identifies and refine their tactics. This brings us back to the parallels between the debate on humanitarian intervention as it developed during the 1990s, and that currently raised by the war on terrorism, including the attempt, in the midst of such chaos and political upheaval, to divert violence away from civilians. I have pointed to the differences, in the sense that one is about protecting the weak from the strong while the other, potentially, involves protecting the strong from the weak. In both cases we keep on being drawn back into the complex affairs of unstable regions and mismanaged states, where are to be found deep social and political cleavages and enduring conflicts that demand intensive diplomatic attention. In the end the central issue remains the same: whether to get involved in difficult and demanding parts of the world, accepting the drain on our resources, our energy and our political skills, on the firm understanding that if we do not these are not only places where people get viciously angry with each other but also provide havens and inspiration for those who are angry with us.

Notes

1 Remarks by the President at the 2002 Graduation Exercise of the United States Military Academy, West Point, New York, 1 June 2002, at http://usinfo.state.gov/topical/pol/terror/02060201.htm.

2 President Bush's State of the Union Address, 29 January 2002, at http://usinfo.state.gov/topical/pol/terror/02012914.htm. On the difficulties faced by US military planners, see William Arkin, 'US Military; Planning an Iraqi War but Not an Outcome', *Los Angeles Times*, 5 May 2002.

3 Ivo Daalder and Michael O'Hanlon, 'Let's Cool Those Terrorism Alerts', *Newsday*, 23 March 2002.

4 A. Oppenheimer, 'Weapons of Mass Destruction: Radiological Devices', *Jane's Terrorism and Security Monitor*, May 2002. This notes that as early as 1993 bin Laden operatives tried and failed to buy enriched uranium, and in recent times appear to have been sold some useless material in the belief that it was weapons-grade.

5 The number was down from 2,000 when 426 had been counted. US State Department, Counterterrorism Office, *Patterns of Global Terrorism 2001*, May 2002, at http://www.state.gov/s/ct/rls/pgtrpt/2001.

6 *The Doctrine of International Community*, 22 April 1999, at http://www.number-10/public/info/index.html.

7 See e.g. the pre-election article by Bush's National Security Advisor, Condoleeza Rice, 'Promoting the National Interest', *Foreign Affairs*, vol. 79, no. 1, Jan.–Feb. 2000.

8 Address by the President to a Joint Session of Congress and the American People, 20 Sept. 2001: 'Every nation, in every region, now has a decision to make. Either

you are with us, or you are with the terrorists': http://usinfo.state.gov/topical/pol/terror/01092051.htm.

9 Michael Howard, 'What's in a Name? How to Fight Terrorism', *Foreign Affairs*, vol. 81, Jan.–Feb. 2002.
10 I took this line in Lawrence Freedman, 'The Third World War?', *Survival*, vol. 43, no. 4, Winter 2001.
11 Richard Caplan, 'International Diplomacy and the Crisis in Kosovo', *International Affairs*, vol. 74, no. 4, Oct. 1998, pp. 753–4.
12 Jeffrey D. Simon, *The Terrorist Trap*, Bloomington, Indiana University Press, 2001.

Finance Warfare as a Response to International Terrorism

MARTIN S. NAVIAS

FINANCE warfare emerged as a major instrument of anti-terrorist strategic operations almost immediately following the 11 September attacks in the United States. It drew upon legislative, regulatory and policing instruments already in place, though these had long been geared primarily to financial battles little connected with terrorist funding. The refinement and development of this stratagem as a means of combating international terror, its implementation and global integration, involve and continue to demand enormous efforts by political, financial and policing authorities.

To be sure, attacks upon an enemy's economic infrastructure and assets have always been elements of grand strategy. Economic targeting is a form of indirect approach whose object is to undermine the opposition's capacity for conducting operations by assaulting one of the key pillars of fighting power and political will. Finance warfare as it has emerged in the context of counterterrorist operations after 11 September is a form of economic warfare whose context is the global financial markets and whose aim is to constrain the enemy's capability both to generate funds and to shift monies across borders for the purposes of supporting and sustaining international operations. The institutions mobilised in this counterterrorist campaign are those very organisations that facilitate and underpin the global markets themselves. The legislative and regulatory means are the means deployed to counter non-political criminal money-laundering activities. Thus finance warfare has achieved a new salience since 11 September, but its strategic pedigree and the tools of its implementation are to be traced back prior to that infamous date.

The early financial emphasis of the broader counterterrorist campaign derived from the fact that the money trail leading from the hijackers not only helped establish their political origins but also served to expose all too clearly the vulnerabilities of the international banking system to terrorist fund generation, money laundering and general financial logistics. The 11 September atrocities were revealed to have been made possible by a sophisticated financial operation, one that relied at least partially on correspondent banking and alternative remittance systems, backed up by a diffuse network of legal and illicit associations consisting of an amalgam of private organisations, corporate shell companies and charitable bodies straddling the globe. The central hub of this network was located in the loose banking arrangements in a number of developing states in North Africa and the Gulf but extended to financial networks situated in Europe and North America.

© The Political Quarterly Publishing Co. Ltd. 2002
Published by Blackwell Publishing, 108 Cowley Road, Oxford OX4 1JF, UK and 350 Main Street, Malden, MA 02148, USA

The interconnectedness of the laxer, less regulated banking and finance frameworks in the developing world with the more orderly complexes in Europe and North America confirmed that internationally the financial system was vulnerable to penetration by terrorist organisations intent upon supporting worldwide operations, including operations in areas where financial controls were thought rigorous.

This chapter reviews a number of the main international, regional and national efforts undertaken both before and since 11 September to constrain terrorist exploitation of the international financial system and to assess continuities and discontinuities in method. In terms of regional and domestic approaches to the problem it will focus on various steps taken in Europe and in the United Kingdom in particular, but will show the linkages to developments in the United States. It will analyse some of the essential legislative and regulatory measures which have been adopted since the terrorist attacks and place them in the context of anti-money-laundering efforts before 11 September. In so doing it will outline the main parameters of operations but also seek to address the question of how measures which have until recently been geared in the main to constraining financial practices in the context of non-political criminal activities have been amended to meet the demands of what amounts to a politically and ideologically driven financing process.

The immediate response: declaring financial war and freezing assets

Prior to the first ordnance being dropped on enemy positions in Afghanistan and well before substantial ground forces were deployed in theatre, financial war was publicly declared by the United States and its allies on international terrorism. The declaratory opening of a financial front against terrorists and their supporters, the explicit characterisation of financial methods as relevant techniques of combat and the drafting into the battle of international financial institutions can be traced to President Bush's executive order on terrorist financing, issued on 24 September, less than two weeks after the attacks on New York and Washington. 'Because of the pervasiveness and expansiveness of the financial foundation of foreign terrorists,' Bush argued, 'financial sanctions may be appropriate for those foreign persons that support or otherwise associate with these foreign terrorists.' The need existed, said the President, 'for further consultation and cooperation with, and sharing of information by United States and foreign financial institutions as an additional tool to enable the United States to combat the financing of terrorism.'[1]

This focus on financial countermeasures certainly served the expedient purpose of demonstrating resolve and commitment to a public expectant of imminent action at a time when military plans were still incubating. It was uncontroversial, as its core argument that finance underpinned terrorist operations and therefore needed to be constrained was well understood. In terms of implementation the policy carried little attendant physical risk or danger, and in the short term at least involved the agreement and assistance of only the more amenable of like-thinking allies. Visible victories and apparent progress could be declared with rapidity.

From the start of the counterterrorist financing operations it was evident that while the focus was on al-Qaeda, the net was cast much wider and sought to capture not only operations supporting al-Qaeda but those of a broad range of Islamic and non-Islamic groups. Terrorist organisations were thus quickly identified and their bank accounts blocked. On 17 September the FBI provided a list of terrorist suspects to various banking supervisory agencies, while all banks operating in the United States were requested to report immediately on any transactions with the specified individuals. On 24 September the US government publicly identified twenty-seven such individuals and institutions, closing their bank accounts and freezing their assets. This was followed shortly thereafter by EU measures which sought to freeze funds held by a similar number of organisations and individuals believed to support terrorist financing activities and aimed at also ensuring that these funds could not readily be shifted around the EU banking system for purposes of evading the freeze. Various alternative remittance systems and charitable organisations believed to have links with terrorist organisations were shut. By 8 January 2002 the United States had frozen more than $33 million in assets belonging to more than 150 individuals and organisations, while a similar amount was frozen by European and other countries.

The US authorities had in fact been interested in identifying and freezing bin Laden's assets since the East Africa embassy bombings in 1998, but lack of political will and sense of urgency meant no steps had ever been taken towards this end. The freezing of terrorist funds after 11 September thus certainly represented an upgrading of financial efforts aimed at terrorist organisations, but it was short-term financial firefighting and was recognised as such. While the measures demonstrated national and international resolve and also cut off funds to terrorists, the amounts involved were relatively tiny, and the effects on terrorist financing capabilities—given their recognised sophistication and complexity as well as their extensive scope—could not be expected to be anything but negligible. What was needed was a more sustained and globally coordinated campaign that addressed systemic vulnerabilities in the international financial system and specifically targeted the generation and accumulation of funding by terrorist organisations, as well as their ability to launder funds and otherwise transfer monies across borders.

At an extraordinary summit in Brussels in October 2001, heads of the EU reached agreement on fast-track measures against terrorist funding. Specifically, the council of finance ministers emphasised the need 'to take the necessary measures to combat any form of financing for terrorist activities'. European countries were called upon not only to implement a framework decision on freezing terrorist assets but also to adopt a new and improved anti-money-laundering directive and to support global initiatives in this regard by signing and ratifying a UN convention on suppressing terrorist financing. In addition, the joint statement indicated that measures would be taken against states identified as having lax controls in relation to their financial systems such that those systems could be readily exploited by terrorist organisations. Concomitantly, EU justice and home affairs authorities agreed to cooperate better in the area of intelligence information exchange as to the sources of terrorist funding and to ensure that the banking system was not used for the transfer of terrorist funds. The European Central Bank made similar declaratory pronouncements. The intent was there to improve coordination and to begin upgrading regulatory controls at a variety of levels, as well as to start closing off regulatory loopholes that could be exploited for purposes of terrorist financing logistics.

Systemic vulnerabilities exposed

Both immediate and medium-term financial responses to the 11 September attacks were conditioned by a recognition of the vulnerabilities in the financial system that made terrorist financing and ultimately terrorist operations possible. The focus on reining in correspondent banking relationships, shutting down alternative remittance systems and paying more attention to fundraising and disbursing organisations of a charitable or other legal nature came from a belated recognition that steps would need to be taken against such systems as they provided access to the North American and west European banking environment. As noted by US Senator Carl Levin in evidence before the Senate Committee on Banking, Housing and Urban Affairs on 26 September 2001, 'The evidence is clear that terrorist organisations are using our own financial institutions against us, and we need to understand our vulnerabilities and take new measures to protect ourselves from similar abuses down the road.'[2] The vulnerabilities were many, but three stood out: the problems posed by correspondent banking systems; challenges related to alternative remittance systems; and the use of legal entities for fundraising and disbursement purposes.

Correspondent banking systems clearly highlighted the vulnerability of Western national banking to external penetration. Correspondent banking involves the provision by one bank of financial services to another bank so as to move funds across borders or carry out a variety of other financial transactions. If, for example, a bank in Saudi Arabia had a client who wanted sterling in the United Kingdom, the Saudi bank would employ a bank in London with which it had a correspondent relationship to make sterling available in the United Kingdom. Undoubtedly, such relationships facilitate and ease movement of capital, but they clearly have their costs. A major weakness of the system was that at least prior to 11 September banks may not have always carried out proper due diligence procedure in respect of the correspondent bank with which they had a relationship, even if such a bank was located in a jurisdiction with known lax regulatory controls. By 'nesting' in a bank with a correspondent banking relationship in a targeted country, a terrorist can access the banking system of that country, a strategy that was facilitated by not only poor but in many cases effectively non-existent investigatory procedures exercised by banks over their correspondent relationships.

If such controls were less effective than expected or required in the formal banking sector, the whole purpose of the informal sector was to avoid them. The term 'alternative remittance systems' refers to the non-bank financial institutions that transfer funds for entities or individuals mainly through their own network. This is an essentially paperless system involving unregistered lenders in at least two countries prepared to move money across borders. As there are no official bank records or statements, there is no proper trail to the source of the funds. Groups such as terrorist organisations intent upon distancing themselves from their money and keeping the finance out of the formal regulated sector found such systems extremely useful. Jeffrey Robinson, for example, has shown how the *hawala* network operating between London and the Punjab and Kashmir has served not only to channel finance in relation to drug trafficking, but also to support Sikh and Kashmiri secessionists.[3]

It should be emphasised that not only was all this well known by Western banking and regulatory authorities prior to 11 September, but it was also well known before 11 September that al-Qaeda engaged in correspondent banking activity and alternative remittance systems as means of transferring funds across borders in order to support terrorist operations. Indeed, by the late 1990s it was common knowledge that bin Laden's main area of technical specialisation was his experience of money transfer techniques in support of terrorist attacks, techniques which had been honed during his involvement in the war against the Russians in Afghanistan and conflicts in East Africa and the Balkans, as well as in relation to the financing of numerous other cross-border terrorist strikes.[4]

The importance of correspondent banking to the al-Qaeda network can be seen by examining the case of the al Shamal Islamic Bank in Khartoum. The bank was capitalised by bin Laden himself in the early 1990s when he provided an estimated $50 million to secure a major shareholding in the new institution. Foreign currency accounts were set up at al Shamal for a number of companies belonging to bin Laden, including the al Hijra Construction and Development Co. Ltd, which was involved in major construction work in Sudan, and a company called Wadi al Aqiq, which served as a holding company for various legitimate businesses including furniture, bakery and cattle breeding. These accounts appear to have been constantly replenished from sources in the Gulf. Then, by relying on al Shamal's correspondent banking relationships with a variety of reputable institutions with global reach—including in the United States, Citibank, American Express and Arab American Bank (since acquired by the National Bank of Egypt); in Africa, Standard Bank of South Africa; in Europe,

KommerzBank in Germany and Crédit Lyonnais in Switzerland; in the Middle East, Saudi Holland in Jiddah (in which ABN Amro had a 40 per cent stake); and in Asia, ING Bank in Indonesia—all of which had their own various correspondent banking relationships, al-Qaeda was able to move money rapidly and relatively unimpeded around the world.[5]

Alternative remittance systems were also important to al-Qaeda's ability to move funds. In relation to a *hawala* known as al Tarqua, a US government source stated that 'we believe that al-Qaeda has been skimming off that [*hawala*] network.' Al-Qaeda was thought to have actually established the network and funded it, as well as getting a percentage of every transaction that it made. Here the *hawala* served the dual purpose of moving finances as well as generating funds.

Finally, and very significantly, bin Laden set up another separate financial system for fund generation and transference, grounded in legal and quasi-legal charitable organisations, businesses and educational foundations. These organisations were originally based upon the al-Qaeda Foundation, a charity established by bin Laden in the 1980s whose purpose was to steer funds to Islamic fighters in Afghanistan and Pakistan. As Bodansky has noted, 'this quasi legal system also quickly evolved into a multitude of seemingly unrelated charities and multilayered organizations that interacted and moved people and funds back and forth as security authorities in the West struggled to untangle the web.' As will be described in greater detail below, a key factor in relation to this system was that it circumvented most banking and anti-money-laundering regulatory controls as they existed during the 1990s.

That a general knowledge of systemic vulnerabilities and an appreciation of the efforts international terrorist organisations were making to exploit these vulnerabilities did not result in successful actions specifically to identify terrorist financing operations and shut them down is partially to be explained by lack of political will at the national level, coupled with bureaucratic inertia when it came to implementing regulatory reforms and the fact that existing anti-money-laundering systems were not particularly appropriate to the particularities of the terrorist financing phenomenon.

The anti-money-laundering roots of the finance war against global terrorism

The roots of the finance war against global terrorism are to be found not in specific anti-terrorist financing measures but in the anti-money-laundering initiatives adopted globally, regionally and nationally during the 1990s. Prior to 11 September, anti-money-laundering procedures were certainly receiving increasing attention from the then G7 countries, though the motivation was not primarily counterterrorism. More significant in making the coordination of anti-money-laundering efforts a major policy objective were the declining revenues arising from taxation and increasing recognition of the massive amount of funds being laundered from the proceeds of criminal drug dealing. It was recognised that the opportunities for criminals to hide the illegal origins of their funds were being radically enhanced by the rapid and apparently inexorable move towards integration of international banking and capital markets. According to the IMF these circumstances were resulting in between $600 billion and $1.5 trillion of funds (equal to 2–5 per cent of global GDP) being laundered each year.

Money laundering is defined as the process by which the proceeds of crime are converted into assets that appear to have legitimate origins so that they can be retained permanently or recycled to fund further crimes. Technically, money laundering involves three distinct stages. First, there is placement— the process whereby unlawful proceeds are inserted into legitimate financial institutions, whether by means of wire transfers, actual deposits or a variety of other means; second, there is layering—the process whereby the launderer begins the intricate task of separating the proceeds of the criminal activity from their origin by means of layers of complex and sophisticated financial transactions; and third, there is integration, the process whereby the launderer employs transactions which appear legitimate to disguise the illicit proceeds. It is by way of a combination of these processes that the monetary proceeds derived from illicit activities are transformed into funds with an apparently legal source. An element of criminality is thus central to this definition of money laundering, and therefore, not surprisingly, anti-money-laundering initiatives in both their regulatory and bureaucratic expressions were from the start grounded in efforts to contain non-political criminal activity.

The institutional centrepiece of the bureaucratic mechanism driving international efforts to tackle money laundering is the Financial Action Task Force on Money Laundering (FATF), an independent international organisation set up in 1989 by the G7 countries with its secretariat in the OECD. It has twenty-nine member states plus the European Commission and the Gulf Cooperation Council, representing all the main financial centres in North America, Europe, Asia and the Middle East, who band together for the purposes of investigating means to combat money laundering in all its forms. FATF coordinates global anti-money-laundering activities by working together with a variety of regional and international organisations. At the same time FATF helped to set up and coordinates anti-money-laundering actions with a number of regional anti-money-laundering bodies located in the Caribbean, central and eastern Europe, Asia and the Pacific, southern and eastern Africa, and South America. Initially, efforts focused on criminal activity such as organised crime gangs and drug cartels and little attention was paid to the specifics of terrorist financing, though the general prescriptions obviously had an impact.

In 1990 FATF published the so-called Forty Recommendations (later amended in 1996) for all states and territories to adopt; these are now regarded as constituting the appropriate international standard for anti-money-laundering behaviour. They include requirements for states to criminalise money-laundering activities, to adopt customer identification and record-keeping practices, and to commit themselves to cooperating with other states and international organisations in anti-money-laundering activities. FATF members are committed to the implementation of these recommendations, and adherence is monitored by way of a combination of self-assessment and mutual evaluation, focusing on the implementation of the key legal, financial and international cooperation measures as expressed in the twenty-eight recommendations that require specific action by member states.

The nature of the problem was identified in the 2001 FATF annual review, which stated that 'the limited statistics available suggest that money laundering is actively investigated and prosecuted in a limited number of countries, but elsewhere, the offence is not frequently prosecuted.' In addition to this general implementation problem, which impacts on anti-money-laundering activities including efforts against terrorist financing, the particular point was noted that while the recommendations were properly implemented in relation to banks, they were not always applied in relation to non-bank institutions such as money remittance companies. This latter weakness appears to have been readily exploited by terrorists.

A major task of FATF which, while originally not directly responding to the terrorist financing challenge, undoubtedly has had implications for anti-terrorist-financing measures is the FATF identification of what are known as non-compliant countries and territories (NCCT). These NCCTs are jurisdictions which do not cooperate in combating money laundering, and FATF members are obliged to take financial countermeasures against them. FATF currently blacklists as NCCTs nineteen jurisdictions (including Russia, Egypt, Ukraine, Nigeria, Guatemala, the Philippines, Dominica, Indonesia, Hungary and Lebanon). In order to be removed from the blacklist the NCCT must be able to demonstrate that it has undertaken specific actions in financial supervision, criminal law, customer identification, suspicious transaction reporting requirements and international cooperation. Not surprisingly, the NCCT focus has sometimes strained relationships between FATF and regional organisations, thus demonstrating the political/ideological element that complicates proper implementation of FATF anti-money-laundering prescriptions—something that is particularly acute in relation to political terrorist as opposed to non-political criminal organisations.

For FATF recommendations to have bite, implementation and enforcement must be effected at the national level. Two jurisdictions which have above average FATF records are the United States and the United Kingdom. In both the focus has until recently been on criminal rather than terrorist activities.

The United States undoubtedly possesses the most complex and diverse anti-money-laundering system in the world.[6] As noted in a FATF report, there exist in the United States 'a large number of law enforcement and regulatory agencies, [a] huge number of financial institutions, [and] a diversity of federal and state laws'. The anti-criminal focus of this system is certainly evident, but not surprising since about 60–80 per cent of federal money-laundering cases in the United States involve narcotics proceeds—though significant proceeds are also generated by offences connected with organised, white-collar crime and foreign crimes. Prior to 11 September, efforts to enhance the system included measures such as a new and improved 'suspicious activity' reporting system, modifications to the currency transaction reporting system, new funds transfer record-keeping rules, and efforts to encourage improved cooperation between government and industry and between states: measures which, it can be argued, improved the United States' capability to deter, detect and punish terrorist money-laundering activities. Where, however, the United States approach remained weak—due to, *inter alia*, the pressures of both banks and civil liberties groups—was in the area of client and beneficial ownership identification, a lacuna that terrorist groups could exploit. It was also recognised that effective anti-money-laundering measures needed to be extended to non-bank financial institutions which, as noted above, were of the kind exploited by terrorist organisations.

To point out all this is not to argue that the US authorities did not recognise that terrorist groups laundered money. Indeed, in the Terrorism Prevention Act of 1996 the list of money-laundering predicate offences was extended to cover terrorism as well. To make such an extension is, however, not the same as adopting specifically sensitive counterterrorist financing measures. Consequently one government analyst writing in May 2001 described money laundering as being defined 'Legally . . . as any attempt to engage in a monetary transaction that involves criminally derived property. To convict, prosecutors must show that the defendant engaged in financial transactions . . . that involved funds from a "specified unlawful activity".'[7] This, as will be argued below, was not necessarily appropriate to the problem posed by terrorist financing.

While not as complex as that of the United States, the anti-money-laundering systems of the Europeans and the United Kingdom in particular reflected similar values and priorities. Specifically, British efforts aimed at countering terrorist financing also had their foundations in anti-money-laundering legislation primarily dedicated to constraining the activities of criminal organisations such as drug cartels (legislation, for example, such as the Drug Trafficking Act 1994, which makes it an offence to conceal or transfer the proceeds of drug trafficking) rather than global terrorist networks. Indeed, prior to the Proceeds of Crime Bill (see below) becoming law, the centrepiece of UK primary legislation dealing with money laundering has for some time been the Criminal Justice Act 1988 as amended by the Criminal Justice Act 1993. In respect of money laundering the legislation focused on the handling of the proceeds of crime and creates offences relating thereto. The core offences were those in relation to the knowing acquisition of proceeds of criminal conduct, abetting arrangements facilitating the retention of proceeds of criminal conduct, failure to disclose the provision of financial assistance for criminal conduct and the tipping off of money launderers of any investigation into their activities. The nuts and bolts of constraining money laundering in the United Kingdom are centred on the Money Laundering Regulations 1993, issued pursuant to the 1993 Criminal Justice Act, and in continued implementation into English law of the 1st EU Directive on Money Laundering. These regulations apply to institutions such as banks and building societies carrying on relevant financial business and require the institutions to deter money launderers from using the financial system and catch those that do. The three main methods employed are: (1) the 'know your customer' requirement, which demands that the financial institution be able to identify positively the original source of funding that is entering their business; (2) the identification and reporting of transactions that appear to the financial institution to be suspicious; and (3) the need for the financial institution to consider the requirements of subsequent money-laundering investigations by ensuring the creation of an audit trail. Failure to comply with these requirements is a criminal offence.

There is no doubt that these methods and rules, while not originating in an anti-terrorist framework, provided an appropriate base for dealing specifically with terrorist money laundering. In theory they should have helped identify terrorist funding and made its prosecution easier, though it should be noted—certainly on the basis of experience with the al-Qaeda network—that of all the organisations employing money-laundering techniques, terrorist organisations are probably the most trained and adept at disguising their own origins as well as those of their funds.

Unfortunately, even in relation to their traditional objectives the impact of anti-money-laundering initiatives has been questionable. Studies have shown that outside the United States very little wealth has been interdicted and permanently put beyond the reach of criminals. For example, it has been noted by one UK legal academic that only a third of cases where there has been a conviction on indictment for a crime that involves a profit motive result in a confiscation order. Furthermore, the amount confiscated is usually extremely small. In cases not involving drugs it has been estimated that the sums taken out of criminal circulation are less than 0.0001 per cent of the amounts that theoretically are subject to the law.[8] While this in itself does not indicate that the actual impact on the targeted organisation is negligible, it must raise questions as to the usefulness of the method itself—especially if it is to be used against terrorist organisations whose objectives are not ultimately financial gain and who are presumably less sensitive to financial setbacks.

Part of the problem can no doubt be traced to laxities and inefficiencies in implementation of existing legislation due to complexity, confusion or tardiness rather than to any conceptual failure inherent in the legislation itself. However, at the same time, while the smuggling of illicit narcotics and the laundering of the extensive profits that result from that lucrative trade are international crimes par excellence, they differ in their functioning from practices of global terrorism in that the genesis, motivations and objectives of the former are at root neither political or ideological in character but rather mercantile. For terrorists, on the other hand, the pecuniary consequences of their actions are secondary, while the methods by which they raise and distribute finance sometimes differ from those of criminal organisations.

The terrorist financing typology

The question then arises as to whether relevant statute, regulation and bureaucratic structure primarily geared to constraining financial practices in the context of non-political criminality are those best suited and most responsive to the demands of what amounts to a politically driven finance process which is both broader and independent of money laundering as presently construed. An analysis of the financial underpinning of the 11 September attacks demonstrated that the financial war against terrorist financing was at least partially being hampered by the inappropriateness of the tools at hand. For money laundering as a concept does not encapsulate the problems posed to the integrity of the international financial system by terrorists, while extant anti-money-laundering measures could not cope with their operational strategies.

There is little dispute that major terrorist operations involve a significant financial element. Terrorist organisations are of course known to tap into illegal sources of funding such as drug trafficking, extortion, kidnapping, robbery, fraud, gambling and smuggling of contraband goods. The Peruvian Shining Path has long funded its activities with sales of cocaine, and other groups such as the Revolutionary Armed Forces of Colombia, the National Liberation Army and United Self Defense Forces of Colombia have engaged in similar activities. The advantages of drug trading were not unknown to al-Qaeda. In this, terrorist funding practices are indistinguishable from those of various large-scale non-political criminal organisations. In theory, then, there should be little difficulty in expanding the scope of domestic and international anti-money-laundering measures and other relevant legislation to cover the funding and laundering activities of terrorist networks. Indeed, there is an argument that there exists a critical nexus between terrorism and organised crime, and that many of the skills and equipment needed to combat the financing of organised crime are applicable in combating the financing of international terrorism; all that is required is improved coordination and implementation.

While such a nexus does of course exist—methods of generating and transferring funds may in some circumstances be similar—and enhanced coordination between agencies and governments and improved implementation will lead to better results, the fact remains that there are significant differences between terrorist groups and criminal organisations engaged in money laundering. One key factor here is the important role played by 'legitimate sources' of financing within the broader funding operations of terrorist organisations. This analysis, if it is correct, or indeed even partially correct, immediately calls into question the relevance of anti-money-laundering legislation as a tool for combating terrorist financing as such legislation is essentially based on the assumption that the funds in question are illicit. Thus, for example, where sources of funding are legal there may be few if any indicators that would identify any individual financial transaction, or even a series of such transactions, as being linked to terrorist operations.

Three sources of funding do appear unique to terrorist organisations and serve to complicate the picture severely from a control point of view in that they do not in themselves constitute criminal activity in a domestic context.

First, there is the issue of state financial sponsorship of the terrorist organisation. There are a number of examples of nation-states in the developing world providing support and succour to terrorist organisations for political and/or military reasons. Indeed, each year the US State Department provides Congress with a list of these countries and there may well be others. This support is given in the form not only of training and logistics but also of finance—and not only in supplying funds but also in providing financial services and integrating state and terrorist financial services (for example, in the cases of al-Qaeda and the government of Sudan and the former Taleban government of Afghanistan) or using state financial services to cloak those of the terrorist organisation. Obviously, such action breaks no domestic law, and by providing the full range of complex and integrated state-controlled financial services to support the terrorist organisation large sums of money may readily be integrated on behalf of the terrorist organisation into the international financial system, whether the origin of that funding be the state itself or some other legal or illicit source. The use of state apparatus both to provide and to launder money poses serious challenges to efforts aimed at constraining such financing, both in terms of foreign policy considerations and in terms of actual control mechanisms.

Second, as noted above in relation to al-Qaeda, terrorist organisations can rely on donations and contributions from supporters as a means of funding activities. Because of their political and military objectives, terrorist groups are able to attract funds from supporters—some central, some peripheral—of the organisation. This is unlike criminal organisations, which where they seek to acquire such funds need to do so by coercive techniques such as protection rackets which are themselves illegal (though this is not to argue that coercion of some kind is not present when terrorists generate funds, for example by so-called 'revolutionary taxes'). Significantly, such funds may be generated in terrorist host states or in states that are the target of the terrorist group's activities or are at least hostile to them. In this latter situation, the resort to funding is often abetted by the terrorist organisation's strategy of disguising (from the authorities and in some cases even from the contributors) the true object of the finance. This is done by differentiating between political and military arms of the organisation, the political wing often having a legal basis, or by creating charitable or educational foundations which appear as the object of the contribution (this often being at least partially the case) and which also act as a means of siphoning the funds to the true object, the terrorist organisation itself. By adopting such techniques terrorist groups seek to minimise the suspicion and intervention of the local authorities, escape asset-freezing measures, take advantage of various tax concessions and also establish a means useful in any later money-laundering process. In addition, and importantly, as noted above in relation to al-Qaeda, the establishment of charitable and educational organisations serves the additional purpose of enhancing local support for the terrorist group by actually providing services of the kind to which it is ostensibly directed. Anti-money-laundering techniques have not always been entirely relevant to such strategies, being as they are directed at activities more ostensibly and unqualifiedly criminal. The legal funding approach is beyond the radar screen of much of the anti-money-laundering legislation in place before 11 September.

Third, terrorist organisations may engage in legitimate business activities for purposes of raising and distributing funds. While other criminal organisations may of course seek to move from illegitimate activities into legitimate business activities for both financial and security reasons, it is sometimes the case with terrorist organisations that the businesses themselves may be legitimate from the start and that only the purposes to which the funds generated are ultimately put are illegal. The obvious example here is the al-Qaeda network, whose source of funding was originally based not upon the proceeds of crime but upon a legitimate bin Laden family inheritance (estimated at anywhere between $50 million and $300 million) and legitimate construction, engineering and other corporate concerns. Again, traditional criminal and anti-money-laundering approaches have not been best suited to dealing with such kinds of activities as their focus is elsewhere.

The problem lies not only in the different sources of terrorist funding but in the purposes to which the funding is put and the manner in which it is done. The funding needed to finance even a large-scale terrorist operation may be small and the associated transactions supporting such operations may not be complex. Much of the funding received by the 11 September hijackers was carried out in transactions valued at under $10,000. Some terrorists were ostensibly students who, it appeared, were receiving money to support their studies. The transactions would not be either quantitatively or by category of the type requiring, without other indicators, additional scrutiny by those financial institutions involved in the transaction. Indeed, it should be noted that a US bank filed reports to the relevant authorities on transactions undertaken by the leader of the 11 September hijackers, Mohammed Atta, but these reports did not lead to an investigation.

As argued above, it would be wrong to state that the international community was unaware of the particular need to combat this specific typology of financing. The UN definitely played a role in this area throughout the latter half of the 1990s. The Declaration on the Occasion of the Fiftieth Anniversary of the United Nations contained in General Assembly Resolution 50/6 of 24 October 1995 referred to the problem; General Assembly Resolution 49/60 of 9 December 1994 and its annex on the Declaration on Measures to Eliminate International Terrorism included a general condemnation of terrorist activities and called for a review of international legal measures to combat its outbreak. It provided the framework for approaching terrorist financing issues. Most significantly, General Assembly Resolution 51/210 of 17 December 1996 recognised the specific nature of terrorist financing itself when in paragraph 3 it called upon states to take appropriate domestic legislative measures to prevent the financing of terrorism, not only where it was linked to drug dealing, arms trafficking and other criminal methods, but also where the financing was associated with ostensibly legal and non-criminal institutions of a charitable, cultural or social nature. General Assembly resolutions were additionally backed up by those of the Security Council. UN Security Council Resolution 1373 (2001) called for member states to freeze or block terrorist funds or assets.

This UN focus was given primary expression in 1999 in the International Convention for the Suppression of the Financing of Terrorism.[9] The convention aimed less at defining the specific typology of terrorist financing than at enhancing cooperation between states in adopting effective measures specifically in relation to terrorist financing and its suppression through the prosecution and punishment of its perpetrators. It called upon state parties to adopt domestic measures for the purposes of identifying, detecting, freezing or seizing funds used for committing the (defined) terrorist offences; and also to ensure that financial institutions within their territories 'utilise the most efficient measures' for the identification of their customers and to 'pay special attention to unusual or suspicious transactions'. It further required state parties to establish regulations prohibiting the opening of accounts for unidentified holders or beneficiaries, and to rely upon verification procedures in relation to clients and legal entities. 'Unusual large transactions and unusual patterns of transactions, which have no apparent economic or obviously lawful purpose', were to be reported to the relevant authorities, while financial institutions were to maintain for at least five years all relevant records of their transactions. Significantly, there was also a demand that there be licensing of all money-transmission agencies.

In 2001, prior to the September attacks, and for the first time, FATF too started to take an interest in terrorist financing. It began to investigate the terrorist financing typology and how specifically terrorist groups moved or concealed their funds. One of the main objects of the investigation was to determine whether the reliance by terrorists on legal sources of funding impacted on countries' ability to employ existing anti-money-laundering measures to target terrorist-related money laundering. The conclusions of these discussions revealed a definite lack of consensus. Material discussed by the experts appeared to indicate that there were more similarities than differences in the sources of funding for both types of groups. The report noted that 'there is little difference in the sources used for both terrorist and organised crime groups.'[10] Of the ten identified sources of funding of terrorist organisations, six (drug trafficking, extortion and kidnapping, robbery, fraud, gambling, and smuggling and trafficking in counterfeit goods) were identical to those funding criminal organisations. Four, however, were unique: direct sponsorship by states, contributions and donations, sale of publications and funds derived from legitimate activities. The 2001 report further argued that there was a decline in state sponsorship of terrorism (though no evidence was made public of this assertion) and that in fact 'terrorist groups have increasingly resorted to criminal activity to raise the funds needed to support their activities.' Less controversially, the report argued that there were similarities in money-laundering methods between terrorists and criminal groups.

Some FATF experts argued that what terrorists were in fact doing did not actually constitute money laundering per se as the source of funding was not criminal. Following therefrom it was reported that 'There [was] no agreement on whether anti-money-laundering laws could (or should) play a direct role in the fight against terrorism' as '[s]ome countries, for example, are not able to use anti-money-laundering legislation for tracking or restraining suspected terrorist money if the source of the funds was a voluntary contribution and not a criminal act.'[11] In addition, there was a recognition by FATF of the political problem of definitions as to what constituted a terrorist.

In the final analysis there appeared significant differences of opinion among experts as to how to categorise and deal with the problem of terrorist financing. The details of the discussions were not made public, but there was no disguising the fact that consensus was lacking. Thus it was reported that 'Certain of the FATF experts were of the opinion that terrorist related money laundering is a distinct sub-category of money laundering. Others held the opposite view and believed that terrorism can be adequately targeted under existing laws.' As we shall see, this latter approach was to change dramatically following the events of 11 September.

Of course, it was one thing passing UN resolutions and FATF proposals which recognised the particular nature of terrorist financing and called attention to its particular attributes. It was another to put these, with all their imperfections, into action both domestically and internationally. The events of 11 September were to focus attention on the terrorist typology in a dramatic fashion and to act as a powerful spur to the implementation of ideas that were already being considered.

Enhancing global cooperation

The need to focus specifically on terrorist financing as a specific typology and to develop particular countermeasures to deal with the terrorist financing threat was given obvious urgency by the events of 11 September. Previous debates as to whether existing laws were adequate for the purpose of dealing with terrorist financing or whether in fact such measures should be used at all to combat terrorist financing were rapidly resolved. Problems of definition relating to who or what constituted a terrorist group were in many cases pushed aside—at least temporarily and perhaps superficially—as the United States forced through its own definitions of terrorist organisations. Both the EU and the G8 finance ministers recommended that the lead in the global campaign against terrorist financing be taken once more by FATF and within the context of international effort already taken to combat money laundering.

At an extraordinary plenary on the financing of terrorism held in Washington on 29 and 30 October 2001, FATF delegates demonstrated their intention to use existing anti-money-laundering initiatives as a basis for tackling terrorist financing while at the same time implicitly recognising the inadequacy of the measures for dealing with the specific problem. It was now unequivocally stated that 'FATF [has] expanded its mission beyond money laundering. It will now focus its energy and expertise on the world-wide effort to specifically combat terrorist financing.' An additional 'Eight Special Recommendations' setting new international standards to combat terrorist financing were adopted by FATF and were to be appended to the existing Forty Recommendations. These new recommendations not only committed FATF members to be more expeditious in terms of adopting and enforcing new legislation and enhancing cooperation with other states, but broadened the scope of the regulatory ambit by specifically targeting terrorist financing in terms of funds generation and transfer. At their core was a recognition that terrorists may rely upon legal sources of funding but at the same time utilise financial networks in similar ways to other criminal groups. Specifically, FATF members are now called upon to ratify and implement the 1999 UN International Convention for the Suppression of the Financing of Terrorism, as well as relevant UN Security Council Resolutions; initiate domestic legislation to criminalise terrorist financing, with such offences to be designated predicate offences for money laundering; freeze and confiscate terrorist assets and the assets of their supporters; require financial institutions within their jurisdictions to report suspicious transactions linked to terrorism; commit themselves to engage in cooperation with other countries' law enforcement agencies and financial regulators in terrorist financing investigations; apply anti-money-laundering controls to alternative remittance systems; improve customer identification data transmitted by wire transfers; and take measures to ensure that organisations, especially non-profit bodies, are not abused by terrorist groups.

In November 2001 FATF typology experts meeting in New Zealand sought to provide to financial institutions a means 'to detect transactions potentially related to terrorists and terrorist groups, as well as the persons and entities that support them'. It was intended that the outcome of their discussions would inform the ongoing review of the Forty Recommendations. The substance of their view prior to 11 September was not, however, changed.

The experts continued to reaffirm the view that state sponsorship of terrorism was declining, but without publicly providing evidence for that assertion. Personal wealth was recognised as a source of terrorist financing, but no example other than that of bin Laden was publicly provided. The role of legitimate sources of finance was emphasised, though it was noted that this varied according to the terrorist group and whether the source of funds was in the same geographical location as the terrorist acts. The list of potential legal sources of funding of terrorist groups was expanded and included collection of membership dues and/or subscriptions, sales of publications, speaking tours, cultural and social events, door-to-door solicitation within the community, appeals to wealthy members of the community and donations based upon a portion of personal earnings. According to one expert present, the most effective means of raising funds in his jurisdiction was through community solicitation and fundraising. Examples of legitimate businesses supporting terrorists included publishing, food production, construction and computers. Also reaffirmed was the view that terrorist groups use the same laundering methods as criminal organisations. More specifically, terrorists were relying on cash smuggling, purchases of various types of monetary instruments, structured deposits to or withdrawals from bank accounts, use of debit and credit cards, wire transfers and reliance on *hawala* systems. It was recognised that the identification of terrorists by means of suspicious transactions would be very difficult and that financial institutions would need to be provided with 'other intelligence' as well in order for them to make identifications.

These and other steps taken by FATF received widespread international support. In Europe the need to counter terrorist finance began permeating a wide range of economic discussions. Thus, for example, a commitment was made by the European council of finance ministers (ECOFIN) to reach political agreement on a new proposed market abuse directive 'paying particular attention to the financing of terrorism when it examines the proposed directive'. According to internal market commissioner Bolkestein, this approach 'would be a significant step towards reinforcing safeguards against market abuse, including by terrorists'. A new EU money laundering directive is also construed as having a counter-terrorist-financing objective as it expands the range of predicate offences and seeks to impose additional requirements on professionals working outside the financial services sectors (such as auditors, lawyers and estate agents) whose financing services may be used by terrorists. These professionals will now need to comply with requirements relating to client identification, the keeping of relevant records and the reporting to the relevant authorities of suspicious transactions. This has been made necessary by the fact that as banks have become more stringent in relation to anti-money-laundering controls, money launderers have turned to less regulated sections of the financial services industry such as professionals. Again according to Bolkestein, 'The new directive will be a crucially important measure in the fight against the financing of terrorism and organised crime. [It] will set an international benchmark for the fight against money laundering.'

Certainly, since 11 September urgency has been given to EU efforts in relation to constraining terrorist financing. This can also be seen in ongoing steps, *inter alia*, to extend Europol's mandate to include all types of money laundering, irrespective of the predicate offence underlying the laundering activity; to improve cooperation between national financial intelligence services; and to develop a protocol to the EU Mutual Legal Assistance Convention which would among other matters deal with the vexed issue of banking secrecy and money-laundering reporting. The EU, however, cannot itself monitor compliance with anti-terrorist money-laundering efforts, which has to be carried out at the national level.

Upgrading domestic regulation

The UN and FATF recommendations set the tone and direction for national efforts aimed at reducing the vulnerability of domestic financial systems to terrorist manipulation. Anti-money-laundering legislation was supplemented and buttressed by steps taken specifically to deal with terrorist financing.

In the United States the USA Patriot Act, signed into law by President Bush on 26 October, sought to abet existing US anti-money-laundering measures by targeting terrorist financing in particular. Various other pieces of legislation are currently being reviewed by the House of Representatives and the Senate in support of this objective. The general thrust of the US approach involves allowing for the tracking of information in relation to accounts of foreign persons if there are suspicions that such persons are involved in terrorist financing. Long-arm jurisdiction is established over foreign money launderers. There is also a greater focus on correspondent bank accounts, with requirements for far more enhanced due diligence by domestic US banks when opening correspondent accounts for offshore entities, especially banks situated in jurisdictions where it is known there are in place weak anti-money-laundering controls. This has been complemented by efforts on the part of customs to target *halawas* and by the US Treasury better to track and monitor international terrorist financing. FATF recommendations therefore play a central role in helping US financial institutions prevent, detect and report instances of terrorist and other money laundering.

In the United Kingdom, there already existed prior to 11 September a stream of legislation that focused directly on terrorist groups but which for many years was aimed primarily though not exclusively at Irish terrorism. The key legislation was for some time the Prevention of Terrorism (Temporary Provisions) Act 1989 (as amended by the Criminal Justice Act 1993). This was replaced by the Terrorism Act 2000 which has been used *inter alia* to implement the UN International Convention for the Suppression of the Financing of Terrorism and which was in turn amended by the Anti-Terrorism, Crime and Security Act 2001. This latter new Act includes measures to give police powers to freeze funds under investigation, monitor accounts and seize assets. It also incorporated some of the provisions in the Proceeds of Crime Bill, including the negligence test.

The Proceeds of Crime Bill, which at the time of writing is in legislative passage, is arguably even more significant from the perspective of the finance war against international terrorism. The bill does not amend the 1993 Money Laundering Regulations but consolidates provisions in the Drug Trafficking Act and the Criminal Justice Act. Legislation as currently drafted applies only to laundering the proceeds of serious crime, but this is to be widened to include any criminal conduct. One of the bill's most important contributions, however, is its emphasis on suspicious transaction reporting requirements and its attempt to increase the importance and seriousness accorded to such requirements in financial institutions. It does this by the establishment of a negligence test in relation to failing to report cases where a person has 'reasonable grounds for knowing or suspecting that another person is engaged in money laundering'. An individual who fails to report such suspicions (in the context of reasonable grounds showing that he or she *should* have known that a money-laundering offence was being committed) to a money-laundering reporting officer who would then pass the information on to the National Criminal Intelligence Service (NCIS) could be subject to the imposition of a five-year custodial sentence—a severe sanction indeed. It is irrelevant that the person who should have reported the activity did not actually know that money laundering was taking place. It is, of course, hoped that the authorities will be able to absorb and process increased numbers of suspicious transaction reports, which can now be expected to rise substantially as financial institutions submit defensively.

New legislation has also been complemented by the introduction of new regulatory structures, though again plans for this were already in place prior to 11 September. Certainly for some time efforts were being undertaken in the United Kingdom to modernise the regulatory framework and to include within the new and strengthened regulator's objectives the goal of reducing financial crime. The new regulatory activities of the Financial Services Authority (FSA) are set out in the Financial Services and Markets Act 2000, which came into force on 1 December 2001. In line with the regulatory objective of reducing financial crime, a specific focus on money laundering was also introduced, the significance of which was reinforced by the terrorist attacks. Under section 146 of the Financial Services and Markets Act 2000 the FSA was given the responsibility to make relevant rules for the purposes of the prevention and detection of money laundering. It was also tasked with monitoring compliance by banks and other authorised financial institutions with respect to money-laundering matters. Specifically, financial crime is defined in the new Act to include fraud and dishonesty, misconduct and misuse of information relating to a financial market, and handling of the proceeds of crime. Failure to comply with these rules is a regulatory offence and the FSA can impose fines, withdraw authorisation or publicly censure the relevant party. At the same time the 1993 Money Laundering Regulations remain in force and the FSA now has the authority to prosecute for breaches of these regulations. The FSA is certainly cognisant of the particular problems posed by terrorist financing; indeed, 'within the FSA the term "money laundering" is now short-hand for money laundering and terrorist finance.'

Bureaucratic and specifically intelligence capabilities are being enhanced in terms of both funding and interdepartmental coordination. In October 2001 it was announced that the NCIS would focus increasingly on the specific issue of terrorist financing. Furthermore, a new 'multi-agency terrorist finance unit' would be set up within the NCIS. This financial intelligence unit would be backed by 'additional special branch investigative resources' and would employ academic, financial and commercial expertise to review various relevant banking regulatory matters. In February it was announced that the Treasury is to chair a money-laundering advisory committee to oversee the UK's anti-laundering strategy. New anti-terrorist financing legislation and regulation are to be given teeth.

Conclusion

Despite all these massive national and international efforts, there continue to be reports that terrorist fund generation capabilities remain in place. Thus, for example, there are indications that numbers of *halawas* are still able to function outside national control, while accounts and funds in various jurisdictions, although identified, remain active. Nor is there as yet any suggestion that national intelligence authorities have a full grasp of either the scale or the scope of terrorist financing networks and practices.

The response to the terrorist attacks on the United States involved the creation not only of international military and political coalitions but of a global financial coalition as well. It was recognised from the start that the goal of constraining terrorist fund generation and distribution demanded a level of international cooperation far greater than that required even at the military and diplomatic levels, where disparities in military and political power allowed Washington a more generous freedom of action. National unilateralism in such a finance war, even by the strongest economic power, could never be effective in the context of interconnected global capital markets that increasingly bypass national boundaries and limit the interventionist efforts of local authorities.

Tensions as a result of unilateralism exist but have never had the significance they attained in the military and political spheres. Conversely, the requirement for effective global cooperation has made counterterrorist finance warfare just as strong as its weakest national links. Technical problems stem from the inability of many states actually to identify, control and enforce measures against terrorist financing in their less regulated financial systems, though these difficulties are in many (though not all) cases being addressed with US and European assistance. The conceptual problems are obviously more serious and are linked to the definitional issues that inevitably arise whenever there are attempts to identify and categorise what constitutes terrorism. Without agreement as to such definitions effective cooperation at the financial level spheres is difficult, as it becomes subject to other, more powerful, political and ideological considerations.

Disputes between the US and various Middle Eastern and Islamic countries are unsurprisingly the most public of these definitional debates. For example, there are arguments in relation to the desirability of shutting off Hizbollah funds, especially in the Lebanese banking system, while Saudi Arabia has been criticised for not acting vigorously in relation to certain accounts and funds identified by the Americans.

Even where there may not be great differences in definitions, resentments have arisen over Washington's attempt to set the pace in the finance war. Thus, strains have emerged between the United States and a number of European allies, including Germany and France, over what Washington regards as tardiness when it comes to closing down accounts and constraining funds flow. While some of these latter difficulties are a result of differing legal and bureaucratic practices rather than conceptual variations, they nevertheless still hinder effective counterterrorist operations by creating loopholes through which terrorist finances may pass.

Even more fundamentally, the general principles of counterterrorist campaigning which are embodied in the various FATF recommendations and UN resolutions and conventions are not all uncontroversial, either as principles or as effective counterterrorist tools. This can be seen in the attitude of many international financial institutions, the structural linchpins of the global markets and the frontline soldiers of the anti-terrorist finance campaign, which have found themselves mobilised in a war for which they are both practically and conceptually unprepared. This is not to say that the financial services industry objects to the anti-terrorist focus of the political authorities. On the contrary, the industry recognises the dangers that terrorist financing poses to the integrity of the global banking system and financial markets. However, there is scepticism in relation to the potential effectiveness of some of the new measures and the practicalities of implementation. There is concern as to the costs, in terms of both money and efficiencies, that the anti-terrorist financing measures entail. Thus the practicalities of significant reporting requirements in relation to suspicious transactions (especially where there is an objective test for such reporting), issues of customer identification (which touch upon highly sensitive client confidentiality) and fears as to loss of competitiveness (to less regulated jurisdictions) make this a difficult period for these organisations.

Ideologically, the counterargument in its most general construction, at both the political and the institutional financial level, is that market abuse and organised crime will never be totally removed from the global markets and the extent of regulation required to serve such a goal actually undermines the functioning of those very markets that the regulation seeks to protect. The essence of this type of perspective is that regulatory measures must not be allowed to impede the movement of legitimate capital. If they do, the costs to the global political economy will be enormous and the terrorists, as a result, would succeed in their aim of subverting the international financial system.

Finance warfare remains a critical component of the global struggle against international terror, as the logistical infrastructure of international terrorist organisations must be destroyed if ultimately their operational capabilities are to be degraded. While to date many successes have been claimed in the counterterrorist finance campaign, these in reality represent small battles in what promises to be a long-drawn-out and complicated war where success cannot in any way be guaranteed. The ongoing finance war against non-political money laundering is not a source of optimism in this regard, but in the war against terrorism the stakes are arguably far larger and therefore the war must continue to be prosecuted with vigour. Technical, bureaucratic, political, conceptual and coordinational obstacles will nevertheless need to be overcome before terrorist financing capabilities can be seriously eroded.

Notes

1 For use of war terminology to describe the financial battle, see also statements by Jimmy Gurule, Treasury Under Secretary for Enforcement. According to Mr Gurule, 'The Treasury Department is now waging a multi-lateral battle to break the financial backbone of terrorist groups and their financiers . . . [it] is playing a key role in this new and unconventional war with respect to dismantling the maze of money that makes these atrocious acts possible.' The establishment by the Treasury of the Foreign Terrorist Asset Tracking Center was described as 'a new proactive, preventative strategy for waging financial war': 'Treasury's Gurule on Strategy to Fight Money Laundering', in *US Department of State: International Information Programs*, 22 Oct. 2001.

2 'Sen. Levin Testifies on Money Laundering and Terrorism', *US Department of State: International Information Programs*, 26 Sept. 2001.

3 Jeffrey Robinson, *The Laundrymen*, New York, Pocket Books, 1998, p. 18.

4 For a survey of these issues see Yossef Bodansky, *Bin Laden: The Man Who Declared War on America*, California, Prima, 2001.

5 Anita Ranasastry, 'Follow the Money and Follow it Fast', *Findlaw's*, 15 Oct. 2001; John Willis, 'Trail of Terrorist Dollars that Spans the World', *Financial Times*, 29 Nov. 2001.

6 For a description see Paul Bauer, 'Understanding the Wash Cycle', in *Economic Perspectives: The Fight Against Money Laundering*, vol. 6, Washington DC, US Department of State, May 2001. The main legislative pieces of US anti-money-laundering legislation prior to 11 September include the 1970 Banking Secrecy Act, the 1984 Racketeer Influenced and Corrupt Organisations Act, the 1986 Money Laundering Act, the 1988 Anti-Drug Abuse Act, the 1992 Annunzio–Wylie Anti-money-laundering Act, the 1994 Money Laundering Suppression Act, the 1996 Health Insurance Portability and Accountability Act, and the 2000 Civil Asset Forfeiture Reform Act. Also, the National Money Laundering Strategy for 2001 was mandated by the Money Laundering and Financial Crimes Act of 1998.

7 Bauer, 'Understanding the Wash Cycle'.
8 Editorial comment by Professor B. Ryder in *Money Laundering Monitor*, no. 25, Oct. 2001.
9 International Convention for the Suppression of the Financing of Terrorism, United Nations General Assembly Resolution 54/109 of 9 Dec. 1999.
10 *FATF-XII Report on Money Laundering Typologies (2000–2001)*, p. 19.
11 Financial Action Task Force on Money Laundering, *Annual Report 2000–2001*, 22 June 2001, p. 16.

Responding to 11 September: Detention without Trial under the Anti-Terrorism, Crime and Security Act 2001

HELEN FENWICK*

IT has often been pointed out that terrorist attacks place democratic values under pressure. Indeed, terrorists may well have the aim of forcing democracies to reveal their lack of commitment to such values and their readiness to embrace authoritarian measures. This chapter will argue that the Anti-Terrorism, Crime and Security Act 2001 (ATCSA), introduced by the Labour government as a response to the 11 September attacks, satisfies this aim since it comes into conflict with a number of the guarantees of the European Convention on Human Rights received into domestic law under the Human Rights Act 1998. Indeed, the tension between those rights and the ATCSA measures is such that in order to introduce the latter the government had to derogate from the fundamental guarantee of the right to liberty of the person. The mounting tension discerned by commentators between the Labour government's increasingly authoritarian measures and the Human Rights Act that it itself introduced currently reaches its climax, it is argued, in Part 4 of ACTSA. An exploration of that tension forms the central theme of this chapter.

The legal context

The ATCSA builds upon the Terrorism Act 2000 (TA), which already provides an extremely extensive range of coercive and investigatory powers. When compared to its predecessors it is apparent, it is argued, that the TA is itself an immensely controversial and draconian piece of legislation. Consideration of the UK's previous counterterrorism legislation reveals some acceptance of the principle that emergency measures should be adopted only in the face of immediate, actual and severe need. When the then Home Secretary Roy Jenkins introduced the first Prevention of Terrorism (Temporary Provisions) Act in 1974, he referred to the powers it granted as 'unprecedented in peacetime' but 'fully justified to meet the clear present danger'. The level of IRA violence was very high at the time: in 1972 103 soldiers and 321 civilians had died; in 1973 there had been 86 explosions; and in 1974 20 people had been killed and over 150 injured even before the Birmingham pub bombings

* I am grateful to my colleague, Professor Colin Warbrick, for his extensive comments on an earlier draft. Part of this chapter draws on a forthcoming article in *Modern Law Review*.

of that year, in which 21 people died and over 180 were injured—and soon after which the Act was introduced. The argument in favour of adopting extraordinary rights-abridging measures looked relatively plausible in the early 1970s.

The Northern Ireland (Emergency Provisions) Act (EPA) was introduced in 1973. As well as providing special powers for the security forces, the 1973 Act established different arrangements, including mode of trial, for terrorist cases. It was also made subject to annual review and to renewal by parliamentary debate. Features of the earlier pre- and postwar anti-IRA measures were found in the EPA, which provided a model for the 1974 Act and was similarly extended (amended in 1975, consolidated in 1978, amended again in 1987 and consolidated with further amendments in 1991 and 1996): 'One of [the EPA's] features has been a steady increase in size and scope.'[1] Thus the more draconian measures were confined to Northern Ireland. Where the threat was perceived to be most obvious, therefore, the measures were more far-reaching. This is not to suggest that the measures were justified or effective. It has been said that '[the EPA's] real purpose is to placate the electorate, as well as some of the elected, who demand that some steps must be taken by the law to counteract terrorism, regardless of how effective these might prove in practice.'[2]

The original emergency provisions under the 1974 Act had a renewal period of six months. This was soon extended to one year under the Prevention of Terrorism (Temporary Provisions) Act 1976. The Prevention of Terrorism (Temporary Provisions) Act 1984 included 'international terrorism' for the first time among its provisions. It was to be regularly reviewed and was to expire in five years. It was replaced by the Prevention of Terrorism (Temporary Provisions) Act 1989, also subject to annual renewal, but without the five-year time limit. After 1989 additional powers were added by a number of statutes—the Criminal Justice Act 1993, the Criminal Justice and Public Order Act 1994, the Prevention of Terrorism (Additional Powers) Act 1996 and the Criminal Justice (Terrorism and Conspiracy) Act 1998. By 2000, when the 1989 Act was renewed for the last time,[3] the 'temporary' measures had been in existence for twenty-six years.

The Northern Irish provisions followed a similar pattern, culminating in the passing of the Northern Ireland (Temporary Provisions) Act 1998. Paradoxically, although the level of violence had dropped over the twenty-five years since the first Act was passed, its successor by 1998 represented a much enlarged version of the first Act. Extension was not discouraged by the ceasefire in September 1994 (which broke down in 1996) or the peace process in 1998. Thus, the notion that such far-reaching provisions could be justified only by a severe emergency, such as the one which appeared to exist in 1974, was gradually abandoned. The reality behind the 'temporary' provisions appears to be that for much of the twentieth century UK governments have kept emergency legislation on file or in suspension, ready to be brought into law at short notice under a supine Parliament. This brief sketch of the recent history of counterterrorism legislation indicates that successive governments have demonstrated not only that they are willing to move quickly to cut down freedoms in situations perceived as emergencies, but that they then show little inclination to repeal the measures adopted, preferring instead a process of normalisation, extension and accretion.

In 1998 the peace process in Northern Ireland, culminating in the British–Irish Agreement reached in the multiparty negotiations, had been in existence for some time. As the Labour government consultation paper on the future of anti-terrorism laws, *Legislation against Terrorism* (1998), put it, 'subsequent progress including elections to the Northern Ireland Assembly mean that the outlook in Northern Ireland is changing, and suggest that the days of widespread violence and terrorism may soon be gone for good.'[4] Repeal of the Prevention of Terrorism (Temporary Provisions) Act 1979 might therefore have been expected. The consultation paper, which was intended to address the question of the rationale of retaining 'emergency' anti-terrorism laws in the face of the peace process, was based on a report prepared by Lord Lloyd of Berwick in 1996.[5] In 1995 Lord Lloyd had been asked by Michael Howard, the then Home Secretary, to consider the future of anti-terrorist legislation on the assumption that a lasting peace was achieved. He recommended in his report that a new, permanent anti-terrorist law should replace the temporary provisions. The policy adopted in his report formed the background to the consultation paper and in turn to the Terrorism Bill 2000. When the TA came into force, it repealed the PTA and EPA.[6]

The Terrorism Act 2000 has four key hallmarks. It is permanent; its main provisions apply equally across the UK, although there are special transitional provisions for Northern Ireland; it retains almost all the draconian special powers and offences adopted under the previous 'temporary' counterterrorist scheme, while adding new incitement offences; and, perhaps most significantly, it applies those powers to a far wider range of groups (see below). The justification for the new provisions is that they are needed to combat the threat from three groups. The first of these comprises those Irish splinter groups opposed to the peace process.[7] The second comprises 'international terrorists'. The paper noted that across the world there has been a rise in terrorism motivated by religious idealism.[8] Both these groups were already covered under the existing legislation, although not all the special provisions were applied equally to international terrorism. The new threat is apparently from the third group, on which the case for new legislation must largely rest. This group comprises a wide and disparate range of domestic groups other than those connected with Irish terrorism, such as animal rights or environmental activists and, possibly, anti-abortion groups.[9] The paper accepted that the level of violence associated with such groups is low compared with the level of IRA violence in the early 1970s. However, it argued that these groups pose a continuing threat and that other single-issue groups may be set up and may use violent methods 'to impose their will on the rest of society' (para. 3.12). Thus, the paper switched the focus of concern from the need for measures to combat a high and rising level of violence to the need to be ready to combat the possibility of violence in the future. The threat of violence from environmental, animal rights or anti-abortion activists may be a real possibility, but it has not yet materialised on anything like the scale previously thought of as necessary to justify the draconian anti-terrorist laws. Moreover, it is unclear that the ordinary criminal law would be inadequate as a response to the activities of such groups. The paper merely provided assertions rather than evidence as to the need for special counterterrorist measures, as opposed to a more effective use of the existing criminal law. No effort was made to analyse the need for the extension of the special provisions to a very wide range of new groups. The paper did not, for example, draw on experience from other countries, including European ones, also faced with threats from extremist groups. The problems experienced in the United States were mentioned, but no study was made of the efficacy of the means used to combat them.

The conclusion of the government in the consultation paper was that a threat comparable to that existing in 1974 can be discerned: 'In the language of the then Home Secretary introducing the PTA legislation in 1974, the Government believes that there exists now a clear and present terrorist threat to the UK from a number of fronts' (para. 2.7). But if these examples of group violence are compared with those available in 1974, it is immediately apparent that they are far more uncertain and speculative. The keynote of the paper was the need to safeguard the UK from future threats from indigenous groups, most of which had not arisen and may not do so. In comparison with the climate in 1974 or even, to a lesser extent, in 1998, in the wake of the Omagh bombing, the case for new legislation based on the threats indicated, was not, it is argued, made out.

The Terrorism Act 2000 is permanent; this has the advantage, as the consultation paper points out (para. 2.8), of being 'transparent'—that is, no pretence is made that the legislation will be repealed. This is a strong argument, given the spurious nature, indicated above, of claims that the legislation was temporary and passed only in response to a current emergency. But it abandons even the pretence that temporary and regrettable emergency measures, involving an ordinarily unacceptable infringement of civil liberties, require adoption. The paper noted that the vast majority of criminal law is permanent, implying that this provided a reason for abandoning the temporary nature of the counterterrorism legislation and thereby blurring past distinctions between criminal law and special measures adopted to meet specific emergencies.

Parliamentary scrutiny of the new legislation was also virtually abandoned, although the government did accept concerns expressed in the second reading of the bill, to the extent of agreeing to an annual report to Parliament.[10] A new clause supported by the Liberal Democrats making the legislation renewable was rejected by the government,[11] and no provision for the full review of the legislation was included. Therefore the permanent powers will receive even less scrutiny than the temporary ones did. The clause was withdrawn after the Home Office minister had pointed out that the Human Rights Act would provide 'an important new safeguard'.[12] The justification offered in the consultation paper for abandoning the review process was that it 'does not reflect the current reality that such powers are likely to be needed for the foreseeable future' (para. 2.8). This bland statement, based on little evidence, failed to take account of the fact that these powers were adopted and extended over a long period of time, (apparently) to meet the serious threat posed by a particular group of highly organised terrorists, commanding a range of arms. It also failed to take account of the need for parliamentary scrutiny to oversee the workings of the new powers, leaving their use far more overtly in executive as opposed to parliamentary hands. If certain of the new powers are not in practice used they should be repealed; an annual review would have provided a forum for arguing for such repeal. This appears to be precisely what the government is seeking to avoid, presumably in the interests of saving parliamentary time and avoiding political controversy. In other words, human rights appeared to be viewed as a commodity which could be afforded value only when convenient. While it may be argued that the previous review process achieved little, it is at least possible since the passage of the Human Rights Act that some MPs would have used such a process to afford a stricter scrutiny.

The main provisions of the Terrorism Act 2000 apply equally across the UK. This on its face represents a more satisfactory approach than passing more draconian legislation for Northern Ireland, which has in the past been the case, or, in effect, trying out such legislation in Northern Ireland first and then transferring it to Britain. But once again it erodes the principle that special powers should be as narrow as possible; if the threat is greater in one locality, it justifies the introduction of further powers confined to that locality. Although that justification has been attacked as doubtful, in the sense that counterterrorist legislation appears to have been adopted in Northern Ireland for reasons other than its efficacy in countering terrorism,[13] it is undeniable that the threat of terrorism has been greater in Northern Ireland than in the rest of the UK. The universal application of the new legislation is in any event only an aspiration of the new statute, since under Part VII of the Act it will retain for five years a number of differentials between the powers applicable respectively to Northern Ireland and to mainland Britain.[14] The government stated in its consultation paper that its objective was 'progressively to transform the security environment as appropriate, and achieve complete normalisation as part of the implementation of the [Belfast] Agreement as a whole'. Once that is achieved, the government's position is that there will be no need for any temporary Northern Ireland specific powers (para. 1.3). The temporary provisions are subject to annual review and to Parliament's approval of the Home Secretary's orders of renewal.[15]

Thus, the established model for counterterrorist legislation prior to the TA relied on actual terrorist activity to justify the adoption of draconian laws, on incremental development and a nuanced approach. Particular temporary measures were adopted for periods of time and on a localised basis, to answer to particular threats. Graduation was, in a sense, achieved since where the threat was perceived to be most severe, more severe measures were adopted to meet it. Had the TA introduced greater graduation, depending on different offences and levels of threat, together with a more specific and limited definition of terrorism, its permanent nature might have been less objectionable. But it adheres to an absolutist approach in failing to introduce graduation while abandoning each of the features of the previous legislation. It is more coherent and bold than the previous legislation; it has spurned the hypocrisy of the past which pretended that these measures were temporary. But, it is argued, its adoption shows an even greater degree of cynical opportunism than that which has such a marked pedigree in the long history of counterterrorist measures. The government seemed to fail to understand that the reluctance to take each step reflected some adherence to democratic principle and explained why the previous legislation was piecemeal, anomalous, incremental and localised.

The introduction of the Terrorism Act 2000 can therefore clearly be viewed as representing a decisive break with the past and as paving the way for its more narrowly focused but more draconian successor. It is notable that in debate on the bill of 2000 the main proposals made by the Conservative opposition were more draconian than those of the government, including the reintroduction of internment and the extension of detention by executive, not judicial authorisation.[16] Those proposals have now been realised in the ACTSA. It is an indication of actual and impending significance that now that the TA is established as the basis for the use of counterterrorist powers, its extensive and draconian provisions can continue to be extended. In introducing the ATCSA the government claimed that the TA did not provide it with sufficient powers. It stated that it needed a power to detain non-British citizens suspected of international terrorism, without trial, as a response to 11 September. The government considered that the new provisions would be incompatible with Article 5(1) of the European Convention on Human Rights, which protects the right to liberty and security of the person, afforded further effect in domestic law under the Human Rights Act (HRA), and therefore, as discussed below, entered a derogation to Article 5, under s. 14 HRA, within the terms of Article 15 of the Convention.[17] Although there is an exception under Article 5(1)(f) allowing for detention of 'a person against whom action is being taken with a view to deportation or extradition', it would not cover the lengthy detentions envisaged during which deportation proceedings would not be in being.[18] Thus, before the TA had been in force for one year, it came to be viewed as inadequate.

The derogation

The problem faced by the government was presented to Parliament and a number of parliamentary committees in the following terms: the government was confronted by a dilemma in respect of persons who are suspected of being international terrorists but who cannot be placed on trial due to the sensitivity of the evidence and the high standard of proof required, and cannot be extradited, or deported to their country of origin, because there are grounds to think that they would there be subject to torture or inhuman and degrading treatment, and consequently to do so would violate Article 3 of the Convention.[19] The dilemma arose due to the decision of the European Court of Human Rights in *Soering* v. *UK,* confirmed in *Chahal* v. *UK,* in which it found that a breach of Article 3 will arise where a country deports a person to another country, knowing that he or she will face a substantial risk of Article 3 treatment in that other country.[20] Article 3 imposes an absolute obligation on signatory states. Further, the UK has ratified Protocol 6 and therefore cannot deport persons to countries where there is a real risk that the death penalty will be imposed.[21] It should be noted that in explaining this dilemma the government did not refer only to members or supporters of al-Qaeda, the terrorist group which probably carried out the 11 September attacks.

These new provisions must be placed in the context of the derogation and the thinking that appeared to inform it. As indicated, it was apparently possible to declare the 2001 bill compatible with the rights enshrined in the Convention and in domestic law under s. 19 HRA only by derogating from Article 5(1) of the Convention, providing 'a right to liberty and security of the person', in respect of the clauses in question. The derogation was made by giving notice to the Secretary-General of the Council of Europe under Article 15(3) of the European Convention on Human Rights. Article 15 provides that 'in time of war or other public emergency threatening the life of the nation' any of the contracting parties may take measures derogating from its obligations under the Convention, 'provided that such measures are not inconsistent with its other obligations under international law'. No derogation from Articles 3, 4(1) and 7 or 2 ('except in respect of deaths resulting from lawful acts of war') can be made under Article 15. Article 15 is not included in the rights afforded further effect in UK law under the HRA. The validity of the derogation is a matter of international law in the sense that the interpretation of Article 15 is a matter for the European Court or (previously) Commission of Human Rights. It is a matter of national law in the sense that the derogation instrument itself is made under national legislation and, as indicated below, it can be questioned in domestic courts.

Before giving notice to the Secretary-General the government made an order under s. 14 HRA, the Human Rights Act (Designated Derogation) Order 2001.[22] The schedule to the order, which takes the form of a draft letter to the Secretary-General, points out that the UN Security Council recognised the 11 September attacks as a threat to international security and required states in Resolution 1373 to take measures to prevent terrorist attacks, which include denying a safe haven to those who plan, support or commit such acts. The schedule argues that on this basis there is a domestic public emergency, which is especially present since there are foreign nationals in the UK who threaten its national security. On this basis, therefore, it argues, the measures in Part 4 of ATCSA are clearly and strictly required by the very grave nature of the situation. It may be noted that the government has also derogated from Article 9 of the International Covenant on Civil and Political Rights as a further method of safeguarding the derogation from challenge.[23] Otherwise it could have been argued that the measures taken were inconsistent with its other obligations under international law—one of the requirements of Article 15. Clearly, the derogation itself is not part of ATCSA, but it was considered that Part 4 could be passed only after the derogation had been entered. The derogation, which can be considered in the Special Immigration Appeals Commission (see below) and, of course, at Strasbourg, is considered below, along with the compatibility of the Part 4 provisions with the Convention rights, since the two questions are linked.

The detention provisions

The detention provisions in Part 4 are clearly the most controversial part of the Act. Detention depends on certification by the Home Secretary as a substitute for a trial. Under s. 21(1) the Home Secretary can issue a certificate in respect of a person on the basis of (a) a reasonable belief that the person's presence in the UK is a 'risk to national security' and (b) reasonable suspicion that he or she is a terrorist. The term 'belief' denotes a lower standard than suspicion. Since the decision in *Rehman* v. *Secretary of State for the Home Dept*,[24] the Home Secretary has been accorded, as discussed below, a broad latitude in determining when a risk to national security arises.

Under s. 21(2) a 'terrorist' is a person who 'is or has been concerned in the commission, preparation or instigation of acts of international terrorism' or (b) is a member of or belongs to an international terrorist group or (c) has 'links' with such a group. Under s. 21(4) such links will exist only if the person 'supports or assists' the international terrorist group. The word 'assists' is broad, but 'supports' is broader still, since it could include expressing a favourable opinion about the group. Section 21 (5) states that 'terrorism' has the meaning given to it in s. 1(1) of the Terrorism Act 2000. Thus the TA and ATCSA must be read together. The TA s. 1(1) provides that 'terrorism' means the use or threat, 'for the purpose of advancing a political, religious or ideological cause', of action 'designed to influence a government or to intimidate the public or a section of the public' (s. 1(1)(b))[25] which involves serious violence against any person or serious damage to property, endangers the life of any person, or 'creates a serious risk to the health or safety of the public or a section of the public, or is designed seriously to interfere with or seriously to disrupt an electronic system'. The requirement of a threat to the established order contained in the words 'to intimidate or coerce a government', the key limiting factor under the definition initially proposed by the government in its consultation paper on terrorism (para. 3.17), was watered down in the bill which emerged to 'influence'. This definition applies to action of the types listed in s. 1(2) occurring anywhere in the world; this is made clear under s. 1(4)—the public may be the public of any country and the government may be the government of any country. There is no requirement that the government should be of a democratic country. Threats of action to be taken of one of the types listed in s. 1(2) to be aimed at, for example, the Iraqi government, would be covered.

This definition was attacked in Parliament as creating a 'fatally flawed' bill. It was also said that 'it is utterly perplexing that we should apparently be wedded to a definition that threatens to undermine so sweepingly civil liberties and the credibility of governance itself.'[26] However, the amendments put forward by the Liberal Democrats, which would have narrowed it down, were overwhelmingly defeated, Labour and Conservative MPs (with a few exceptions) voting together.[27] The new definition allows the activities of many groups to be redesignated as 'terrorism'. The definition now expressly covers threats of serious disruption or damage to, for example, computer installations or public utilities. The definition therefore blurs the distinction between direct action forms of protest and terrorism. Danger to property, violence or a serious risk to safety that can be described as 'ideologically, politically, or religiously motivated' may arise in the context of many demonstrations and other forms of public protest, including some industrial disputes. Obviously the new detention provisions in the 2001 Act do not apply to all those persons who fall within the definition in s. 1(1) TA; the power to detain applies only to 'suspected international terrorists' who are non-British citizens. Under s. 21(5) a 'suspected international terrorist' is a person who falls within the definition of terrorism in s. 1 of the Terrorism Act 2000 and who has been certified under s. 21(1).

It is crucial that the definition of a 'suspected international terrorist' should be precise, since such a person can be subject to lengthy—perhaps indefinite—detention without trial. But, as indicated, the definition of 'terrorism' under s. 1 TA, on which it is centrally based, is itself immensely broad and imprecise. No full definition of an 'international' terrorist is contained in the Act, but s. 21(3) provides that an international terrorist group is a group subject to the control or influence of persons outside the UK and one which the Home Secretary suspects (not qualified by 'reasonably') of being concerned in the commission, preparation and instigation of acts of terrorism. The failure to include the need for reasonable suspicion may be contrasted with the inclusion of the requirement of reasonableness in s. 21(1), which may require the courts to read that requirement into s. 21(3). Further, a person can be termed a 'suspected international terrorist' on the basis that he or she has 'links' with an international terrorist group. The power of certification is, it is suggested, deeply flawed in its dependence on these imprecise definitions.

The power of certification can be exercised in respect of persons who, under s. 22, can be subject to immigration control in terms of a refusal of leave to enter or remain, or a variation of a limited leave to enter or remain in the UK under ss. 3–3B Immigration Act 1971, or to a recommendation to deport under s. 3(6) of that Act, or a decision to deport or an order to deport under s. 5(1), refusal to revoke a deportation order, a cancellation of leave to remain, a direction of removal under paras 8–10 or 12–14 of that Act, or a direction of removal under s. 10 of the Immigration and Asylum Act 1999, or the giving of a notice of a decision to deport under the 1999 Act. Persons subject to these actions and decisions can already be detained, briefly, under existing powers under the 1971 Act.[28] Section 22(1) allows these steps to be taken 'despite the fact' that they cannot be deported or otherwise removed due to 'a point of law which wholly or partly relates to an international agreement or a practical consideration', terminology also used, as discussed below, in s. 23. Where any such action has been taken at the point when the person is certified, it will be deemed, under s. 22(3), to have been taken again immediately after certification.

Under s. 23(1) persons falling within s. 21 can be subject to detention in respect of the above immigration controls *'despite the fact* that the action [specified in subsection (2) cannot result] in their removal from the UK either temporarily or indefinitely by '(a) a point of law which wholly or partly relates to an international agreement *or* (b) a practical consideration' (emphasis added). No definition or explanation of these terms is offered. Provision under (a) presumably relates to Article 3 and other equivalent provisions, while the 'practical consideration' could relate—it must be presumed—to the fact that there appears to be no safe third country which will take the person, or to the fact that Britain does not have an extradition agreement with the country from which the person came. Such persons can then be detained under the existing provisions of the 1971 Act allowing for detention of persons liable to examination or removal and detention pending deportation. The provisions therefore discriminate against non-nationals since they lose the right to a trial before prolonged detention. If a British citizen fell within the definition of a 'suspected international terrorist' he or she would have to be brought to trial before the possibility of detention could arise. In other words, the normal due process safeguards, including the presumption of innocence, would have to be in place. All those safeguards can, however, be discarded in respect of non-British citizens falling within ss. 21 and 23.

Even a cursory reading of s. 23, the central provision of Part 4, reveals that if it was intended to allow the government to escape from the dilemma it outlined in the parliamentary debates and to the relevant committees,[29] it is deeply ambiguous and misleading. In particular, it is unclear why the provisions of s. 23(1)(a) and (b) operate disjunctively. In accordance with the provision of a way out of the dilemma one would have expected them to operate conjunctively. The use of the word 'or' implies that where the possibility of Article 3 treatment abroad does *not* arise, the person can be detained rather than deported, so long as a 'practical consideration' is present. The words 'despite the fact that' create additional ambiguity. Presumably they were intended to capture the idea that a person can be detained as a result of being subject to immigration control despite the fact that he cannot be deported for a reason within s. 23(1)(a) or (b). But, crucially, they do not make the existence of a factor falling within either (a) or (b) an essential ingredient of detention. Afforded their natural meaning, they imply that factors within (a) or (b) are *incidental* to the detention: they are merely relevant in the sense that they are not a barrier to it. Thus, these words appear to imply that a 'suspected international terrorist' who *could*, or could arguably, be deported or otherwise removed could in fact be detained instead, without trial.

On the face of it, the reach of the s. 23 power clearly goes beyond those persons who cannot be deported to their own or a third country due to the risk of Article 3 treatment, and a number of expected qualifying provisions are notable by their absence. In particular, there is no express provision allowing such persons to leave if they are prepared to take the risk of incurring that treatment. Indeed, there is nothing to require the Secretary of State to take into account the desire of detainees to leave the country. There is no provision requiring that they must be deported or removed, if they wish to be, when and if a safe third country can be found, or indeed imposing any duty at all regarding the possibility of finding a safe third country. There is no requirement that the Home Secretary should ascertain whether there is genuinely a risk that the person would be subject to Article 3 treatment if removed. Obviously, the provisions are aimed at persons who are likely to be asylum-seekers and strongly wish to remain in Britain due to the risk of Article 3 treatment in their own countries. Nevertheless, they appear to leave open the possibility of detaining some persons who in fact wish to leave. Other omissions are even more disturbing. There is no express provision allowing for the release of the detainee if, for example, the group to which he allegedly belongs, or has links, renounces terrorist activity. It is not necessary prior to certification for the Home Secretary to receive an assessment from legal advisers regarding the feasibility of bringing any of the potential detainees to trial rather than relying on this scheme.[30]

Prima facie it appears that four categories of person could be subject to the new detention provisions: (1) persons falling within s. 21 who are at risk of Article 3 treatment in their own country and in respect of whom there appears to be no or little prospect that they could be deported to a safe third country; (2) persons falling within s. 21 who are at risk of Article 3 treatment in their own country but who could be deported to a safe third country; (3) persons falling within s. 21 who are unlikely to be at risk of Article 3 treatment in their own country; (4) persons falling within category (1) who are willing to take the risk of Article 3 treatment either in their own or another country, rather than be detained indefinitely. Thus, as the Joint Committee on Human Rights pointed out, the provisions go beyond answering to the dilemma the government claimed to be addressing.[31]

In terms of the policy underlying the bill, the most defensible of these is category (1); but even if the scheme allowed for the detention only of persons within that category, it would still cover a range of persons unconnected with al-Qaeda. It would cover those who pose a threat only to other countries, such as the Tamil Tigers, and also those who merely have links with a group of suspected international terrorists. In theory they would cover an obscure Kurd who, say, supports the PKK and has come to Britain to hand out leaflets about them; or a person who supports an international environmental group advocating direct action and has come to Britain to support the group in threatening to destroy GM crops in, say, Russia. In fact, the first of these could be arrested and charged with one of the proscription-linked offences under the TA.[32] The second arguably has not committed any existing offence. Therefore, disturbingly enough, ss. 21 and 23 allow for the detention not only of those who—apparently—cannot be brought to trial due to the sensitivity of the evidence, but also of those who could not be brought to trial in any event.

Four central objections may be made to this scheme. First, Part 4 does create the possibility of internment since quite straightforwardly it provides for the indefinite detention without trial of non-British nationals subject to specified immigration controls and falling within s. 21, if the Home Secretary decides to certify them. Depending on the interpretation placed on the ambiguously worded s. 23, the decision to detain some of those persons is entirely unregulated by Part 4 itself: it is a matter left to the discretion of the Home Secretary, although a subsequent challenge may be mounted. There is no independent check on the Home Secretary's decision at all *prior* to the decision to detain. Second, not only is due process entirely discarded by allowing for the detention without trial of such persons, but this occurs on a racially discriminatory basis. The level of suspicion is—of necessity—well below the 'beyond reasonable doubt' standard, and since the necessary 'evidence' for the formation of the suspicion is not subjected to the check of a trial process, the risk that miscarriages of justice may occur is very high: some persons may be wrongfully detained, perhaps for a number of years. Since a power of *indefinite* detention is provided, the need for such a check is especially apparent. Third, this power of internment is not confined to suspected members or supporters of al-Qaeda but extends to a wide range of other persons, as indicated. Fourth, the power to detain may be used even though the person in question could be deported or otherwise expelled from the country.

It may be noted that where the Special Immigration Appeals Commission cancels the certificate, as discussed below, whether on the ground that the detainee states that he now wishes to leave the country, or because there is in any event little or no risk that he will be subject to Article 3 treatment abroad, or on some other ground, the Home Secretary can issue another certificate on any ground. This is an extremely significant provision. It arises under s. 27(9), which provides that the Secretary of State may issue another certificate 'whether on grounds of a change of circumstance *or otherwise*' (emphasis added). Since it is implied that this provision merely relies on the application of ss. 21 and 23, and itself says nothing about taking into account the fact that the detainee now states that he wishes to leave the country, there is nothing to prevent the re-issuance of a certificate. Clearly, the Home Secretary might be minded to recertify where it was clear (although it was considered that the person could not be brought to trial) that the person represented a threat to a friendly nation such as the United States or to the UK itself. It is understandable that it would seem very strange to release such a person to continue plotting terrorist attacks from, say, Iraq. However, tempting as it might be to continue to detain such a person, that was not—apparently—what the detention provisions were intended to allow. Arguably, the true solution to such a difficulty should be sought at the international level; or, as argued below, greater efforts should be made to bring such a person to trial. If these provisions are in fact aimed in part at the general problem of international terrorism in the sense that there are a number of persons in various countries involved in such terrorism who can rarely be brought to trial, they appear to represent a muddled compromise.

These draconian powers are subject to 'sunset' clauses contained in s. 29: they will expire at the end of fifteen months (calculated from 14 December 2001) unless the Home Secretary revives them by order for a period not exceeding one year or provides that they are not to expire, in which case they will continue in existence for that period of time (s. 29(2)). The order is subject to approval by Parliament. The derogation itself is expressed to subsist until it is withdrawn, but for HRA purposes it will cease to have effect after five years unless its extension is approved by the positive resolution procedure in both Houses of Parliament (s. 16 HRA). The powers were used immediately to detain a small number of persons in Belmarsh Prison in London. Two of them have since stated that they are prepared to leave the country and have done so.[33]

The role of the Special Immigration Appeals Commission

The Special Immigration Appeals Commission (SIAC) plays a crucial role in this scheme, since in most instances it will represent the only means of challenging the decision to detain. SIAC was established under s. 1 of the Special Immigration Appeals Commission Act 1997 (SIACA) after the European Court of Human Rights, in the *Chahal* case,[34] held that judicial review and habeas corpus were inadequate remedies to deal with cases where the Secretary of State was making a decision on whether or not someone should be deported from the country on the grounds that it was conducive to the public good. Under s. 21(8) ATCSA the Secretary of State's decision in connection with certification can be questioned only under ss. 25 or 26, which deal with challenges to the certificate or reviews of it in SIAC. Thus ATCSA seeks to rule out judicial review of the Home Secretary's determinations that persons are involved in international terrorism and his decisions to detain. It also appears to rule out habeas corpus. Derogation matters may be raised only in SIAC under s. 30(2). Judicial review of SIAC's decisions appears to be ruled out since it is now a superior court of record under s. 35, which inserts s. 1(3) into SIACA. The compromise of affording SIAC the status of a superior court of record was arrived at in response to amendments carried in the Lords which would have allowed for judicial review of the Home Secretary's decisions and those of SIAC.[35] A new s. 1(4) is inserted into the 1997 Act under s. 35 ATCSA providing that decisions of the Commission can be questioned only in accordance with s. 7 of the 1997 Act or in accordance with s. 30(5) ATCSA, which covers leave to bring appeals and provides that the appropriate appeal court can only 'consider and do those things which it could consider and do in an appeal from the High Court or the Court of Sessions in proceedings for judicial review'. Section 7 provides a right of appeal on a point of law only to the Court of Appeal and thence, with leave, to the House of Lords. Section 27(1)(b) ATCSA applies s. 7 of the 1997 Act, providing for appeals on points of law, to ss. 25 and 26 of ATCSA. Thus most issues that could be raised on judicial review could be raised as points of law.

There are two methods of judicial control enshrined in Part 4. Under s. 25 a detainee may appeal to SIAC, which has the power to cancel the certificate of the Home Secretary if it finds that there were no reasonable grounds for a belief or suspicion of the kind referred to in s. 21(1)(a) or (b), or that for 'some other reason' the certificate should not have been issued. There is also a distinct power of review of the certificate, which is not instigated by the applicant and which must occur in SIAC. The first review occurs as soon as is reasonably practicable after six months from the issue of the certificate under s. 26(1). However, if there is an appeal this will delay the point of the first review, under s. 26(2), which will occur six months from the point at which the appeal is finally determined. After the first review, reviews must then occur at three-monthly intervals under s. 26(4). The detainee can ask for an intermediate review due to a change of circumstances, under s. 26(4). It is clear that the two procedures differ significantly. An appeal can occur once only in respect of one certification and must be commenced within three months of the issuance of the certificate, although the SIAC can give leave for that period to be extended under s. 25(5). The appeal must be instigated by the detainee, whereas the reviews take place automatically.

The procedure is now governed by SIAC's rules of procedure, as amended.[36] The rules allow for hearings in the absence of the person bringing the proceedings and his or her legal representative. In such instances a special advocate (SA) will be appointed who has had security clearance. The SA cannot take instructions from the appellant and is therefore not in the position that an ordinary lawyer would be in—a normal client–lawyer relationship—

although she is not in a neutral position since the intention is that she should represent the appellant's interests. The procedure is divided between closed and open sessions. Under SIACA s. 5(3)(b) and rule 19 of the rules of procedure, the appellant and his or her advocate are excluded from the closed sessions, but these may be attended by the special advocate. The benefit of the closed sessions is that the government can put forward the facts on which it bases its case. The Commission can allow the appeal and cancel the certificate but, as indicated above, the Home Secretary can then issue a further certificate.

As indicated above, the detention power is not confined to those who are at risk of facing Article 3 treatment in their own countries. But SIAC could cancel the certificate if it viewed the lack of a risk of such treatment abroad, or the level of risk, or the detainee's willingness in any event to leave the country, as a matter falling within s. 25(2)(b), which provides that 'for some other reason'—apart from the belief or suspicion referred to in s. 21(1)—the certificate should not have been issued. The fact that the detainee asserts that he could leave the country and wishes to do so, even if a risk of Article 3 treatment exists, should be treated as an 'other reason' since the government has presented the new provisions as being intended for use only where a person cannot be removed due to the risk of such treatment. However, given that the introduction of these provisions was predicated on the assumption that the UK wished to deport or extradite rather than detain the persons in question, it is decidedly strange, to say the least, that this whole matter was not placed on a statutory basis but left to be determined by SIAC without any further guidance under s. 25(2)(b).

Clearly, the position of the applicant is weak before SIAC. Bearing in mind that in relation to Part 4 its procedure is—in effect—a substitute for a trial, it cannot be viewed as satisfactory in due process terms. The difficulty with commissions or tribunals of this nature is that the constraints under which they operate, which limit the opportunities of the defence to challenge evidence, detract from their efficacy. The extent to which the evidence can genuinely be tested is questionable. As C. White has put it in relation to the Northern Ireland tribunal set up under the Northern Ireland Act 1998 and modelled on SIAC: 'the central difficulty with the type of Tribunal set up by the 1998 Act is that it attempts to create an adversarial forum where one of the parties is severely hampered in presenting his or her case.'[37]

Tension between Part 4 and the rights to liberty and to freedom from torture or inhuman or degrading treatment

All the persons administering Part 4 ATCSA are public authorities under s. 6(1) HRA and therefore must abide by the rights laid down in the European Convention on Human Rights, unless, following s. 6(2), as the result of a provision of Part 4 which is incompatible with the rights it was not possible to act differently or where the authority was acting to enforce such a provision. The following arguments, based on the Convention, would have to be raised initially in SIAC.

The Part 4 detention scheme can be compatible with Article 5(1) only if it is covered by the derogation order, necessitating consideration of Article 15. Therefore two questions arise in respect of the derogation. The government has not claimed that this is a time of war, and therefore the first is whether a public emergency threatening the life of the nation, within the meaning of Article 15, exists. It may be noted that the European Court of Human Rights has never found that a claim for a derogation is unjustified on the basis that such a state of emergency does not exist.

In *Lawless* v. *Ireland* the Court of Human Rights considered whether Ireland was justified in entering a derogation under Article 15 to Article 5.[38] It found that any terrorist threat must affect the whole population, must be in being or be imminent, and must have produced a situation in which the usual law enforcement mechanisms are unable to function. It found that these conditions were satisfied in 1957 due to the existence of a 'secret army' operating in Ireland and in the UK, and because of the alarming rise in terrorist activities in the previous year (para. 28). The introduction of special powers in Ireland, including internment, in 1971 was found to be justified by an upsurge in terrorist activity together with serious and prolonged rioting.[39] The requirement that the whole population should be affected has not been strictly applied: it has been accepted that it covers events occurring in one part of a state only which may be assumed to have an effect on the population in general.[40] A derogation from Article 5 was upheld in *Brannigan and McBride* v. *UK* in the context of 3,000 deaths attributable to terrorism, caused by over 40,000 terrorist shooting or bombing incidents between 1972 and 1992.[41] In *Aksoy* v. *Turkey* the court accepted that there was a state of emergency in south-east Turkey on the basis that there had been on average 3,000 deaths a year related to terrorism.[42]

In all these instances there was little dispute as to the facts: the only question was whether they disclosed a state of public emergency. However, in the *Greek* case the threat was largely imminent rather than actual;[43] and the European Commission on Human Rights found that the derogation was not justified. The Greek government had argued that there had been a steady decline in public order which had brought the nation almost to a state of anarchy, necessitating the adoption of various measures, including the derogation, in order to prevent a communist takeover. The Commission, abjuring a stance of deference to the state in this instance, disagreed with the government's assessment of the situation, finding that the life of the nation was not threatened. However, the stance of the Commission in this exceptional situation was out of accord with that of the court in *Aksoy* and *Brannigan*. Indeed, where terrorist activity is already occurring in a state, as in those instances, it can more readily be argued that an objective assessment can be made. While the court may be prepared to make its own assessment of such situations, albeit while conceding a wide margin of appreciation to the state,[44] which means that it makes little attempt to gather independent evidence, it is placed in a particularly difficult position where a government enters a derogation—as in the instant case—on speculative grounds, based on very sensitive intelligence. The court may be unable to make any real assessment if the intelligence is viewed as largely undisclosable. In other words, ironically, it may be easier to make an assessment where terrorist activity has already occurred and is continuing, than when intelligence sources suggest, on the basis of circumstantial evidence, that it may occur. Thus, the previous instances discussed may not be entirely in point in relation to the current situation in the UK, since the assessment that an emergency exists is based on speculation rather than actuality. These suggestions lead to the unpalatable conclusion, contrary to the view of the Commission in the *Greek* case, that a broader margin of appreciation should be afforded to the state when it claims that a state of emergency is imminent as opposed to actual.

In introducing the ATCSA the Home Secretary said that the government held secret information suggesting that members of some international terrorist groups are currently in Britain,[45] and this was also suggested in the schedule to the derogation order. Presumably some of them may be members or supporters of al-Qaeda. Thus the government took the view that, taking into account the 11 September atrocities and Britain's support for America, a state of public emergency affecting the life of the nation could be said to exist. The Joint Committee on Human Rights, however, expressed concern in its second report about the lack of specificity in the reasons given for taking this view (para. 29). It examined the Home Secretary in oral evidence on the reasons for thinking that a state of emergency existed differing from that facing the country when the TA 2000 was enacted; he replied that the current threat is greater than that posed by the IRA since the 1970s because the terrorists in question are thought to have access to weapons of mass destruction.[46] The committee found that there might be evidence of a state of public emergency but that no evidence of it had been disclosed by the Home Secretary. It therefore recommended that each House of Parliament should look carefully at the question whether, under the criteria of Article 15, there was a state of emergency (para. 30).

As the joint opinion prepared for the group Justice pointed out, the situation in the UK following the attacks of 11 September is significantly different from each of those circumstances in which states have successfully claimed that a state of emergency justifying derogation exists in the past, since there have so far been no al-Qaeda attacks on British soil. Nevertheless, Justice took the view that a court would be likely to find that a public emergency currently exists due to the threat created by al-Qaeda.[47] In making the assessment as to the existence of a state of emergency it cannot be assumed that SIAC would apply the same tests as have been applied at Strasbourg. SIAC might apply a somewhat stricter standard of review, since as a domestic court it would not concede a margin of appreciation to the executive (see note 44). However, it would be likely to accept that the executive had a discretionary area of judgement in determining whether a public emergency exists.[48] The differing standards of scrutiny connoted by the two terms might mean that claims of a threat to national security would receive a somewhat stricter scrutiny in SIAC than at Strasbourg. On the other hand, the view taken by the House of Lords in *Secretary of State for the Home Dept* v. *Rehman* of the meaning of a threat to national security may be broader than the view Strasbourg would be likely to take since Strasbourg might not accept that threats to other countries should be taken into account.[49] In *Rehman* it was found that such a threat should be broadly defined to include the possibility of future threats, including those to the UK's allies. Following these findings SIAC is likely to accept a broad interpretation of a state of emergency. Taking into account the breadth of this definition and the fact that SIAC would have to assess, on the basis of very sensitive intelligence, not an overt but a covert, implicit and speculatively imminent state of emergency, it may be concluded that it will find that one is currently in existence in the UK, although such an assessment would clearly be open to future revision if al-Qaeda's operational effectiveness were apparently to diminish. The fact that at a number of points in recent years when terrorist activity has been especially serious, such as after the Omagh bombing, the government has not sought to derogate from the Convention is, it is suggested, beside the point. Failures to derogate in the past are not directly relevant to this assessment of the current derogation. The existence of a state of public emergency is a necessary condition for derogation, but it does not mandate it, and a state which seeks to adhere to the Convention despite the fact that it could probably defend a derogation at Strasbourg deserves credit for doing so.[50]

The second question to be asked under Article 15 is whether the derogation applies 'only to the extent strictly required by the exigencies of the situation'. In determining this issue SIAC will rely on the Strasbourg jurisprudence, but again it is likely to concede that the executive has a discretionary area of judgement in settling on the measures necessary to combat the public emergency. The most significant issue SIAC is likely to examine is that of the necessity of introducing the Part 4 detention scheme, bearing in mind the other available measures which have not themselves necessitated derogation.[51] The most significant of these is the Terrorism Act 2000; but that does not allow for detention without trial, and the government's argument is, as indicated above, that the difficulty of bringing suspected international terrorists to trial, coupled with the impossibility of deporting some of them, demands such a measure. Such arguments have previously been accepted at Strasbourg.[52] Some evidence supporting the claim that this measure is indeed necessary will have to be put forward to SIAC in closed session. Such evidence will presumably seek to demonstrate that it is almost impossible to procure the conviction of certain suspected international terrorists given their operational methods and the dangers of exposing informers and of undermining intelligence operations. It may be noted that the Joint Committee on Human Rights concluded in its second report that even if the requisite state of emergency exists, it doubted whether the measures in the bill could be said to be strictly required, bearing in mind the array of measures already available to be used against terrorism, and the fact that no other European country had derogated from Article 5 (para. 30). It returned to this issue in its fifth report on the bill, finding that the case for adopting the emergency measures had still not been made to Parliament (para. 4). Other legal opinion on this issue is at present quite firmly to the effect that the derogation is unjustified on the basis that it goes further than is required by the exigencies of the situation.[53]

If, notwithstanding these expressed reservations, SIAC shows some deference to the government in accepting the necessity of introducing detention without trial, it will go on to consider the separate question of the proportionality between the emergency situation and the detention scheme in Part 4.[54] Bearing in mind the doubts that have been expressed as to the existence of a public emergency, it is fair to argue that if one it exists it can only marginally fall within that term. Therefore, it is suggested, the government should have viewed itself as circumscribed in its choice of the measures to be taken, and should have chosen the less repressive among the possible measures which could have been adopted. The choice in fact made fails, it is argued, to satisfy the requirements of proportionality in the use of the extraordinarily broad definitions, of 'terrorism' and of national security, on which the power of certification and therefore detention depends. As indicated above, a number of persons who are suspected to be part of international terrorist organisations but have no links with al-Qaeda are covered by s. 21, as are—still less justifiably—persons who have 'links' with such organisations. The 'emergency' is apparently imminent due to the 11 September attacks. Therefore a measure allowing for the detention without trial of those who were uninvolved in any way in those attacks appears to be disproportionate to the demands of the situation in the wake of 11 September. Disproportionality also arises from a further feature of Part 4, since on the face of it the detention scheme allows such persons, as well as suspected members of al-Qaeda, to be detained, even where they could be returned to another country. Admittedly, the government could merely have introduced a new power of detention without trial for all those falling within s. 21, regardless of whether they were subject to immigration controls. Arguably, such a measure would have represented an even more repressive response than the current one, since the possibility of deportation rather than detention would not have arisen in respect of many detainees.[55] But the rejection of this more draconian alternative does not in itself mean that the demands of proportionality are satisfied. The government, as indicated above, appears to have reserved for itself the right, exceptionally, to detain some persons rather than allow them to go to certain countries even where they are willing to do so.

Assuming, then, that the derogation is found to be valid in the sense that it is accepted that a public emergency is in being, there appears to be a strong argument that the measures taken go further than strictly required by the exigencies of the situation. If SIAC takes this view it could find a breach of Article 5(1) in respect of both the powers and their application on the basis that the power under s. 23 goes further than the derogation would allow. Under s. 3(2) HRA, SIAC cannot strike down ss. 21 and 23 as incompatible with Article 5(1) even if they are not covered by the derogation. It could seek to render them compatible with Article 5(1) by interpretation, under s. 3 HRA, but this would be very difficult, given the plain wording of s. 1(1) TA. Since SIAC is a superior court of record it is able to make a formal declaration of the incompatibility under s. 4 HRA.[56] If it did so, the detainee would not be benefited since the incompatible provisions would be unaffected by the declaration and therefore the detention under them could continue (see s. 6(2) HRA). A declaration of incompatibility could then be appealed to the Court of Appeal, and if necessary to the House of Lords, by either party. Ultimately, if the certificate was not withdrawn the detainee could make an application to the European Court of Human Rights, challenging the validity of the derogation and alleging a breach of Article 5(1).

It is also possible that the detention scheme is incompatible with Article 3, which guarantees the right to be free from torture or inhuman or degrading treatment. It is arguable that subjecting a person to indefinite detention without trial in itself breaches Article 3, as found in *R. v. Offen*.[57] There is also the possibility that the application of the scheme itself amounts to Article 3 treatment where the only means of escape from indefinite detention without trial is to accept the risk of Article 3 treatment abroad. Assuming that a person might consent to go to her own country to face a risk of Article 3 treatment there rather than be indefinitely detained, and assuming that SIAC therefore cancelled the certificate and the Home Secretary did not re-issue it (accepting that she should be deported there once she expressed herself as willing to take the risk), might it be said that to confront a person with such a dilemma in itself amounts to Article 3 treatment? In other words, having been detained without trial for, say, three years, such a detainee might feel, with mounting anguish, that she has no real choice but to take that risk, since she sees little prospect of release otherwise. If the deportation or extradition of a person to a country where they will face Article 3 treatment is in breach of Article 3, it is arguable that one could say the same, in principle, of forcing a person to choose between indefinite detention without trial and accepting the risk of Article 3 treatment abroad, since the 'choice' is so circumscribed. The application of Part 4 can place—and is intended to place—some detainees in the position of being forced to choose between two fundamental rights. It is therefore arguable that ss. 21 and 23 combined are incompatible with Article 3 since they are so deeply opposed to the values it enshrines. In this instance, since the scheme was precisely set up to place certain detainees in this position, it is possible that the Court of Appeal may eventually have to make a declaration of incompatibility between Article 3 and ss. 21 and 23.

Conclusions

The better solution to the dilemma faced by the government, it is contended, would have been to charge persons covered by s. 21 with one of the extraordinarily broad offences introduced by the Terrorism Act 2000.[58] As indicated above, the introduction of the TA was justified in part on the ground that it was needed to combat the threat from extremist Islamic groups. Section 1 of the TA, as pointed out above, covers those who have only engaged in terrorist activity abroad. Once an organisation falls within the definition of terrorism under s. 1 TA, or supports an organisation within that definition, the Home Secretary has a completely unregulated discretion to proscribe it under s. 3 TA. Al-Qaeda is already proscribed, as are a number of other similar organisations.[59] Given the breadth of the proscription-linked offences under ss. 11–13 TA, which include an offence of belonging to a proscribed organisation, and the breadth of the terrorist offences, such as that under s. 56—to direct a terrorist organisation at any level—it might be thought that one of them at the least would cover many, if not all, of those persons within s. 21 ATCSA. These offences are themselves readily open to criticism due to their breadth and the imprecision of the definitions on which they depend.[60] Nevertheless, this solution is preferable, since the standard to which it must be proved that a person has committed an offence equivalent to that of being a 'suspected international terrorist' is higher, overt racial discrimination is avoided, the presumption of innocence is preserved and the detention is dependent on the outcome of a judicial rather than an executive process.

Clearly, the government would counter this argument by claiming that a number of suspected terrorists cannot be brought to trial due to the sensitivity of the evidence and the required standard of proof. There is the possibility of revealing the identity of undercover security service agents or informants in the UK and abroad, and there is also the problem that material deriving from the interception of phone conversations is inadmissible in evidence under s. 17 of the Regulation of Investigatory Powers Act 2000 (this was formerly the case under s. 9 of the Interception of Communications Act 1985). The government would contend that if it could have brought those within s. 21 to trial it would have done so, and that this was the very *raison d'être* of Part 4 ACTSA. If one accepts this argument,[61] the solution would be to introduce a much more limited detention scheme covering only members or supporters of al-Qaeda and other violent groups with similar aims within the first category put forward above. To meet the criticisms detailed above and to minimise its oppressive effects, such a scheme would also have to include a statutory right to leave the country, provisions regarding the conditions of the preventive detention, which should be higher than those applicable to remand prisoners, and provision for an independent assessment of the possibility of bringing the suspected terrorists to trial.

Democratic governments are perfectly entitled to take extraordinary measures if faced with a threat of atrocities on anything like the scale of those which occurred on 11 September. But since it is unarguable that counter-terrorist measures such as detention without trial are opposed to human rights norms treated as fundamental by liberal democracies, they should be subjected to the most rigorous tests for proportionality: an immediate and very serious threat should be evident; the measures adopted should be effective in combating it and should go no further than necessary to meet it. The limited detention scheme suggested above would have had a reasonable chance of meeting these demands. This chapter has contended that the Anti-Terrorism, Crime and Security Act 2001 fails these tests and in so doing comes into conflict with two of the most fundamental guarantees respected in democratic societies.

Notes

1 S. H. Bailey, D. J. Harris and B. Jones, *Civil Liberties: Cases and Materials*, 4th edn, London, Butterworths, 1995, p. 283.

2 B. Dickson,; 'Northern Ireland's Emergency Legislation: The Wrong Medicine?', *Public Law*, 1992, pp. 592–624 at p. 597.

3 The Prevention of Terrorism (Temporary Provisions) Act 1989 (Continuance) Order 2000. See *House of Commons Debates*, 15 March 2000, col. 474.

4 Home Office and Northern Ireland Office, *Legislation against Terrorism: A Consultation Paper*, Cm 4178, London, Stationery Office, 1998.

5 Lord Lloyd of Berwick, *Report of an Inquiry into Legislation against Terrorism*, Cm 3420, London, Stationery Office, October 1996.

6 Commencement occurred on 19 Feb. 2001: Terrorism Act 2000 (Commencement No. 3) Order 2001, SI 2001, No. 421. The PTA was renewed for the last time on 15 March 2000 (see note 3 above). The EPA was renewed for the last time on 24 August 2000. The special measures it provides for Northern Ireland are provided in Part VII of the Act of 2000.

7 In the paper the government finds that 'there are small numbers who remain opposed to peace and wedded to violence. So, even though the context is of a general movement towards lasting peace in Northern Ireland, it is too soon to be confident that all terrorism has been abandoned' (*Legislation against Terrorism*, para. 2.3).

8 Lord Lloyd's report draws attention to 'possible future changes in the terrorist threat' and to lives and property in the UK; changes which mirror what is happening across the world'(*Report of an Inquiry*, para. 2.4). Examples are given of the rise of 'Islamic extremism' and of the use of sarin nerve gas on the Tokyo underground in 1995 by the Aum Shinrikyo religious cult, which killed twelve people and affected up to 5,500.

9 'The threat from some marginal but extreme elements of the animal rights movement continues to be of more concern to the Government [than Scottish or Welsh nationalist groups].' The consultation paper notes that animal rights extremists have in the past sent letter bombs to the leaders of major political parties, attacked Bristol University's Senate House with a high-explosive bomb, targeted a veterinary surgeon and a psychologist with car bombs and caused

millions of pounds' worth of damage. 'The shape of new counterterrorist legislation needs to reflect the possible threat from indigenous groups too' (*Legislation against Terrorism*, para. 2.5). In chapter 3 of the paper the concerns regarding these groups are given some further substance. It is noted that in 1997 more than 800 incidents were recorded by the Animal Rights National Index (ARNI) and 'these included attacks on abattoirs, laboratories, breeders, hunts, butchers, chemists, doctors, vets, furriers, restaurants, supermarkets and other shops' which resulted in injuries (although not in deaths) and in damage done in 1997 estimated at more than £1.8 million (para. 3.10). The paper speculates as to the possibility that anti-abortion groups will adopt terrorist methods in the UK: 'In the United States, for example, there is an increasing tendency by individuals and groups to resort to terrorist methods. Some of those opposed to the USA's laws on abortion have bombed clinics and attacked, and, in a number of cases, killed doctors and nursing staff employed by them. Although there have been no comparable attacks in the United Kingdom, the possibility remains that some new group or individual could operate in this way in the future' (para. 3.12).

10 See *HC Deb.* 15 March 2000, col. 360. This provision is now s. 126.

11 Ibid., cols 352–6.

12 Ibid., col. 363.

13 See Dickson, 'Northern Ireland's Emergency Legislation', p. 597.

14 Under s. 112(4) the additional temporary measures for Northern Ireland only are time-limited to five years.

15 This was promised in the consultation paper (para. 1.4) and is now contained in s. 123(4)(f).

16 A new Schedule 2 and a new clause which would have effected this were proposed: *HC Deb.* 15 March 2000, cols 331–7. Both were defeated, Labour and Liberal Democrat MPs voting together: *HC Deb.* 15 March 2000, col. 347. See also ibid., col. 431.

17 Sections 14(1)(b), 14(4) and 14(6) provide power for the Secretary of State to make a 'designation order', designating any derogation from an Article or Protocol to the Convention; it can be made in anticipation of the making of the proposed derogation.

18 See *Chahal* v. *UK* (1996) 23 EHRR 413, para. 113. Deportation proceedings should be in being and it should be clear that they are being prosecuted with due diligence.

19 Home Affairs Select Committee, *The Anti-Terrorism, Crime and Security Bill* (HC (2001–02) 351, 10 Nov. 2001), First Report.

20 (1989) 11 EHRR 439 paras 90–1; (1996) 23 EHRR 413 para. 74.

21 *X* v. *Spain* D R 37 (1984) p. 93; *Aylor-Davis* v. *France* (1994) 76-A DR 164; *Raidl* v. *Austria* (1995) 82-A DR 134. Protocol 6 prohibits the death penalty in time of peace: it was ratified by the UK on 27 Jan. 1999.

22 SI 2001 No. 3644. It was laid before Parliament on 12 November 2001, coming into effect on the following day. It designates the proposed derogation as one that is to have immediate effect.

23 Under Article 4(1) of the Covenant: see *UK Derogation under the ICCPR*, 18 Dec 2001.

24 [2001] 3 WLR 877.

25 These words were not included in the original bill; they were added as a Lords' amendment, reluctantly accepted by the government. See *House of Lords Debates*, cols 1443–51, 4 July 2000.

26 Mr Simpson MP, *HC Deb*. 15 March 2000, cols 399 and 394.

27 *HC Deb*. 15 March 2000, col. 415.

28 In the Immigration Act 1971 Schedule 2, para. 16(1) and (2). See *R*. v. *Governor of Durham Prison ex parte Hardial Singh* [1984] 1 WLR 704; *R. (on the application of Saadi and Others)* v. *Secretary of State for the Home Dept* (2001) 145 SJLB 246; (2001) 151 NLJ 1573.

29 For a full list see *Anti-Terrorism, Crime and Security Bill: Further Report*, the Fifth Report of the Joint Committee on Human Rights (2001), para. 1.

30 It may be noted that if this procedure were instituted in future, the person in question could be detained while the necessity of certification as opposed to trial was being assessed under the existing powers.

31 Joint Committee on Human Rights, Fifth Report, para. 6.

32 Section 12(1) TA would provide the obvious one.

33 See *Guardian*, 15 April 2002.

34 (1996) 23 EHRR 413.

35 Amendment no. 32 passed in the Lords left out clause 30, the ouster clause excluding judicial review of the decision of the Secretary of State. The amendment was then defeated in the Commons.

36 SI 1998 No. 1881, amended by SI 2000 No. 1849.

37 For discussion see C. White, 'Security Vetting, Discrimination and the Right to a Fair Trial', *Public Law*, 1999, pp. 406–18 at p. 413. See also C. Walker, *The Prevention of Terrorism in British Law*, 1st edn, Manchester, Manchester University Press, 1986, p. 82; he advocates an inquisitorial system for such tribunals.

38 A 3 para. 28 (1961).

39 *Ireland* v. *UK* A 25 (1978) para. 23.

40 See *Ireland* v. *UK* A 25 (1978).

41 As pointed out by D. Pannick QC in the legal opinion on the derogation prepared for Liberty. For *Brannigan and McBride* v. *UK* see (1993) 17 EHRR 539.

42 (1996) 23 EHRR 553.

43 12 YB 1 (1969).

44 The European Court of Human Rights has stated that the role of the Convention in protecting human rights is subsidiary to the role of the national legal system (*Handyside* v. *UK* A 24, para. 48 (1976)) and that since the state is better placed than the international judge to balance individual rights against general societal interests, Strasbourg will operate a restrained review of the balance struck. See further D. J. Harris, M. O'Boyle and C. Warbrick, *Law of the European Convention on Human Rights*, London, Butterworths, 1995, pp. 12–15.

45 See *HC Deb*. 15 Oct 2001 col. 924; evidence of the Home Secretary given to the Joint Committee on Human Rights, Second Report, questions 3–7 and 9.

46 Second Report, para. 29, and oral evidence appended to the report, questions 3–7 and 9.

47 Memorandum from Justice, Joint Committee on Human Rights, appendices to the minutes of evidence, para. 1.7.

48 See *R*. v. *DPP ex parte Kebeline* [1999] 3 WLR 372; *Secretary of State for the Home Dept ex parte Rehman* [2001] 3 WLR 877 (also known as *Rehman* v. *Secretary of State for the Home Dept*).

49 [2001] 3 WLR 877, HL; [2000] 3 All ER 778, CA; [1999] INLR 517 (SIAC).

50 As the opinion for Justice pointed out, the fact that a state of emergency could be viewed as currently in being may not *continue* to justify the existence of the

derogation since the assessment is based on the continued operational effectiveness of al-Qaeda (paras 10–11). At the time of writing it appears that certain al-Qaeda leaders and fighters are engaged in last-ditch resistance to US and UK troops in eastern Afghanistan and may be defeated within a matter of weeks. If a large number of al-Qaeda's leaders are captured or killed, or in some other respect it becomes apparent that it is not likely to carry out atrocities in future, the justification will disappear, or at least diminish.

51 See *Lawless* v. *Ireland* A 3 para. 36 (1961); *Ireland* v. *UK* A 35 para. 212 (1978).

52 This occurred in both cases cited in the previous note.

53 David Pannick wrote a legal opinion for Liberty; David Anderson QC and Jemima Stratford wrote one for the group Justice on this issue (memorandum from Justice to the Joint Committee, appendices to the minutes of evidence). Both came to the conclusion, on different grounds, that the derogation was unjustified. The opinion for Justice considered that Part 4 goes beyond what is strictly required by the exigencies of the situation in covering a wide range of suspected international terrorists.

54 The tests of *both* necessity and proportionality must be satisfied: *Lawless* v. *Ireland* A 3 para. 36 (1961); *De Becker* v. *Belgium* B4 (1962) para. 271.

55 'Arguably' since such a measure would not have been racially discriminatory.

56 It was accepted in Parliament that SIAC's new status made it a clear part of the High Court: *HC Deb.* 2001, vol. 376, col. 920. The High Court can make declarations of incompatibility: s. 4(5)HRA.

57 [2001] 1 WLR 253, CA.

58 Technically—apart from the offences of inciting terrorism abroad under ss. 59, 60 and 61—they were not introduced by it: they already existed but were applied to a far wider range of groups.

59 SI 2001 No. 1261, The Terrorism Act 2000 Proscribed Organizations (Amendment) Order 2001. The organisations added to Schedule 2 of the TA are: al-Qa'eda, Egyptian Islamic Jihad, Al-Gama'at al-Islamiya, Armed Islamic Group (Groupe Islamique Armée) (GIA), Salafist Group for Call and Combat (Groupe Salafiste pour la Prédication et le Combat) (GSPC), Babbar Khalsa, International Sikh Youth Federation, Harakat Mujahideen, Jaish e Mohammed, Lashkar e Tayyaba, Liberation Tigers of Tamil Eelam (LTTE), Hizballah External Security Organisation, Hamas-Izz al-Din al-Qassem Brigades, Palestinian Islamic Jihad–Shaqaqi, Abu Nidal Organisation, Islamic Army of Aden, Mujaheddin e Khalq, Kurdistan Workers' Party (Partiya Karkeren Kurdistan) (PKK), Revolutionary People's Liberation Party–Front (Devrimci Halk Kurtulus Partisi-Cephesi) (DHKP-C), Basque Homeland and Liberty (Euskadi ta Askatasuna) (ETA), 17 November Revolutionary Organisation (N17).

60 See H. Fenwick, *New Labour, Freedom and the Human Rights Act*, London, Longman/Pearson, 2000, ch. 3; N. Whitty, T. Murphy and S. Livingstone, *Civil Liberties Law: The Human Rights Act Era*, London, Butterworths, 2001, ch. 3, esp. pp. 126–7.

61 One further possibility, which might allow for the trial as opposed to detention of at least some of those covered by s. 21, would be to repeal s. 17.

American Hegemony: European Dilemmas

WILLIAM WALLACE

THE tragedy of 11 September 2001 demonstrated both America's vulnerability and its overwhelming power. The American response—the skilful application of military force, backed by active diplomacy, leading to the rapid collapse of the Taleban regime—demonstrated that the United States remains the global hegemon in the projection of power: capable of responding to a distant threat through instruments unavailable to any other state, without more than marginal assistance from any other state. The immediate impact of the American success in Afghanistan—achieved without significant assistance from other states, through carefully calibrated projection of force from the continental United States—has, indeed, strengthened the perception of global American supremacy, both inside and outside the United States. Subsequent announcements of increases in US defence spending have widened the gulf between American capabilities and the collective capabilities of its allies.

West European states, the closest allies and formal 'partners' of the United States in the Western international order established after 1945, found themselves sympathetic spectators, in spite of their immediate gestures of alliance solidarity and subsequent offers of military assistance. The United States dispatched the Taleban regime with assistance from forces within Afghanistan and from a number of neighbouring states. The Bush administration resisted any repetition of the experience of Bosnia and Kosovo, where the need to consult with allies had, it seemed to US policy-makers, needlessly inhibited American freedom of action for little compensating gain in military contribution from partner states.

In the wake of this immediate triumph, confirming longer-term trends in American approaches to foreign policy, the United States's European allies are thus faced with a range of strategic and tactical choices. Do they assume that American dominance within the post-Cold War global order is likely to remain unchallengeable for the foreseeable future? Do they accept, and work within, a global framework of American hegemony, attempting to *bandwagon* as far as they can on established ties to the United States through pursuing influence at the margin; or should they seek to *balance* American dominance by building up European institutions as a competing centre of power? In either case, do their relations with the United States depend on the provision of particular types of power—military, as well as economic—or is it possible (and acceptable to their American ally) to maintain mutual trust and cooperation between the self-consciously 'civilian power' of institutionalised Europe and the militarily dominant United States? Is 'partnership' within the

© The Political Quarterly Publishing Co. Ltd. 2002
Published by Blackwell Publishing, 108 Cowley Road, Oxford OX4 1JF, UK and 350 Main Street, Malden, MA 02148, USA

framework of multilateral institutions established over the past half-century—in almost all cases on American initiative, and with active American support—still meaningful, when the historical circumstances that under-pinned these transatlantic institutions have now disappeared?

There are, of course, limits to American dominance. The speed with which the Taleban regime collapsed, with scarcely any Western casualties in the campaign, has created a second 'unipolar moment' in US foreign policy, comparable to that which followed the success of the 1991 Gulf War. Subsequent campaigns, for example to force a change of regime in Iraq, might well prove more difficult. The resolution of conflict between Israel and Palestine or between India and Pakistan, and the political and economic stabilisation of Central Asia, present far more complex challenges, only partly responsive to the projection of American hard power. The 'war against terrorism' cannot be won by the United States alone; it requires active cooperation from the intelligence and police services of many other countries. The current mood of American self-confidence would be badly affected by a subsequent setback—just as the confidence which followed the Gulf War victory was dented by the fiasco of military intervention in Somalia. Nevertheless, the underlying divergence of US and European military capabilities represents a long-term reality which will shape American attitudes to the European allies, and European attitudes to the United States, for years to come. The United States will remain beyond question the imperial global power; but will it also remain the developed world's accepted hegemon?

Hegemony—and liberal hegemony

Antonio Gramsci's concept of 'hegemony', now widely accepted in conventional political discourse, emphasised the combination of coercion and consent which maintains structures of dominance, both within states and within systems of states. Stable structures of power depend on both material resources and ideology—dominant systems of belief. States can secure temporary supremacy over their neighbours through the use of overwhelming force and superior technology, underpinned by the expenditure of the necessary economic resources; longer-term supremacy, however, depends upon at least a degree of acceptance from those dominated of the legitimacy of the dominant power. All formal or informal empires have proclaimed legitimising ideologies, with greater or lesser degrees of success. Islam provided the motivating force and rationale for Arab conquest of North Africa, Persia and Central Asia, and maintained a succession of regional orders over the centuries that followed. Napoleon Bonaparte's modification of the ideology of the French Revolution into a doctrine of popular mobilisation and administrative modernisation provided the legitimacy which recruited divisions of German, Polish and Dutch troops to march with the Grand Army to Moscow in 1812. The absence of any broader rationale for German hegemony was a crucial weakness in the Nazi regime: outside its borders it could depend only on coercion, apart from a handful of would-be collaborators, provoking resistance which tied down its forces and dissipated its resources.

Theories of liberal hegemony—from Arnold Toynbee, Charles Kindleberger, Robert Gilpin and others—have provided a rationale for American engagement in the construction and maintenance of global order since 1945. Toynbee looked back to a succession of previous international orders, in which dominant powers had established structures of custom, law and institutionalised diplomacy which prolonged dominance and enabled the dominant power to maintain its position through prestige and authority as well as through the distribution of resources and the threat—and use—of force. Kindleberger and Gilpin focused more directly on the nineteenth-century period of British dominance, as historical precursor for the American role after the Second World War. The English-defined gold standard and the English doctrine of free trade briefly nurtured global (or at least European) economic expansion, while the British navy suppressed piracy and the slave trade, and British political leaders and lawyers laid down rules for international diplomacy and crisis management. Competing imperialist ideologies—Russian, French, German, Italian, Japanese—brought a reversion to economic protection and international rivalry. Germany's rapid growth to industrial and scientific leadership in the final decades of the century, followed by a military and naval expansion which was a clear challenge to Anglo-Saxon pre-eminence, then brought the long peace of nineteenth-century Europe to a catastrophic end in the Great War of 1914–18.

Nineteenth-century Britain, however, was never as unchallengeable in terms of economic or military supremacy as the United States is today. Militarily, the collapse of the Soviet Union has left the United States without any competitor, in terms of either investment in advanced technology or deployable forces. The long timescale of military research, development and deployment implies that no serious challenger to the United States is likely to emerge within the next fifteen to twenty years—at least in terms of the provision of conventional, organised forces. 'Asymmetric' warfare by state-sponsored terrorist groups remains, of course, an active threat; but America's ability to project military force across the globe is likely to remain unique. There is no indication of any other state, or group of states, being willing to make the sustained investment needed to acquire such capabilities, or able to marshal the resources to support such sustained investment.

British hegemony was undermined partly by its loss of markets, and of industrial and technological leadership, to Germany. After the sustained economic growth of the 1990s, supported by technological innovation across a range of sectors, the United States also appears unchallengeable within the global economy, at least within the medium term. With the United States skirting recession in 2001–2, however, and with the flow of inward investment which has supported a strong dollar slowing, it is worth remembering the rapidity with which economic recession and a weak dollar have brought shifts from optimism to pessimism in the past, and might do so again. In the late 1980s, budgetary and trade deficits, accompanied by slow growth, provoked a succession of studies of American 'decline' and of the dangers of imperial 'overstretch', of which Paul Kennedy's *The Rise and Fall of the Great Powers* (1988) was the most widely read. The Japanese economy, widely seen as the strongest and most technologically advanced national economy in those years, has since then fallen back to apparent stagnation, in a remarkably rapid reversal.

There *are* a number of structural weaknesses in the American economy, most notably the scale and persistence of its trade deficit and its increasing dependence on imports of energy. A shift in the balance of economic growth between the United States and Europe, accompanied by a shift in the dollar–euro exchange rate, might well bring a parallel shift in perceptions of economic strength and weakness. As this goes to press, such a shift appears to be under way. It may be noted that the last period of European optimism and American pessimism accompanied (and in part reflected) the surge in economic integration launched by the Single European Act in 1986. Continued economic growth within China may also have a cumulative impact on American economic competitiveness and confidence. US economic hegemony is thus not as secure as US military supremacy over the medium term.

Liberal hegemony, however, also depends heavily on the consent that comes from acceptance of the legitimacy of systemic leadership. The Western international system established under US leadership after 1945 embedded political and economic values in multilateral institutions, accepted as authoritative by America's allies and partners. The US administration at the end of the Second World War engaged, as John Ikenberry put it in the *European Journal of International Relations* (1998), in 'constitutional politics in international relations'. Washington officials deliberately encompassed America's dominant position in military and economic terms within the constraints of an institutional order that reassured its dependent allies that the United States would remain committed to multilateral cooperation and to political and economic stability, and provided those dependent allies with a voice to influence American decisions through these institutions. American dominance was to some extent diffused through the United Nations, the International Monetary Fund, the World Bank, the Atlantic alliance and the many other global and regional agencies established under US leadership. For twenty years after 1945, it was almost unthinkable within any of these institutions for American policy-makers to find themselves outvoted; American assumptions and perspectives continued to set the agenda, while allowing political leaders from other states a sense of participation in joint decisions. West European economies recovered under benign American guidance and economic assistance; west European armed forces were rebuilt with transferred US technology, within NATO guidelines.

American prestige retained its aura as the countries of 'the free world' in western Europe and east Asia recovered from wartime devastation to become less dependent, partners who might share America's global burdens in resisting communist expansion and assisting the economic development of the southern hemisphere. The Kennedy administration in 1961–2 launched its 'Grand Design' for a strengthened Atlantic Community, together with the transformation of the Organisation for European Economic Cooperation into the broader Organisation for Economic Cooperation and Development, and with the declaration that the 1960s were to be 'the decade of development', in the confident expectation that America's partners would accept the rationale for its initiatives and continue to follow its lead.

By the early 1960s American economic domination had weakened, as a consequence of US-assisted dynamic growth within western Europe and Japan. The challenge to American international *political* leadership came from outside these close allies, however, as the new states whose case for independence US diplomacy had vigorously supported flocked into international institutions, forming the caucus of the Non-Aligned Movement (and later the G-77), and allied with the Soviet bloc in challenging the US-led multilateral agenda. The deepening US involvement in Vietnam further weakened the United States' confidence, balance of payments and international reputation. Nevertheless, Robert Keohane's classic study, *After Hegemony* (1984), was mistitled. American leadership persisted through the 1970s and 1980s, in spite of the decline of US economic dominance and the apparent decline (post-Vietnam) of US military supremacy, because American ideas about governance and markets retained their authority, both within international institutions and within other advanced democracies. Within the third world, authoritarian governments and revolutionary movements rejected US domination as they saw it, looking to Soviet or Chinese models for alternative inspiration; but as the sclerosis of the Soviet system became apparent, and the Chinese themselves rejected the brutalities of the Cultural Revolution, even the flawed qualities of the American model regained their appeal. Joseph Nye, in *Bound to Lead: The Changing Nature of American Power* (1990), rightly drew attention to America's reserves of 'soft power', reflected in the wide international acceptance of 'Western' values and market principles, the prestige and influence of American universities and research institutions, and the broader cultural influence of the largely American English-language media. American power might be more effectively exerted indirectly than directly, through the half-conscious acceptance by elites within other states of American assumptions about domestic and international order.

Is the United States still a liberal hegemon?

Part of the paradox of the resurgence of American economic and technological supremacy in the 1990s, together with the demonstration (first in the Gulf War, and then again in the intervention in Afghanistan) of American military dominance, is that these have been accompanied by a weakening of American 'soft power'. American prestige, both abroad and at home, has suffered (as in the 1970s) from domestic political and economic scandals. The disappearance of the Soviet Union deprived the United States of its most easily accepted rationale for global engagement, which also legitimised American leadership of the Atlantic alliance and the broader 'free world'. Between the Gulf War of 1991 and the Afghan intervention of 2001, the visible hesitancy with which American policy-makers approached the deployment of US power, in Somalia, Bosnia and Kosovo, and the preoccupation with 'exit strategies' from the point of entry on, weakened the respect of America's allies for its military and political leadership. A further paradox of American supremacy is that what is perceived within the United States as 'resentment' at its liberty and prosperity, as 'anti-Americanism' from hostile outsiders, has partly flowed from the spillover of domestic controversies on to the inter-national stage. The 'global' NGOs which demonstrated against US domina-tion of the global economy at the WTO meeting in Seattle were largely American-led. The narratives of anti-globalisation and the corruption of free-market capitalism have drawn upon American critiques as well as on diatribes from other countries, and have been disseminated across the world through English-language media.

A yet further paradox is that the collapse of state socialism, with the apparent 'victory' of market democracy as the model for political and economic order, has led not to the 'end of history' that Francis Fukuyama proclaimed but to a greater emphasis on the differences among approaches to market democracy. The Malaysian prime minister and others laid great stress in the immediate post-Cold War period on the claimed superiorities of the 'Asian model'. The most delicate and difficult dialogue on the values which underpin market democracy has, however, been across the Atlantic: between an American model which emphasises free markets and a limited role for government in social welfare, and European 'social market' models which—in differing ways—lay greater stress on the regulation of employment and on the provision of welfare. American charges that European social democracy has led to 'Eurosclerosis' have been met by European charges that American-style capitalism carries unacceptable social costs. The symbolic importance of capital punishment as an issue in transatlantic relations is that it encapsulates the differences of approach: the American belief in a more vigorous culture of success and failure, of reward and punishment, against the European concern with social harmony and community as necessary components of a liberal economy—or the Old Testament certainties of good and evil, reward and punishment, within America's religious culture against the secular culture of urban Europe.

Here again, the division of opinion is partly a reflection of differences *within* the United States, as well as between the United States and other democratic states. The Republican attack on 'big government', which in many ways defined the issues of American politics during the 1990s, attracted limited support within Europe. Most European right-wing parties remained closer to the traditions of Christian democracy and state-centred conservatism; from the mid-1990s onwards, furthermore, the majority of European governments were centre-left rather than centre-right. The international spillover of the Republican attack on Democratic 'big government' and Democratic 'internationalism' was that American 'values' have come to be rhetorically presented—by leading Senators and members of Congress, as well as by the Washington intellectuals who dominate the op-ed pages— as distinct from those of America's partners and allies, rather than as universal.

Geir Lundestad has described the US-led Atlantic 'community' of the past half-century as *Empire by Integration* (1998). The United States, as a self-consciously liberal hegemon, operated through multilateral institutions which disguised, legitimised and moderated its dominance, and provided a narrative (or rationale) of common values shared by the 'free world' which were declared to be universal in their application. A central difficulty for the United States's European partners, in responding to the current re-establishment of American military and economic dominance, is that the rhetorical justification for this dominant position is more often couched in realist than in liberal terms: with reference to US national interests rather than to shared global values and concerns, with self-conscious unilateralism rather than US-orchestrated multilateralism. The consensus within Congress and within the Washington think-tank community turned against global institutions in the course of the 1980s, as images of corruption and anti-American bias replaced earlier assumptions about cooperation in pursuit of shared values in the face of communist obstruction (see Edward Luck, *Mixed Messages: American Politics and International Organizations*, 1999). In the 1990s the consensus appears to have been moving also against cooperation with allies, against disguising the hard realities of US preponderance within the softer clothes of multilateral partnership, in favour of a determined—even hard-nosed—assertion that US interests come first, and that there was nothing that America's partners had to contribute to the definition of America's short-term or long-term interests.

Walter Russell Mead, in a widely accepted conceptualisation of the contending traditions of US foreign policy (*Special Providence: American Foreign Policy and how it Changed the World*, 2001) has described this shift of emphasis as the victory of the Jacksonian tradition of hard-nosed and self-righteous promotion of American interests over the Wilsonian tradition of the promotion of an American-led international community. He notes the greater strength which the Jacksonian tradition drew from the pioneers who settled the western lands across the Alleghenies, against the moralists, internationalists and international traders and financiers of the east coast. The Jacksonian tradition, linked to the Christian fundamentalism which sustained the pioneers as they pushed west, carries its own tone of moral certainty; far more than the Wilsonians of the Atlantic seaboard, it also represented a deliberate rejection of the old continent which they had left behind, even a denial that Americans shared the same values as the effete and corrupt Europeans.

This anti-European undertone has been sharpened by the alliance between Christian fundamentalists and Jewish conservatives over policy towards the Israel–Palestine conflict, rejecting European criticisms as antisemitic in what EC Commissioner Chris Patten has described as the 'Likudisation of American foreign policy'. The journals of American neo-conservatism, from the *Weekly Standard* to the *Washington Times*, now convey an anti-European bias as pronounced as the anti-American bias of the old European left—linked to rejection both of the applicability of treaties and international law to US domestic legislation and of the relevance of attitudes of other governments and 'the international community' to the shaping of US foreign policy. The rhetoric is imperial, of forceful imposition of US interests, rather than hegemonic, of persuasive leadership couched in multilateral terms, backed by force only when necessary. There is no room for partnership in this more forceful assertion that American interests come first; only for followers prepared to accept America's right to lead.

Bandwagon or balance?

European governments are therefore faced with a harsher choice in responding to the reassertion of American leadership than their predecessors were in responding to President Truman's formulation of shared values across the 'free world', or to President Kennedy's grand design for 'Atlantic partnership', or even to the first President Bush's 1991 evocation of shared values within a 'new world order'. The current rhetoric of 'American values' and 'national interest' is far less inclusive. European governments are offered a choice between 'followership' behind assertive American leadership, or resistance to American leadership—which necessarily implies a search for an alternative focus for power and influence sufficiently strong to demand American attention.

Over the past forty years, British governments have characteristically adopted a bandwagonning stance: declaring their firm support for American strategic goals, while attempting from within that overall stance to influence American policy at the margin. French governments, on the other hand, have characteristically resisted American strategy, while at the same time attempting to persuade their European partners to combine in a caucus which could collectively hope to counterbalance American dominance of Western diplomacy. The dependence of west European states on American military commitment during the Cold War limited the attractions of this balancing strategy to other states, most of all to the then West Germany. Nevertheless, over Middle East policy, in 1973–4 and again in 1981, European governments deliberately diverged from the line set by American leadership—provoking sharp transatlantic disagreements and subsequent retreat from the autonomous approaches briefly adopted. Even before the outbreak of transatlantic differences on the Middle East in 1973, Henry Kissinger's 'Year of Europe' speech had spelt out to America's European allies the realist doctrine that military power and economic cooperation were intrinsically linked, and that western Europe's continuing dependence on the United States to extend security required its governments to bend their international economic policies to American preferences.

British and French approaches have to some extent converged since the end of the Cold War. Both were, for example, determined to provide ground, air and naval forces to support the US-led coalition to expel Iraq from Kuwait in 1991, to demonstrate their significance as American allies. The experience of Bosnia, however, demonstrated to British and French policy-makers alike that a greater capacity for autonomous military operation was needed to avoid being forced to follow US policy without gaining significant influence over its direction: that a balancing caucus was needed to counter US domination. This led to the 1998 Franco-British initiative on European defence, which set out the objective not only of achieving a much greater degree of integration among European military forces but also of establishing a degree of 'auto-nomy' for EU member states within NATO—an objective which successive US administrations had firmly resisted. At the Helsinki European Council in December 1999 the EU heads of government committed themselves to a series of 'headline goals' for deployable military forces, to be operational by 2003. By the summer of 2002, however, progress towards achieving these goals in practice appeared modest.

In the wake of the attacks of September 2001, not only the British but also the French and German governments chose explicitly to bandwagon rather than to balance: to declare their active support for the American response, and to offer military contributions towards it. (The French government, it should be noted, took this stance in the face of considerable opposition in the domestic media.) Tony Blair, the British Prime Minister, went furthest in declaring active sympathy for the American predicament and support for the American response. This gained him immense visibility and popularity within the United States. It remains unclear, however, how far he gained any significant influence over aspects of American policy. All three European governments appear to have chosen explicit support for current US policy in the hope of gaining some degree of leverage over future American options. Their calculation has been that, after such a display of support for current policy, a subsequent threat of withdrawal of support from the United States's most active allies might serve to tip the balance among Washington policy-makers—over further military action against Iraq, for example; that is, they are bandwagonning now in the hope of improving the chances of successful balancing later.

Transatlantic economic relations have, of course, been for many years much more a matter of balance among relatively equal powers than of leadership and followership. The EU is an effective force in global trade negotiations, a standard-setter in international regulation, and a challenge to the extra-territorial reach of American anti-trust policy towards multinational companies—and therefore a necessary partner in developing global competition policies. Successive rounds of world trade negotiations have revolved around transatlantic bargains between the EU and the United States, to rising discontent from other parties to the negotiations. The supremacy of the dollar—and the close links between the Washington-based international financial institutions and the US Treasury—have, however, maintained American dominance over crucial areas of global economic management. In the shadow of the attacks on the World Trade Center and the Pentagon, it is possible that the successful launch across twelve of the fifteen EU member states of the euro, now visibly and tangibly available as an alternative reserve currency and store of value, may prove in the long term to have given the EU the capacity to balance the United States in another major area of global public policy.

For that to happen, however, it will be necessary that the current Jacksonian 'America-first' mood which characterises Washington's approach to politico-military issues does not extend into the politico-economic realm. Rejection of the Kyoto Protocol and of an energy conservation policy, alongside the simultaneous pursuit of a geopolitical strategy towards the control of oil supplies from Central Asia, suggest a similar unilateralism in this sphere. Imposition of steel tariffs, and the commitment to reintroduce substantial subsidies for American farmers, have—at least temporarily—reversed the US commitment to multilateral bargaining through international institutions as a framework for reconciling American interests with those of other states within an open world economy. In trade policy, global competition policy, monetary management and economic stabilisation, European states collectively have balanced the United States for several decades, in a blend of cooperation and competition which has satisfied both sides. European governments may find it difficult to maintain that balance when faced with a more aggressively self-confident United States, wishing to trade off its military dominance by demanding concessions in other spheres.

Currencies of power

One of the most difficult issues for America's European partners to address is that of the balance to be struck between military power, diplomatic activity and economic influence—and how to respond to the greater emphasis American policy-makers characteristically place on military power. West European governments depended on the United States for security throughout the Cold War. The US maintained twelve divisions, two fleets and substantial air forces in and around the European theatre, backed by strategic and tactical nuclear weapons. Institutionalised European integration developed, within this Atlantic security framework, as a self-consciously 'civilian' power, using the instruments of financial assistance and trade concessions to persuade neighbours and partners to cooperate.

The enlightened self-interest which led US administrations to underwrite the economic and political recovery of western Europe after 1945, and to extend an American security guarantee, lay partly in the expectation that the rebuilding of European state structures and economies would in time enable those states to shoulder a larger share of the 'burden' of global order and global development. American policy-makers saw burden-sharing both in military and in economic terms, anticipating that within NATO the European allies would progressively replace the conventional US contribution to the common defence, and that within the UN system and through bilateral economic assistance they would provide a progressively larger financial contribution to the pursuit of shared Western objectives. The question of potential linkages between burden-sharing and policy-sharing remained unexplored; US policy-makers appear to have assumed that their European partners would continue to accept the rationales for American policy, and thus to follow American leadership, even as they shouldered a larger and larger proportion of the costs of the defence and promotion of Western values.

In practice, the United States continued to provide by far the largest contribution to Western defence throughout the 1970s and 1980s, while becoming more and more discontented with its national contributions to economic development in other countries and to international institutions. Since then the continuing shrinkage of US aid programmes, along with congressional resistance to contributions to multilateral institutions accompanied by active support for high levels of military expenditure even after the Soviet threat had disappeared, has tipped the budget for American foreign policy heavily towards military power rather than instruments for economic influence. European governments, in contrast, took their 'peace dividend' in the form of deep cuts in military expenditure, while largely maintaining expenditure on non-military aspects of foreign policy. As a result the United States's share of global military expenditure is now rising from 40 per cent to 50 per cent, while the EU collectively accounts for less than 25 per cent. The United States is battling to reduce its 25 per cent contribution to the budgets of the UN and UN agencies, while EU states collectively contribute 40 per cent of the UN's regular budget, and 50 per cent of agency budgets and the costs of peacekeeping.

There is, however, no basis for mutual understanding across the Atlantic on the appropriate exchange rate between these different currencies of power and influence. The realist conception of foreign policy which underpins the Bush administration emphasises the determining importance of military power, effectively demonstrated once again in its projection over Afghanistan. The logic of this position is that European states must invest a great deal more in deployable military forces if they wish either to balance American dominance or to exert greater influence over the direction of American policy; that the instruments of 'civilian power' are the small change of global influence. There is, however, little domestic support within any European state for significant increases in defence spending—and there is substantial frustration among political elites that substantial expenditure on international economic development, even when (as in Palestine) in support of declared US objectives, has not gained significant influence over the policies which the hegemon pursues.

In summary, the United States has moved towards a foreign policy biased towards coercion, while European states have moved further towards dependence on foreign policy instruments focused on the generation of consent. From the predominant European perspective, American policy-makers over-emphasise the politico-military dimension of international politics; from the predominant American perspective, European governments place far too much faith in diplomacy and economic aid. Divergent attitudes to the threat posed by a new wave of revolutionaries who reject the Western model of modernisation reflect these opposing biases in their approaches to world politics. The rhetoric of the Bush administration, of Congress and of the US media is that the United States is 'at war' with global terrorism: that there is a clear target, which must be attacked and defeated. The understanding of European governments, informed by the bitter experiences of combating terrorism within Europe over the past generation—in Ireland, in Italy, in Germany, in Spain—is that terrorism cannot be defeated through military means alone: that a combination of state reconstruction, economic develop-ment, negotiation, policing, intelligence and military power is necessary to 'drain the swamp' within which terrorism breeds.

Is partnership possible?

American rhetoric about transatlantic partnership was always a little disin-genuous, offering junior partnership within an American-led community rather than an effective partnership of equals. Multilateral rhetoric, and multilateral institutions, nevertheless made it easier for European govern-ments to accept American leadership, and to persuade their domestic publics that they had gained a degree of influence over American policy in return. The United States resisted any moves towards an autonomous European group within NATO, from the 1960s through to the 1990s; but successive US presidents paid lip-service to the multilateral character of NATO, participat-ing in regular summits and bilateral consultations of a quality which persuaded all but Gaullist France that the consultative partnership offered was a bargain worth maintaining. Partnership in global economic policy has become much more substantial—with the partial exception of global financial regulation, where US administrations have remained determined to maintain their key role within the IMF. The most difficult test for continuing hege-mony—that is, for continuing acceptance by America's dependent partners of the legitimacy of its dominant role—thus lies in the politico-military domain.

The United States has now demonstrated, in Afghanistan, that it can go it alone in managing a crisis and defeating a distant but weakly armed opponent. American policy-makers were determined to avoid their Afghan operations becoming entangled in the multilateral coils of NATO, permitting only a handful of forces from a small number of allies to assist the American-led effort. But it has not yet demonstrated that it can build a stable peace within West, Central and Southern Asia without a broader coalition to sustain a longer-term strategy. The implication of administration rhetoric and requests for assistance from allies has been that the long-term process of rebuilding domestic order and a working economy can be shouldered primarily by others, after the United States has defeated the immediate threat. Such a division of responsibilities is unlikely to be welcome or acceptable, however, without both some appearance of continuing consultation and some definition of shared objectives and values sufficient to legitimise the demands the United States wishes to make. A world in which American policy-makers proclaim that 'superpowers don't do windows', or that 'it is not the job of the 101st Airborne to help children across the road', while expecting their allies to shoulder the burden of such essential but subordinate nation-building tasks, is one in which American power is likely to be increasingly resisted rather than welcomed. US power can be successfully exerted in a crisis without waiting for the consent of other friendly states; but if the consent of those friendly states is taken for granted over an extended period it will cease to be offered so willingly, and may in time be withdrawn.

The dilemmas European governments face in the aftermath of 11 September in responding to the expectations of their American hegemon are acute. They have to recognise that Europe as a region now matters far less to the United States than it did over the previous half-century, as American attention has turned to the western hemisphere and Asia. They have to weigh up the arguments for greater investment in military power, partly in response to US expectations and partly as a means of counterbalancing US power. They have to pursue opportunities to influence the direction of US policy, in circumstances in which American tolerance for multilateral channels of consultation has declined. They have to respond to American requests for support and assistance, without having had the opportunity to share in formulating the policy which has set the context within which those requests are made. They will need to learn how to persuade American audiences to accept the legitimacy of European interests, and the credibility of European values. After a period in which European political leaders have invested relatively little in influencing the American political debate, a concerted effort at public diplomacy both in Washington and across the United States will be required.

There are, however, dilemmas for the United States as well. Hegemony rests on consent as well as on coercion, as has been argued above; and consent has to be generated and maintained, through the provision of persuasive leadership and through reference to a universal set of values. Liberal hegemony requires dominant powers to present the pursuit of their enlightened self-interest as being in the common interests of civilisation as a whole. Explicit references to direct and immediate national interests, a rationale for foreign policy which stresses the exceptional and exclusive interests of the United States compared to those of its partners, resistance to multilateral regimes which diffuse American leadership within frameworks of shared rules and obligations, all weaken the 'soft power' of American prestige and reputation on which the informal empire of this hegemonic world order depends.

The founding fathers recognised that 'a decent respect for the opinions of men' outside the North American continent required them to frame the rationale for independence in terms which foreign as well as domestic audiences might accept. US political leaders and intellectual elites in the post-Cold War world have found it easier to address their domestic audience than their partners and allies beyond North America in providing a framework for foreign policy—not recognising that in the long term this may threaten the ability of the US to generate the 'coalitions of the willing' needed to support US objectives across the globe. Where economic and financial instruments are required, America's European partners are essential to such coalitions; where peacemaking and nation-building operations follow the resolution of immediate crises, they have greater resources and skills than any other group of states. Those instruments and resources will continue to be readily available in support of American interests only if American policymakers continue to invest in a multilateral rationale for US dominance, rather than to assert that dominance as a reality which other states must—willingly or unwillingly—accept. Hegemony rests upon a range of resources: hard military power, economic weight, financial commitments, and the soft currency of hegemonic values, cultural influence and prestige. Soft power costs political time and investment, rather than massive expenditure of budgetary resources; imaginative leadership, to persuade those states in the shadow of the hegemon that they share in a common enterprise, rather than being coerced to follow an agenda set over their heads.

This is an extended and updated version of 'Living with the Hegemon: European Dilemmas', chapter 6 in Eric Hershberg and Kevin W. Moore, eds, *Terrorism and the International Order: Global Perspectives on Sept. 11th and its Aftermath*, New York, New Press/SSRC, 2002.

The Eleventh of September and beyond: NATO

ANNE DEIGHTON*

THE US military retaliation against al-Qaeda was not a NATO action. Yet since 11 September, decision-makers have struggled to redefine NATO in a world that is absorbed by the phenomenon of global terrorism. Some predict NATO's demise; others its transformation. It may evolve as a defence and anti-terror alliance, as a regional security community, as both, or perhaps as neither. It is not clear who will be its members, or how it can and should operate as a politico-military organisation. During the 1990s the focus of the NATO reform debate settled around three issues: the strategic and capabilities agenda, its relationship with the EU, and enlargement. All three remain at the core of the NATO debate. What the terrorist attacks have done is to intensify these debates.

All for one?

On 12 September 2001 the North Atlantic Council decided that, if it could be shown that the suicide attacks against the United States had been directed from abroad, they should be considered to constitute an action covered by Article 5 of the North Atlantic Treaty.[1] On 2 October the Council was given evidence to prove this, and it then announced that Article 5 was operational. Indeed, on 27 September NATO defence ministers had offered their military support, but were told by the US Deputy Secretary of Defense, Paul Wolfowitz, that the United States did not require a NATO operation. This was a crucial moment: Article 5 failed to trigger a NATO-led military response. Instead, the galling memories of bad coordination and planning, ill-preparedness and lack of suitable European capabilities that had marked the Kosovo military campaign of 1999 made an unencumbered US military operation a *sine qua non*. The United States preferred to operate with what Secretary of Defense Donald Rumsfeld called 'floating coalitions'. It asked for enhanced intelligence sharing, blanket overflight clearance and access to facilities worldwide, security for US facilities and 'backfilling' by NATO allies to give the US greater operational freedom, by which it meant that it might draw down units involved in Balkan operations.

On 7 October the US swung into action in Operation Enduring Freedom, which was initially a bombing campaign directed from US Central Command

* I am grateful to Paul Lettow, Tim Noetzel, Anna Vassileva and Stephanie Willmann for information and helpful comments.

119

in Tampa, Florida; it received direct military support from Britain alone, although the number of contributing countries grew as the campaign turned from the air to the ground. These US decisions—first to work outside the NATO framework, and then to operate by building bilateral coalitions at head of state level, rather than through multilateral organisations—have been one of the most noticeable features of its military performance, fuelling doubts about the long-term commitment of the United States to multilateral solutions.

That the US response would initially be virtually unilateral was perhaps to be expected, but it was doubly ironic for NATO. In 1949, everyone had assumed that the all-important Article 5 would cover an attack by the Soviet Union on western Europe, not one on the United States by a terrorist group. Further, it was US decision-makers who had crafted the wording of the Article in such a way as to forestall their being automatically drawn into a military conflict in Europe. The global application of Article 5 had been considered during the Cold War (over Algeria and Vietnam) and during the Gulf War, but the Article had not been invoked. Now, the ill-conceived decision of 12 September exposed the conditional nature of Article 5. In the interests of fighting an effective war, the Americans decided not to bring NATO into the battlefield.

The military contribution that NATO made was not in the combat zone. Instead, five (then eight) of NATO's twenty-four airborne warning and control systems (AWACs), with multinational crews, were deployed to patrol US airspace, to allow the Americans greater operational flexibility and enable the United States to deploy its own AWACs to the Indian Ocean. This NATO operation ended in mid-May, when the aircraft returned to their duties over south-eastern Europe (which had been covered by France for the previous seven months). NATO further deployed nine vessels from its Standing Naval Force Mediterranean to the eastern Mediterranean, to give a presence in that area and to demonstrate NATO's 'resolve and loyalty'.[2]

Behind the scenes, NATO was also engaged in talks with Russia about nuclear, chemical and biological technologies. The initial reaction to an attack on the United States that involved no sophistication in terms of tools has developed into a concern about control of and countermeasures against the acquisition of tools of mass destruction by non-state actors and those members of the American-designated 'axis of evil'. Thus, in general, disarmament and non-proliferation, the threats posed by the proliferation of weapons of mass destruction (WMD) and their means of delivery, conventional arms reductions, transparency and confidence- and security-building measures have been high on the NATO agenda, operating through the WMD Centre. This work on NATO's part, along with deterrence and defence, was stressed as playing an essential role in enhancing security against these new threats.

NATO's battlefield role was not marginal through want of trying. Hasty plans were drawn up for NATO to deploy peacekeeping forces in Afghanistan when the first phase of fighting was completed. However, when the Petersberg Conference was convened in Bonn in December 2001, the UN stalled any opportunity for NATO to lead the follow-up operations in Afghanistan. This decision was taken in part because the Afghan representatives themselves did not in fact want any follow-on peacekeeping force. For NATO, however, it represented another blow to the chance to use the Afghan operation as a means of engaging NATO forces, while the United States was able to continue with its chosen way forward, with a growing ad hoc coalition. NATO tried to put a brave face on this, announcing:

We reiterate our determination to combat the threat of terrorism for as long as necessary. In keeping with our obligations under the Washington Treaty we will continue to strengthen our national and collective capacities to protect . . . from any armed attack, including terrorist attack, directed from abroad . . . Meeting this challenge is fundamental to our security . . . we will examine ways to adapt and enhance Alliance military capabilities. We will deepen our relations with other states and international organisations . . . We stress that military tools alone are not sufficient to combat terrorism effectively. The response must be multi-faceted and comprehensive . . . In this context, NATO and the European Union are exploring ways to enhance cooperation to combat terrorism.[3]

Fine words.

However, the peacekeeping efforts in Afghanistan were conducted through the International Security Assistance Force (ISAF) and not coordinated by NATO, although reportedly there were more European national contingents serving in this force than there were American soldiers in the country. NATO's own peacekeeping operations were confined to the continuing effort in the Balkans (from which the Americans had withdrawn several thousand of their own troops) and a mission in Macedonia. This latter was led and manned by Europeans, and had the imprimatur of NATO, rather than the use of US troops. However, it was before 11 September that the United States had suggested that they would not send personnel to Macedonia for the follow-up operations there.

Does this story of relative NATO inactivity from 11 September now spell the end for NATO? The answer is no—at least, not of itself. NATO's failure to engage fully is symptomatic of a malaise that has existed for more than a decade, and indeed, quarrels between allies were part of the fabric of the alliance during the Cold War. As the Cold War ended, many thought that NATO would cease to have a role. Others claimed that NATO had always been a transatlantic security community that bound its Western partners together, as well as having a defence role, and would therefore survive a major system change.[4] Meanwhile, the 1990s were characterised by a transatlantic 'drift': the emergence of different cultural preferences (over, for example, gun control and the death penalty), and disputes over the US commitment to international institutions.

Debates on the future of NATO also took place in the context of greater military instability and insecurity than Europe had known since 1945. While some states had been able to re-emerge or re-invent themselves in the 1990s (Germany, the Baltic states, the Czech Republic, Slovakia, Slovenia), in others, particularly in the Balkans, state-building was accompanied by bloodshed. It was in this context that NATO actually undertook its first major military operations—and they were not under Article 5—with air strikes over the Bosnian towns of Sarajevo and Pale in 1995. NATO took to the air after first EC and then UN diplomacy had failed in the years after 1991. NATO then led the peacekeeping operations in Bosnia with the creation of the International Force (IFOR). These operations attracted participation from non-member states, including Russia, in 1996. However, the Kosovo operation of 1999 stretched both American patience and European capabilities to their limits, and was to inform and shape American decision-making about the role of NATO in its armed struggle after 11 September.

All for what? And how?

So what should NATO now do, and how should it do it? Even in the 1990s, questions of strategy, missions and capabilities were problematic. The 1991 New Strategic Concept did not provide a durable tool. The primary difficulty was that of the relationship between the Atlantic and the European sides of the alliance, and in particular the formation and equipping of forces that would be better suited to a rapidly changing strategic landscape. The European Security and Defence Identity, Combined Joint Task Forces, the Allied Rapid Reaction Force concept, and then the Defence Capabilities Initiative of 1999 all pointed to a demand for greater flexibility, mobility and interoperability. It was envisaged that any operations would probably take place outside alliance territory. They might last for many years; and they would involve troops of many nations working closely together—principally from member states but also, in some instances, from partner countries. Moreover, it was already appreciated that crisis management tasks demanded different skills from those required for fighting wars.

The possibility of worldwide operations with coalitions that extended beyond NATO members' territory was thus under consideration as part of the remodelling of NATO well before 11 September 2001. It was a debate in which the Clinton administration had favoured global operations, and the Europeans did not. Article 24 of the 1999 Strategic Concept, however, stated that alliance security interests must also take account of the global context. This constituted an admission that alliance security risks could be affected by other risks of a wider nature, including acts of terrorism, sabotage and organised crime, and by the disruption of the flow of vital resources. The uncontrolled movement of large numbers of people, particularly as a result of armed conflicts, could also pose problems for security and stability affecting the alliance.[5] Yet, when George W. Bush came into office, this dimension to the NATO debate was temporarily dropped.

Now a global role for NATO in support of the new US grand strategy is back on the agenda. In his speech to the German Bundestag in May 2002, Bush argued that 'America and Europe need each other to fight and win the war against global terror.' Reaffirming his own belief in the 'axis of evil' as the basis of the strategic challenge to the United States, he went on to say that 'NATO needs a new strategy and new capabilities' and to be 'able and willing to act whenever threats emerge . . . We do not know where the next threat may come from, we really don't know what form it might take.'[6]

In an important recent *Foreign Affairs* article, Rumsfeld has accentuated that fear of surprise ('It's like dealing with burglars,' he said), which has prompted the United States to focus upon its ability to respond to and pre-empt further attacks. The eleventh of September is portrayed as only the beginning of a new phase: as the new adversaries 'gain access to weapons of increasing range and power, the attacks could grow vastly more deadly than those we suffered on September 11'. A capabilities approach by the United States envisages the potential to engage in four theatres, backed up by the ability to defeat two aggressors at the same time, while preserving the option for one massive counteroffensive to occupy an aggressor's capital and replace its regime. Pre-emptive defence and massive new defence investments, particularly in the areas of conventional forces and missile defence, characterise the US approach to the defence needs of the United States, and these are the ideas that are driving the current NATO capabilities debate.

In keeping with the priorities of the new US Quadrennial Review, Rumsfeld (who did not even mention NATO in his article), proclaimed that the United States would accept help from any country, on a basis that is comfortable for its government, and that the United States could 'benefit from coalitions of the willing'. But the 'mission must determine the coalition, the coalition must not determine the mission', and war by committee is out of the question.[7] It is not made clear whether this is a reflection on NATO's or the United States's own chain of command during the Kosovo air strikes, but the implication is clearly that Europeans should be thinking about preparing to retool NATO in a way that is compatible with US global policies. If they do not, the United States will continue alone, or with ad hoc coalitions. The US expectation is now that if NATO is to be part of the US global campaign against terror, NATO's rapid reaction forces could no longer expect to operate only within Europe, but on the contrary must be ready to deploy almost anywhere that member states feel themselves threatened. The British and Spaniards have led a response to this US thinking, which echoed the global role they felt NATO should additionally be able to perform. The gloss put on this by one British official was as follows:

the way I would see this manifesting itself in reality is that NATO would be able to play a role in areas where it looked efficient for NATO to go and do the job, which certainly comprehends as far as Afghanistan and I would say well down into central Africa . . . it was terribly important that we didn't set a limit on how far we went because that just encourages terrorists to set up somewhere else outside that area.[8]

NATO must thus redefine its objectives; but in the eyes of the United States, that alone will not be enough. Since Kosovo, the Europeans' capabilities gap has entered the catalogue of NATO's woes, and after 11 September the capabilities issue has rarely left the centre of the debate. First, the Defence Capabilities Initiative of 1999, with its fifty-eight new spending priorities, has had to be rewritten.[9] The United States points out that the Europeans simply did not have many of the military tools to enable them to launch a NATO operation. The US defence budget is $380 billion and has just received a $48 billion increase. The US view is that it may not be possible for the Europeans to keep up with the United States's continuing revolution in military affairs—even if they spend a great deal more on defence than they are doing now. As one official has put it, while 'the U.S. Air Force is studying the first flight of Boeing's newest X-45A Unmanned Combat Aerial Vehicle—so advanced it may herald the end of the manned bomber—NATO is asking Bulgaria if it can offer anything more to its rapid reaction forces than the decontamination bath units it has sent to Bagram air base in Afghanistan.'[10]

The Europeans do already spend $150 billion on their defence needs, but the American hope is that they will now both spend what they have more effectively, and also increase those defence budgets. The formula which is dominating the agenda is C4ISR, covering command and control, computers and communications, surveillance, reconnaissance and intelligence. If the Europeans cannot comply, a European credibility gap will develop which, as Lord Robertson has argued, will reveal that in fact the Europeans are more interested in producing bureaucracy than capability. In practical terms, discussions now centre on the extension of the CJTF principle, heavy-lift capacity, and JStar surveillance systems.

Whether the Europeans should buy American, or whether they should develop joint European ventures, raises political as well as capability questions about markets. The need for speedy recalibration of the military machine, and the desire to penetrate the European market, are clearly influencing American policy, although the argument is that compatibility with American armaments and equipment is essential for effective NATO operations. However, European publics are deeply suspicious about increasing defence budgets, despite a stream of exhortations from NATO officials and some leaders of European governments.

However this capabilities debate develops, to find the means of acting as a European security institution NATO itself will require a very substantial overhaul of both its own administrative structures and its capacities. Its administrative budget has been cut by 5 per cent since the end of 2001, making reform an ambitious task, which a possible enlargement will make even harder. NATO's committee structure is cumbersome. Its officials could learn from the experience of the EU, which has, over time—while often nervous about enlargement and policy initiatives—managed to combine enlargement with administrative reform. However, there is as yet no public debate about the nature of NATO decision-making; nor is it likely that the

United States would welcome changes that reduced its own capacity to act. Yet ironically, it was the operational weakness of these very structures that contributed to NATO's frailties over Kosovo, and the subsequent US rejection of NATO as the vehicle for its response to the suicide attacks. NATO has developed rather effective mechanisms for those who are within the Partnership for Peace, and has moved ahead on its civilian dimensions in the Euro-Atlantic Partnership Council (EAPC) in areas relating to civil emergency planning and international disaster relief, but it is not an organisation that is embedded in a set of foreign policies. NATO is thus unable to implement structured security decisions and to project its norms using a range of foreign policy tools.[11]

NATO and the EU

In this respect NATO is very different from the EU. The EU has a large range of security policies, both to consolidate and develop relations between its members, and also for use when it projects power beyond its borders. These range from economic tools (trade, aid, sanctions), to diplomatic activity and legal instruments. Indeed, after 11 September the EU was to legislate, act diplomatically and use its trade tools.

Since the end of the Cold War, competition between the EU and NATO has developed over the sphere of military security. One reason for this was that the EU, which had in effect had a self-denying ordinance on the acquisition of a military role during the Cold War, began to move into the same security space that NATO was also beginning to occupy as the end of the Cold War removed its own obvious *raison d'être*. With the Treaty of Maastricht, which opened the way to closer relations for both NATO and the EU with the Western European Union, the EU began to explore the possibilities of taking a greater role in the provision of its own military security. This came about in part through long-term pressure for an integrated EU to play a wider international role, and in part through Western military failures in Bosnia— and, indeed, because of some Europeans' fears about US foreign policies in the mid-1990s.

In December 1998 the British and the French agreed at their bilateral summit in St Malo that the EU should begin to think about creating a small EU rapid reaction force for certain security tasks. While the French saw this as part of their long-held ambitions for greater European security autonomy, the British saw it rather as a way of shoring up NATO. After 1998, EU leaders sought to create a military headline goal of about 60,000 troops available for Petersberg tasks of crisis management and peacekeeping, and a civilian headline goal for parallel policing and judicial operations. An EU police force will be deployed in Bosnia in 2003, when the UN mandate for the region ends.[12]

Though neither Britain nor France claimed that St Malo was intended to weaken NATO, and both, in different ways, interpreted it as a means to develop the resources of the EU, the initiative sharpened up the transatlantic debate about its future. Many in Washington were furious. Many others thought that it was high time that the Europeans organised their military capabilities more effectively, particularly after Kosovo. As one Foreign Office official put it, 50 per cent of those in the Pentagon thought that the European initiative would destroy NATO, while the other 50 per cent hoped it might possibly save it. One difficulty has been in achieving a balance in allowing the facilities for the EU to operate autonomously without upsetting the delicate relationship between the United States/NATO and the EU itself. This has been made harder by the fact that NATO actually has very few military assets of its own, and so, in practice, cooperation with the United States for military tools is essential.

However, not all members of NATO are in the EU: Turkey, Norway, Poland, Hungary, the Czech Republic, Iceland and Canada are not. Neither are all members of the EU also in NATO: Austria, Finland, Ireland and Sweden remain outside the alliance. This has increased tensions in an already problematic debate about the civilian ethos of the EU since its inception, and how 'militarising' the EU should proceed. For non-NATO members, there has been an understandable reluctance to allow NATO practices and influence to dominate such a sensitive area of EU policy-making, and therefore a tendency to insist upon privileging the civilian aspects of intervention and peace-keeping. For NATO members, there has been a reluctance to allow assets from NATO to be deployed indiscriminately for EU operations. In the case of Turkey, the so-called Berlin Plus issue of access to NATO assets by the EU has been complicated by Turkey's long-standing and as yet unsuccessful application for membership of the EU. No sooner was a provisional deal reached than the Greeks raised objections to the formula on the grounds of other policy concerns relating to Cyprus.

The ESDP (European Security and Defence Policy) process has continued at its own pace since 11 September, although the question of whether ESDP should be confined to regional security operations, or be harnessed to the wider global operations that the United States appears to have in mind for NATO, is now exercising its decision-makers. There is nothing in the Petersberg tasks that would of itself prevent global operations, but the first priority remains the provision of security tools for the EU's own 'near' abroad'. If it can also organise its military capabilities, it is relatively well placed to deliver as a security institution, not least given the continuing need for some kind of outside military presence in the Balkan region. However, the Americans are developing plans for NATO-based mobile units, plans which could well be seen as rivals to the EU's headline goal, and to the promise of military autonomy in the mid-term.

American views have long been split among those who supported European efforts to organise their security more effectively; those who have argued that the 'Pax Americana' is so unchallengeable by Europeans that the United States can support an EU security identity, as it will simply make the Europeans more useful, not geopolitical competitors; and those who have argued that 'America's days as a well-bred doormat for EU political and military pretensions are coming to an end.'[13] Lord Robertson argues that the ESDP must not stall in the face of 11 September and its consequences, and warns of a return to the 1950s, when the Americans under President Eisenhower threatened an 'agonising reappraisal' if the Europeans did not sort out their military security problems. Robertson is no doubt exhorting the Europeans to spend more money, and to develop capabilities compatible with those used by the United States, to avoid NATO 'lite' by acting before the unilateralists win the day in the United States.[14]

One NATO for all Europe?

Both NATO and the EU are enlarging. The enlargement question was intensely debated in the 1990s, and remains a key component of the debate, despite America's unilateralist impulse. Strategic institutional initiatives to re-imagine NATO were developed through the North Atlantic Cooperation Council (NACC), Partnership for Peace (PfP, which now has twenty-six members), and the reformed NACC, now called the Euro-Atlantic Partnership Council (EAPC), to extend NATO's remit beyond its full members. By 1994, enlargement under Article 10 of the 1949 Treaty was being considered. After considerable pressure from Germany, and from the Czech Republic, Hungary and Poland themselves, the United States took the lead in proposing and pushing through NATO's first post-Cold War enlargement to these three east European states, which joined in 1999. Then, in an important speech in Warsaw in June 2001, President Bush asserted that it was not a question of 'whether', but 'when' the other hopefuls—the Baltic states, Bulgaria and Romania, Slovakia, Slovenia and Macedonia, as well as Albania—would the leave the so-called 'grey zone' of east–central Europe and join NATO.[15]

After 11 September the pace of negotiations accelerated, and there ensued a somewhat undignified scramble by the applicants to accommodate themselves to American interests, not least by offering contributions to the American military effort. The Prague NATO summit of November 2002 was seen as a kind of deadline for decisions, and the maximalist 'big bang' outcome would be for Bulgaria, Estonia, Latvia, Lithuania, Romania, Slovakia and Slovenia to be offered membership. Learning from the experience of the 1999 enlargement exercise, this time Membership Action Plans (MAPs) were drawn up. They committed the applicants to a raft of military, legal and civil-society obligations relating to democratic procedures and human rights, and to an obligation to spend at least 2 per cent of GDP on defence. As with all earlier NATO enlargements, the United States drove this process, which is popular with the political elites in most of the applicant countries: NATO membership carries with it the prospect of greater foreign direct investment, diplomatic prestige and, indeed, legitimacy.

The speed at which the negotiations were taking place carries hazards with it, and risks creating long-term problems through a short-term fix propelled by 11 September and the prospect of the Prague summit. Further, little is known about the import of this NATO enlargement, either among applicants or among existing member states. NATO has maximum leverage over the applicants only in the run-up to their admission; it is essential that the threshold for membership should not be sacrificed in the interests of achieving quick results. (It is possible to expel members of NATO after a warning period of six months.)

For example, the membership of Bulgaria and Romania would seem to make considerable strategic sense, given their geographical proximity to the eastern Mediterranean and beyond to Central Asia, where the United States sees major problems. However, there is not yet incontrovertible evidence that these states are fully prepared and stable democracies. Indeed, as recently as February 2002 there were indications that Lord Robertson was hoping that the EU could be persuaded to admit them until they were ready for NATO membership. (In the run-up to the 1999 enlargement, there were similar American suggestions that the Baltic states should be accommodated in the EU, as the climate was clearly not ripe for their accession to NATO.) There were difficult debates within Latvia concerning the electoral rights of the Russian-speakers there, whose numbers amount to almost 30 per cent of the population. Slovakia was under warning in the run-up to elections.

As they themselves have admitted, none of the applicants has very much to bring to NATO's strategic equation: a 'big bang' enlargement will add 35 per cent more territory to the alliance, but only 2.5 per cent more GDP. (Similar statistics hold for the EU: if the ten applicants join, they will add 23 per cent to its territory, 20 per cent to its population, and 4 per cent to its GDP.) Further, the push to achieve the 2 per cent of GDP requirement on defence spending has proved hard for most of the applicants: indeed, none of the 1999 entrants has yet achieved this level of expenditure. However, the pressure on the Europeans to purchase more weapons and equipment—and to do so from the United States—has intensified over the past year.

Although a 'big bang' enlargement does not imply that all invited states would join at the same time, it does imply another future NATO enlargement: Albania and Croatia, Macedonia and Serbia are eyeing NATO. More significantly, the position of those countries already in the EU, but as yet remaining outside NATO (Austria, Finland, Ireland and Sweden) may well become untenable after the this round of enlargement, as many elites are beginning to recognise. NATO enlargement to some or all of these countries would spill over into the security policy framework of the EU for all its members, including France, as well as making the already fragile position of Canada's NATO membership more complicated.

The current applicants are seeking to join an institution which is itself changing. For example, while post-territoriality is part of the postmodern security discourse, it is not clear that such thinking would carry the day for a new NATO member that experienced territorial violations. Yet the conditionality of NATO's Article 5 was shown after 11 September. Joining NATO is still not a matter of membership of a civilian security community organisation, like OSCE, but carries military obligations and promises, whose contours are still unclear. Many of the NATO applicant countries are also hoping to join the EU, but the two sets of enlargements have not yet been conceived as part of a joint strategy. There is some evidence that applicant countries are already looking over Brussels towards Washington in matters concerning military security, although NATO leaders thought of enlargement as two parallel processes.[16]

There is one area in which the institutional framework of NATO has already changed sharply, and that is in its relations with Russia. As the Cold War ended, it was clear that Russian relations with the West were sensitive, but still vitally important. In 1995 Russia itself joined PfP, and contributed to NATO-led peacekeeping operations in the Balkans, although there was strong and understandable Russian resistance to any NATO enlargement. By 1997, a NATO–Russia Act was agreed, and a Joint Permanent Council was set up. This Council did not prove very active or successful, and Russia's relations with the West took a sharply downward turn after the Kosovo air strikes.

President Putin's sympathetic response to 11 September has opened the way to further institutional change within NATO as well as in Russia's bilateral relations with the United States. For the United States, Russia after 11 September was a partner with expertise to offer—indeed, images of abandoned Russian tanks still occur in footage of Afghanistan, testimony to the disastrous Soviet invasion of 1979. Putin saw that his own problems with terrorism in Chechnya could be recontextualised in the light of America's experience with terrorism, even if this should mean allowing US bases in Central Asia. Progress at the bilateral level has been rapid as Putin sees a unique window of opportunity for Russia to re-establish itself on the international stage. The ride has been occasionally bumpy, but Putin's hostility to the earlier American proposal unilaterally to abandon the ABM Treaty was modified, and in May 2002 he and Bush signed an agreement to reduce the numbers of strategic nuclear weapons each holds by two-thirds, although weapons will not necessarily be destroyed.

Putin commented in October 2001 that 'if NATO takes on a different shade and is becoming a political organisation . . . we would reconsider our position with regard to such expansion, if we are to feel involved in such processes.'[17] This represented a clear shift in the Russian President's thinking on NATO enlargement. In November 2001 Blair began negotiations on an initiative to bring Russia closer to NATO than the Joint Permanent Council had allowed for. For several months, complicated negotiations took place between the Russians and NATO. The Russians sought joint decision-making across all NATO issues; NATO insisted upon 'retrievability' of any subject, which meant that the Russians would not be given full NATO rights, nor would they have any sort of decision-making veto. The 'NATO at 20' agreement, signed at the NATO Council meeting in Rome only one week after the nuclear arms limitation treaty, gave Russia a place at the NATO table. The Russians will move into offices in Brussels, and will meet regularly with NATO as equals when issues relating to terrorism and counter-terrorism, WMD, rescue operations and so on are discussed. But Russia has not joined NATO, and all sides have retrievability rights.

This agreement might not be particularly well received by those countries from eastern Europe that are seeking full NATO membership. Many wish to draw a line under their former relationship with the old Soviet Union. However, for countries such as Bulgaria, which have strong and established trade relations with Russia, this is not an issue. The agreement received some criticism from within the United States, too, by those who feel that it signals too clearly the end of NATO's role as a defensive alliance, or that Russia's political system is still flawed. On the other hand, it has also been argued that the agreement paves the way for enlargement by reducing Russian fears about NATO's intentions and character, and that the United States will also gain in its bilateral relationship with Russia.

Putin has played a difficult hand well thus far, although he is under constant pressure from those among the military within Russia itself who see their country's territorial and decision-making autonomy slipping away. Russian foreign policy remains dominated by notions of balance: just before the NATO agreement was signed, Putin signed a presentational upgrade of a ten-year-old collective security organisation with his six neighbours, for joint initiatives and exercises. The move is clearly an attempt to show that Moscow is doing something to balance the United States in Central Asia. Thus he has pursued a double strategy: on the one hand he has sought to weave Russia more closely into international organisations (although membership of the WTO remains the biggest, and as yet elusive prize for a former superpower which now has a GDP equivalent to that of the Netherlands); at the same time he is seeking to present Russia as a serious great power in a strategic bilateral relationship with Bush. This is based upon his perception of the US interest in dealing with terror, and also looks further east towards the ways in wich relations may develop with China. This realistic approach has suited the United States quite well.

The European reaction to these developments has been largely positive. Yet when taken as part of Bush's preferences for bilateral agreements and heads-of-state diplomacy, the Bush–Putin entente poses problems for existing and new NATO members. They may find themselves more closely woven into a NATO institutional structure that includes new members, and which has a 'place at the table' for the Russians, but in which the United States may take less interest over the longer term.

Conclusion: power, terror and security

Since 11 September, the overwhelming preponderance of US technological, military and economic power is undeniably a 'given'. This phenomenon is not new. During the Cold War, the relative wealth of the United States under-pinned its reconstruction efforts, military developments and its acquisition of a global role.[18] In the early post-Cold War period, fears were expressed—especially in France—about American 'hyperpower', and the United States's apparent growing disregard for the constraining influences of international institutions. However, it was not clear to Americans who or where the enemy was, or if there was actually an enemy at all.

This angst came to an end with 11 September. Paul Kennedy's seminal article in the *Financial Times* set out very starkly the unprecedented relative disparity of US power.[19] When this power was suddenly coupled with a new mission, existing international institutions then appeared rather feeble. Remarks such as those of President Bush—that 'those who are not with us are against us', and his unfortunate early use of the image of an American crusade—signalled that the United States would now act bluntly in its own perceived national interests. During the following year, US grand strategy and its consequences have become clearer.

The first issue is whether the United States, while happy to work with coalition partners who are useful, does not now wish to be bound by partners, particularly within institutions. As NATO was sidelined after 11 September, national leaders took a greater role. Putin seized what he saw as a strategic opportunity. Leading west European figures expressed solidarity through the EU and NATO, but—particularly Tony Blair—also acted unilaterally. Their responses undermined a collective European response (particularly from the smaller states) as the international fall-out of 11 September spread, particu-larly to Israel and Palestine, and as the long-contested issue of policy towards Iraq came back to the top of the international agenda. Bilateral politics and ad hoc coalitions necessarily threaten the cohesion of international institutions, and this affects NATO's role.

Second, the events of 11 September and their consequences tell much about NATO as an institution. NATO has always reflected American hegemony, and has depended upon American military power. US leadership within NATO was needed to animate it as an effective player in any military engagement. This was not forthcoming in September 2001. Subsequently, the United States has moved towards reinventing NATO in a way that focuses upon its own global fight against terror, implying that the Europeans must intensify their efforts to update their military capabilities, and, further, ensure compatibility with the United States' own capabilities. How NATO Euro-peans respond to this is up to them.

There are two issues here: the nature of terror, and the appropriateness of NATO as an instrument with which to challenge terror. How realistic and substantive is 'terror' as the object of a policy strategy, and as a basis for a reformed NATO? This 'war' could be a war without end: for, given the covert nature of terrorism, how will we know when the war is won? Further, the causes of terrorist action are complex. They range from simple moral wickedness through cultural clashes to increasing social and economic despair in a globalising world where the disparities in wealth can be seen by all (terrorism as the weapon of the weak) and to the relationship between terrorist activity and political ends (terrorists as freedom fighters). This phenomenon does not, therefore, invite primarily militaristic responses. Terrorism as war further defies any distinction between domestic and foreign policies, and has thus far enabled governments to act in ways which erode their own democratic values and human rights. This is increasingly adding an alarming twist to the old Cold War concept of the 'national security' state, as civil rights are diminished in the interests of security against terror, although potentially racial or 'civilisational' dimensions have as yet been given less public emphasis than the application of terror as a form of political behaviour. It is, however, essential that civilian and legal processes mediate between the military and terror, not least to prevent the loss of the very freedoms and human rights in whose name counterterrorist actions are undertaken. Indeed, law-based and human rights groups must also mediate between states (and the EU) and the character and implications of anti-terror legislation.

If in the medium term the 'war' against terrorism loses political salience, a re-imagined NATO may have difficulties acting as an international institution and mediating the wider security interests of all its members if it has become a provider of services, including specialised manpower, to the United States. If the United States loses interest, or if the Europeans fail to perform over capabilities in a way that meets Pentagon needs, the institutional base will seem very hollow, as NATO would have little to offer beyond military action.

A broader interpretation of events since 11 September, however, indicates that the United States will, over time, add nuance to its NATO policy, and will remember that NATO can serve US interests in Europe in ways other than as an anti-terror institution. Enlargement and the negotiations with Russia are evidence of this. So the diplomatic, political and economic opportunities that NATO still presents for its influence in Europe are not lost on the Americans, even as they reduce their direct role as a provider of military security in the region. Indeed, such a scenario could give rise to the possibility that the EU's own efforts will be crushed by US insistence upon the reinvention of NATO in their own interests, and that the EU will be relegated to a second-order security institution, with strategic priorities and resources shifting to comply with a NATO configured according to anti-terrorist objectives.

The ESDP and the EU's own ambitious enlargement strategy have moved forward, despite the turbulence of 2001–2. The ESDP, unlike NATO, is firmly anchored within the foreign and security policy-making structures of the EU and its member states. The deliberate ambiguity about the remit of the ESDP does allow for global operations—and Palestine is one area that has been suggested; but with limited resources, regional priorities are also pressing, and there is an obvious role for an effective ESDP, starting in the Balkans. It would be bad for Europeans and for Americans if the ESDP initiative were now lost. But the delicate and sometimes very raw seam of NATO/EU military security provision is under continuous pressure despite efforts to weave a path between US assets, NATO engagement, EU autonomy and NATO/EU cohesion.

The NATO debate is about power in international institutions, the relationship between the United States and Europe, and whether the United States, the preponderant power, will continue to act multilaterally. The United States is free to make strategic choices. The European partners will make their own judgements on their best national and European interests, but they do not have that same freedom of choice, although it is clear that it is in no one's interests that they be left less tightly bound to each other through institutions. Yet as the fall-out from 11 September continues, institutional competition may become more, not less intense, and the Europeans, and the EU itself, are clearly weaker players than is the United States, either with or without NATO. More has happened to NATO in the last year than in any year since it was created, except perhaps 1999. For the Americans, the Europeans, and the shape of the international system, the dust has not yet settled.

Notes

1 Article 5 of the 1949 NATO Treaty states that 'The Parties agree that an armed attack against one or more of them in Europe or North America shall be considered an attack against them all and consequently they agree that, if such an armed attack occurs, each of them, in exercise of the right of individual or collective self-defence recognised by Article 51 of the Charter of the United Nations, will assist the Party or Parties so attacked by taking forthwith, individually and in concert with the other Parties, such action as it deems necessary, including the use of armed force, to restore and maintain the security of the North Atlantic area.'

2 Christopher Bennett, 'Aiding America', *NATO Review*, vol. 49, no. 4, Winter 2001. For an early overview of these events, see Philip H. Gordon, 'NATO after 11 September', *Survival*, vol. 43, no. 4, 2001, pp. 89–106; and for an early assessment, François Heisbourg, 'Europe and the Transformation of the World Order', speech to the IISS/CEPS European Security Forum, Brussels, 5 Nov. 2001.

3 M-NAC 2(2001)158, 6 Dec. 2001, at www.nato.int/docu/pr/2001/p01-158e.htm.

4 Thomas Risse-Kappen, *Cooperation among Democracies: The European Influence on US Foreign Policy*, Princeton, Princeton University Press, 1995; Helga Haftendorn, Robert Keohane and Celeste Wallander, eds, *Imperfect Unions : Security Institutions over Time and Space*, Oxford, Oxford University Press, 1999.

5 'The Alliance's New Strategic Concept'.

6 www.usembassy/de/bush2002/bundestag.

7 Donald H. Rumsfeld, 'Transforming the Military', *Foreign Affairs*, vol. 81, no. 3, May/June 2002, pp. 20–32.

8 Quoted by Peter Almond in 'NATO New Members not a Natural Fit', UPI, 29 May 2002.

9 Stanley R. Sloan, 'Crisis Response', *NATO Review*, Spring 2002, issue 1, at www.nato.int/docu/review/issue1/opinion.html.

10 Quoted by Peter Almond in 'NATO New Members not a Natural Fit'.

11 For a clear overview account of why a wider approach than that of military/ strategic studies is needed to understand contemporary security issues, see Barry Buzan, *People, States and Fear: An Agenda for International Security Studies in the Post Cold-War Era*, Harlow, Longman, 1991 edn.

12 Anne Deighton, 'Militarising the European Union', research paper no. 15, University of Québec, Montreal, at www.er.uqam.ca/nobel/cepes/notes/ note15.html; and 'Why St Malo Matters', in Hall Gardner and Radoslava Stefanova, eds, *The New Transatlantic Agenda: Facing the Challenges of Global Governance*, Aldershot, Ashgate, 2001, pp. 51–64.

13 W. C. Wolhforth, 'Stability of a Unipolar World', *International Security*, vol. 24, no. 1, Summer 1999; John Bolton, *Financial Times*, 11 Feb. 2000. See further Robert D. Kaplan, *Warrior Politics*, New York, Random House, 2002; Nicholas Lemann, 'The Next World Order', *New Yorker*, March 2002.

14 Lord Robertson, 'Defence and Security in an Uncertain World', speech to Forum Europe, Brussels, 17 May 2002, at www.nato.int/docu/speech/2002/ s020517a.htm; 'Robertson Says NATO Must Spend to Remain Effective', Reuters, 5 June 2002.

15 President Bush's remarks, Warsaw University, US Embassy text: www.usembassy/ de/bush2002/bundestag.

16 Antonio Missiroli, *Bigger EU, Wider CFSP, Stronger ESDP?*, occasional paper no. 34, April 2002, Paris, European Union Institute for Security Studies, www.eu-iss.org; Anthony Forster and William Wallace, 'What is NATO For?', *Survival*, vol. 43, no. 4, 2001, pp. 107–22.

17 Quoted in Stuart Croft, 'Guaranteeing Europe's Security? Enlarging NATO Again', *International Affairs*, vol. 78, no. 1, 2002, pp. 97–114.

18 Raymond Aron, *The Imperial Republic: The USA and the World, 1945–1973*, New Jersey, Prentice-Hall, 1974.

19 Paul Kennedy, 'The Eagle Has Landed', *Financial Times*, 2 Feb. 2002.

The Eleventh of September and beyond: The Impact on the European Union

CHARLES GRANT

INTERNATIONAL crises have a habit of embarrassing the European Union. When Iraq invaded Kuwait in 1990, the EU was largely an irrelevance: various member states pursued solo diplomatic initiatives, and then only Britain and France provided troops to fight alongside the Americans. During the collapse of Yugoslavia, which happened shortly afterwards, the EU tried and failed to prevent the outbreak of war. The unfortunate comment of Jacques Poos, then Luxembourg's foreign minister, in June 1991—following an EU peace mission to the Balkans—that 'this is the hour of Europe, not of America,' will never be forgotten.

The EU's response to 11 September, however, was more impressive. In the immediate aftermath of the attacks on New York and Washington, and during the autumn's war in Afghanistan, the EU's fifteen member states were united among themselves and in support for the United States. The Europeans offered a great deal of help to the US-led campaign against al-Qaeda and the Taleban, including diplomatic and military support, the sharing of intelligence and new initiatives to help track down terrorists and their funding. It would be premature to say that, in the decade since the Kuwait and Yugoslav crises, the EU has come of age as an international actor. But it has certainly grown in maturity.

A year after 11 September, the war against terrorism seems to have had little effect on much of the EU's business and many of its priorities. The Union is proceeding with the admission of ten central European and Mediterranean countries, which—so long as an Irish referendum approves the Nice Treaty—are likely to join in 2004. It has established a convention to prepare the ground for another round of institutional reform that is due in 2004. The EU is trying to refine a system for coordinating the budgetary policies of its member states, and to make them mesh with the monetary policy of the European Central Bank. And it is struggling to implement the ambitious plans for economic reform that were sketched out in Lisbon in 2000, when EU leaders pledged to make the Union the 'most competitive and dynamic knowledge-based economy in the world by 2010'.

However, 11 September has affected the Union's embryonic common foreign and defence policies, where its ambitions have been growing. In December 1998 the British and French governments launched a plan for a European Security and Defence Policy (ESDP). The Union has since

Published by Blackwell Publishing, 108 Cowley Road, Oxford OX4 1JF, UK and 350 Main Street, Malden, MA 02148, USA

committed itself to a 'headline goal' of 60,000 soldiers, supposed to be available for peacekeeping missions by 2003. And since September 1999 the EU has had a High Representative for the Common Foreign and Security Policy (CFSP), in the person of Javier Solana. Prior to 11 September he had begun to give the EU a more visible presence in international diplomacy, for example by stitching together—with the help of NATO Secretary-General George Robertson—a peace plan for Macedonia in the summer of 2001.

Events since 11 September have influenced the debate over the future of the EU's institutions, which has become more focused on the way the Union makes foreign and security policy. But, perhaps surprisingly, the Union's plans for the ESDP have changed very little. In fact, the policy area most directly affected by 11 September has been police and judicial cooperation, where the member states have agreed to give the EU a bigger role.

In the months after al-Qaeda struck the United States, the EU's ability to maintain a generally united front was impressive. However, by the summer of 2002, policy shifts in the United States and events in the Middle East were placing increasing strains on European unity—and on the transatlantic alliance. America's propensity to act 'unilaterally', outside the framework of international treaties and organisations, in addition to what appeared to be a growing desire to wage war on Iraq, caused dismay in much of Europe. At the same time the rising death toll in the Israel–Palestine conflict produced very different responses from public opinion on the two sides of the Atlantic, further threatening the unity of the alliance against terrorism. By the summer of 2002 the transatlantic relationship, which had been so warm in the months after 11 September, appeared thoroughly chilled.

Europe, the soft power

The EU is poorly designed to deal with large-scale, intense military conflicts. Such armed forces as it can call upon are controlled by national governments rather than EU institutions. The nature of the EU's decision-making machinery means that it will never be able to deploy force as quickly as a nation-state. Some of the EU's members, like Britain and France, have the capability to fight serious shooting wars, but the EU itself has no such ambition. Even if it succeeds in meeting its targets for the headline goal, the ESDP will merely be able to carry out peacekeeping missions. The EU as such would not be able to contribute very much to a high-intensity conflict such as that in Afghanistan last autumn, or any war against Saddam Hussein.

However, some of the current security challenges in places such as Afghanistan highlight the EU's strengths as much as its weaknesses. For the EU comes into its own when softer forms of power are required. 'Soft power' can be defined as the ability to influence events through means other than military force. The EU can use economic assistance, humanitarian aid and trade agreements as tools to help meet its political objectives. The EU can also enhance its soft power through legislation, for example laws that enable it to clamp down on terrorist funding; or through diplomacy, for example by working to strengthen the international alliance against terrorism.

In the months after 11 September, many European leaders—with Tony Blair, Gerhard Schröder, Jack Straw and Joschka Fischer among the most active—spent much of their time in the Middle East and South Asia, building support for the US-led coalition. And during the Bonn peace conference in December, hosted by the German government, European and US officials worked together to persuade the many participants to sign the agreement on the future of Afghanistan.

The EU and its member states are the world's biggest providers of development aid, contributing 65 per cent of grant aid to poorer countries. They pay for about 80 per cent of the economic assistance that goes into reconstructing Bosnia and Kosovo, and they may end up the largest donors to Afghanistan. In 2001 the EU gave Afghanistan €352 million of food and humanitarian aid, of which €103 million came from the Commission and the rest from the member states. At a donors' conference in Tokyo in January 2002, the EU and its member states pledged a further €600 million for this year. The money is being spent on projects such as the destruction of opium crops and the clearance of mines, as well as the salaries of the Karzai administration. From this year until 2006 the EU has set aside €1 billion for Afghanistan.

The EU has used trade as well as aid to promote objectives such as the shoring up of the anti-terrorist front. Thus in December it combined €100 million of extra aid for Pakistan with a new package of trade measures, to reward the Musharraf government for its help in the fight against the Taleban. The EU has removed all tariffs on clothes imported from Pakistan, and increased quotas for textiles and clothing by 15 per cent.

In November 2001, in an effort to bring the Iranians closer to the international coalition, the Commission proposed the negotiation of a new trade and cooperation agreement with Iran. In June 2002 EU foreign ministers approved the opening of talks with Iran. The EU has set down clear criteria for progress in these talks: Iran must be willing to discuss issues such as human rights, judicial reform, the fight against terrorism and the proliferation of weapons of mass destruction.

This putative agreement with Iran shows that EU support for the US-led coalition does not prevent it, occasionally, from pursuing policies which differ from those of the United States. President George Bush says that Iran is part of an 'axis of evil' and bans American companies from investing there. The Europeans believe that engagement with Iran is more likely to benefit its reformists—and, of course, the interests of European oil companies.

The EU has taken many steps towards tracking down and freezing terrorist funds. All the member states have undertaken to ratify the United Nations Convention on the Suppression of the Financing of Terrorism. The EU's members and the Commission have also played an active role in the Financial Action Task Force, the international body which tackles money laundering.

Meeting in Washington DC in October 2001, the task force produced eight recommendations on how to deal with the financing of terrorism, for example on the reporting of suspicious transactions.

In line with these recommendations, in November 2001 the EU revised an existing directive on money laundering, to extend the obligation to notify suspicious transactions beyond banks to other groups such as lawyers and accountants (the United States still has to pass equivalent legislation). The revised directive also widened the definition of laundering to include the proceeds of all serious crime and terrorism. In December the EU approved a new regulation that makes it easier for governments to freeze terrorist funds and to prevent the provision of funds to terrorists. There is some evidence that all this increased scrutiny is disrupting terrorist networks.

The EU governments have agreed on several lists of terrorist groups to which the regulation on terrorist funds, and other similar laws, will apply. These lists cover not only al-Qaeda and related organisations but also European groups such as the Real IRA, ETA and the Kurdish PKK. By April the EU had frozen over €100 million of assets belonging to named organisations or individuals. The EU has drawn up these lists in cooperation with the United States, which has undertaken to freeze the assets of a similar list of terrorist groups.

However, the United States brands Hamas and Hizbollah, whose members have launched attacks on Israel, as terrorist groups. The EU argues that parts of those two organisations are legitimate; it has therefore blacklisted individuals within those groups, and their terrorist wings, rather than the organisations themselves. There are several other Palestinian groups, such as the al-Aqsa martyrs brigade, on the EU list. Despite such transatlantic differences, the general tenor of cooperation between European and American governments in the fight against terrorism has been positive.

Big against small

For several years there has been a growing tension in the EU between smaller and larger countries, of which the bitter argument at the Nice summit in December 2000 over voting weights was just one manifestation. Since 11 September, with the British, the French and the Germans leading the EU's response, the big–small divide has deepened. The EU's 'big three' twice decided to meet as a group. First President Chirac, Prime Minister Blair and Chancellor Schröder held a brief mini-summit before the official summit in Ghent on 20 October. Then Blair convened a dinner in Downing Street on 4 November, with invitations going initially only to Chirac and Schröder, but ultimately—following much complaining—to the Italian, Spanish, Dutch and Belgian prime ministers (the last representing the EU presidency), plus Javier Solana.

As far as the leaders of the big three were concerned, it was self-evident that when there was a war on and military questions needed to be discussed, they should be able to meet together, without the presence of EU institutions. Neither the European Commission nor the Belgian presidency had great diplomatic or military capacity. Britain, France, Germany and perhaps Italy were the only EU states whose forces could make a fairly significant contribution to a military campaign in Afghanistan.

But the large countries handled these mini-summits insensitively. They failed to reassure the smaller member states that they were not trying to establish a de facto *directoire* to manage the Union's foreign and security policy. The small countries argued that the big three pow-wows had in fact talked about matters of EU competence, such as humanitarian aid for Afghanistan, and therefore that EU institutions should have been represented.

The small member states also made the more general complaint that by acting alone, particularly in dealings with the United States, the big countries had undermined EU institutions. In the months after 11 September, Blair, Schröder and Chirac went separately to Washington. Each was happy to win some glory for his country in standing shoulder-to-shoulder with the United States. They did talk to each other before their visits, to concert their arguments, but none of them made much of an effort to speak for the EU when in Washington.

However, the leaders of these large countries had a strong defence of their solo diplomacy: Bush and his team wanted to see them personally, since they represented real diplomatic and military clout. In December, when the Laeken European Council decided to send the Belgian Prime Minister to Washington, to represent the EU presidency, the results were embarrassing: senior figures in the administration did not find the time to talk to him.

Blair's personal diplomacy, in particular, made a big impact in the United States, where the UK became extremely popular. In Europe, the dynamism and self-confidence of Blair's performance was more controversial. Some on the left regarded him as a warmonger, and some of the less Atlanticist politicians argued that his strongly pro-American line was by definition anti-European. Louis Michel, the Belgian foreign minister and a socialist, accused him of 'grandstanding' and of using 'bellicose' language.

Blair would have ruffled fewer feathers in Europe if, when in Washington, he had talked more often about the EU's as opposed to Britain's role in the crisis. In his speeches in the United States Blair missed an opportunity to get a message to American public opinion that the Europeans were being helpful and supportive to the US-led coalition (most Americans had no idea that, in the spring of 2002, there were roughly as many European troops as US troops in Afghanistan).

Blair may have sometimes got the tone wrong, but the substance of Britain's diplomacy—like that of the French and the Germans—was generally to promote the European interest. In the autumn of 2001, for example, he counselled caution on Iraq, and he urged the United States to take Palestinian aspirations seriously. On both subjects he may have had some influence. In late September and early October, when some voices in Washington were calling for strikes against Iraq, Bush demurred. And in November the President issued a clear call for the establishment of a Palestinian state. Therefore when the leaders of the larger countries presented European views or sensibilities during their trips to the United States, they probably strengthened the Union's external policy.

By the spring of 2002, European criticism of Blair was growing. The thrust of his remarks on Iraq appeared to follow Bush's aggressive line, rather than the general European view that an invasion would be unwise. In May Romano Prodi, the Commission President, attacked Blair in a speech in Oxford, arguing that if the British believed being pro-American increased their clout in Europe, they were wrong. An early version of the speech compared the American–British relationship to a penny-farthing bicycle, with the UK being the small wheel at the back.

One of the Commission's roles in the EU is to act as the friend and protector of the smaller member states. It has therefore always opposed solo diplomacy by the big member states. In May 2002, when Blair and Chirac came out in favour of a new 'European president', a figure to be appointed by the heads of government who would chair the European Council and represent Europe at the highest level, the Commission was upset. The Commission saw the proposal—probably rightly—as an attempt to diminish the role of the Commission President. Many small countries opposed the idea. However, this plan for a European president has gathered momentum among the large countries, Germany excepted. The main argument for such a post is that 11 September and its aftermath highlighted the inability of the EU's existing institutions to represent it effectively.

Redesigning institutions

One positive consequence of 11 September is that the EU is likely to reform the institutions of the CFSP. The EU's 'rotating presidency'—the system whereby a different member takes over the chairmanship every six months—will probably be scrapped. Until recently the rotating presidency looked likely to survive. When the Nice summit of December 2000 set down four institutional priorities for the treaty revision due in 2004, it did not include the presidency in particular or the EU's machinery for making foreign policy in general. But both are now rising to the top of the EU's institutional agenda.

Countries outside the EU have long complained about the rotating presidency. They are fed up with having to adjust every six months to a new set of people and priorities. The EU had never been very concerned about the complaints of Russians, Americans and others. But this changed after 11 September: the EU's institutions were evidently ill-suited to responding quickly or representing the Union forcefully to the rest of the world. As the holder of the EU's rotating presidency in the second half of 2001, Belgium had the responsibility for managing the EU's reactions to 11 September. Being a small country without great diplomatic or military clout, Belgium lacked the credibility or ability to perform that task well. Not taking the Belgian presidency seriously, the United States did not bother to inform the Belgians of its plans. Thus, on 7 October, when the United States was about to start bombing Afghanistan, Secretary of State Colin Powell called Solana to warn him in advance—but not the Belgian government.

The imminent enlargement of the EU is in any case strengthening the case for reforming the presidency system: the ten countries likely to join in 2004 are all, bar Poland, small countries. It is true that some smaller member states have run efficient presidencies, particularly with regard to the EU's domestic agenda. But the EU's diplomatic weight would evidently suffer if countries such as Slovenia, Malta and Latvia took turns to represent Europe to the rest of the world.

Traditionally, the smaller countries have been reluctant to give up their turn at the presidency: they like their six months in the spotlight, and they fear that whatever replaced the presidency would increase the power of the big countries at their expense. However, since 11 September the mood has shifted in many capitals. Small countries such as the Netherlands, Belgium, Finland and Sweden have accepted the case for reform. The rotating presidency is likely to go, at least in the domain of external representation. The High Representative and the Council of Ministers secretariat will probably take over some of the presidency's external tasks.

One way or another, the role of Solana and his successors will probably be enhanced. And there will be pressure for the two sides of EU foreign policy—diplomacy under Solana and economic assistance under Chris Patten, the Commissioner for External Relations—to become more closely integrated. There is widespread recognition that, because these two sides are managed separately, Europe's voice is weaker than it need be. In the Middle East, for example, the EU is the biggest provider of aid to the Palestinian Authority and Israel's major trading partner. But it has never used that economic position to exert much political leverage.

Whatever the reforms that emerge from the Convention and the subsequent treaty revision, Europe is always going to be predominantly a soft power. One of the many challenges for European foreign policy is to find ways of working closely with the United States, a country which displays the opposite bias. Under the leadership of George W. Bush, in particular, the United States is more comfortable thinking about and exercising the hard sort of power. Optimists will argue that these two sorts of power are complementary. The picture in Afghanistan in the first half of this year—with US forces hunting for terrorists in caves, and Europeans keeping the peace on the streets of Kabul—suggests that in some ways, at least, the EU and the United States need each other.

CHARLES GRANT

Military Europe

On 12 September 2001 NATO invoked Article 5 of the North Atlantic Treaty, thereby enabling the United States to call on the Europeans for whatever military help it saw fit. President Bush and his advisers were genuinely touched by this expression of European solidarity. Subsequently many European countries offered military assistance to the United States during the war in Afghanistan. Some of those offers were taken up, and not only from the British. French bombers and German mountain troops played useful roles.

However, the United States did not avail itself of most of the European offers of military assistance. There were two reasons for this. One was that the Europeans had few of the high-tech military capabilities would have been useful to the United States in the fight against the Taleban and al-Qaeda—for example, sophisticated unmanned aerial vehicles, satellite-guided munitions or the ability to mount combat search and rescue missions. The one European capability that the Pentagon was keen to make us of was special forces, and it took up offers of these from several European countries.

The second reason was that the people in charge of the Pentagon were unsympathetic to the idea of working with NATO's organisation or EU countries. The experience of the Kosovo air campaign in 1999, when some decisions on targeting were taken by NATO committees rather than US generals, had left a bad impression on the US military. The Pentagon thought—probably rightly—that in military terms it would be easier and more efficient to run the war through US chains of command, slotting in officers from close allies when necessary.

Al-Qaeda struck New York and Washington when the EU's plans to develop a military role were only halfway to implementation. It is a cliché of history that countries or alliances prepare to fight the last war they were involved in. The rationale of the ESDP was to give Europe the means to cope with the challenges it faced in the Balkans during the 1990s.

Most of the ESDP's institutional arrangements had been sorted out before 11 September. The Western European Union, a military alliance of ten EU members, had been folded into the EU. The EU has the legal competence to run its own military operations—either 'autonomous' missions that would not draw on NATO assets, except for the military planners at the Supreme Headquarters Allied Powers Europe (SHAPE) in Mons, Belgium, or missions that would make use of NATO and American assets. The EU has created a military staff to carry out strategic planning; a military committee consisting of senior officers from the member states, to advise ministers; and a Political and Security Committee of national diplomats, to coordinate foreign and security policy, and to manage crises. All these bodies are situated in the Council of Ministers in Brussels, and come under the aegis of Solana.

But the ESDP is about more than institutions. It is also an attempt to boost Europe's military capabilities. The Helsinki summit of December 1999, in addition to setting the headline goal of a 60,000-strong deployable force, committed the EU to achieving 'collective capability goals in the fields of command and control, intelligence and strategic transport'. The summit also defined 'non-military headline goals' for crisis management, such as the deployment of civilian police to a trouble zone, the training of local administrators and the provision of judges. Subsequently the EU has created an institutional process for building capabilities. There have been two capabilities-pledging conferences in Brussels, the more recent in October 2001. Having compiled a list of 144 capability gaps, the defence ministers claimed at the end of 2001 that they had filled 104 of them. They have now set up seventeen panels of experts—with one member state responsible for leading each panel—to work on plugging the remaining forty gaps.

Cynical Americans will remark that this process has done more to generate paper than real shooting power. Certainly there have been no dramatic improvements in capabilities. In general terms, the ESDP is probably not evolving very differently from how it would have developed if 11 September had never happened. The objectives remain the so-called 'Petersberg tasks', defined in the Amsterdam Treaty of 1997 as 'humanitarian and rescue tasks, peacekeeping tasks and tasks of combat forces in crisis management, including peace-making'.

Have the Europeans been foolish to persevere with their plans for the headline goal, given that the capabilities it has defined would not be of much direct use in the struggle against al-Qaeda and the Taleban? After all, the Afghan war was very different from the kind of operations the Europeans have grown used to in the Balkans. One lesson of that war is that special forces may be crucially important in a military campaign, yet the headline goal says nothing about them. Several governments, including Britain's, are thinking seriously about expanding the numbers of such forces. There may be a case for some modest coordination at EU level, so that the special forces of different countries can learn to work together.

That said, the EU was probably wise to leave the basic design of the ESDP in place. Many of the capabilities that the Europeans are trying to develop for the headline goal—such as transport planes, lightly armoured mobile troops and better communication systems—are highly relevant to a situation such as that in Afghanistan. For example, such capabilities would make it easier for the Europeans to provide effective peacekeeping forces in a place like Kabul, or indeed Baghdad. In any case, other challenges that the Europeans have had to face in recent years, in places such as Sierra Leone, the Great Lakes of Africa and of course the Balkans, remain problematic. The military capabilities they are trying to develop would be useful in such areas.

The Europeans' armies are experienced at peacekeeping, a task which they usually perform well. About 80 per cent of the peacekeepers in Bosnia and Kosovo are from EU countries. The International Security Assistance Force that is maintaining order in Kabul is almost entirely European. Like the NATO force in Macedonia, it contains no American soldiers. The United States does not, as a rule, like to commit men to peacekeeping.

There are other reasons why the EU has not shifted the goals of the ESDP. For one thing, the Petersberg tasks are very flexible. One of them, 'peace-making', could be interpreted to cover EU involvement in a serious military conflict. For another, most EU governments suppose that if they had to commit forces for high-intensity warfare, either NATO would run the show or they would work directly with the United States. It is not self-evident that the EU as such would need to be involved. And finally, some of the EU's non-aligned members would not want the Petersberg tasks to be rewritten in a way that implied the EU was committed to fighting wars.

Unfortunately, 11 September has made little impact on the ESDP's biggest institutional problem: a dispute between Greece and Turkey over the EU's links to NATO. Turkey, in NATO but with little prospect of joining the EU, fears that an EU force could—under the influence of Greece and Cyprus—operate against its interests. So for a year, starting in December 2000, Turkey vetoed agreements which would give the EU assured access to NATO military planning, and presumed access to other NATO assets. Finally, at the end of 2001, with the help of some American diplomacy, and written assurances to the Turks, the Ankara government signed up to the NATO–EU agreements. But then the Greeks refused to accept those agreements, complaining that Turkey had been given too much influence over EU defence policy. Greece fears that Turkey may be able to prevent the ESDP being used to promote Greek interests. Unless Greece lifts its veto on EU access to NATO assets, the EU will in practice find it very difficult to run a peacekeeping mission anywhere.

In one respect 11 September is likely to have a positive effect on the ESDP. Since the United States became involved in Afghanistan it has emphasised that the Balkans are less of a priority. The Bush administration expects the EU to take on more responsibility for the security of the Balkans. Even before 11 September, the United States was thinking of withdrawing troops from Bosnia and Kosovo, and in July 2002 it announced a reduction in their numbers of 2,000. The Pentagon has encouraged the EU to take over responsibility for the NATO force in Macedonia, and may soon be urging it to do the same in Bosnia. The EU has already agreed to take over the policing of Bosnia from the UN, starting in January 2003. There is a growing realisation among European governments that the Balkans is their responsibility. In July 2002, when the new International Criminal Court came into effect, the Bush administration, fearing that American personnel could face prosecution, threatened to block the renewal of UN mandates for a number of policing and peacekeeping operations. The row over the ICC is likely to reinforce EU efforts to prepare units of soldiers—and other essential groups such as police and judges—that can be deployed in the Balkans.

In the short run, however, the Greece–Turkey problem is preventing the EU from expanding its role in the Balkans. Meeting in Seville in June 2002, EU leaders reaffirmed the view they had stated at their previous two summits, that the EU should take over the Macedonia mission. But they made it clear that the problem of EU access to NATO assets needed to be sorted out first. At the time of writing there is little sign of the Greek position softening.

For much of the year that followed 11 September, European defence budgets seemed to be unaffected by the tragedy. The long-term decline in those budgets had bottomed out before the al-Qaeda attacks. Britain, Italy, the Netherlands and Spain had increased defence spending in real terms in 2001, partly because of their commitment to the ESDP, while France had found more money for procurement. Germany, however, was continuing to cut its budget, and its squeeze has threatened the Europeans' plans to build a new military transport plane, the A400M, which would greatly improve their ability to dispatch forces to a place such as Afghanistan (though by summer 2002 it seemed more likely than not that the plane would be built).

Budgets had declined over many years because people felt safe. Politicians did not think that they would win votes by campaigning for more weapons, against schools and hospitals. Since 11 September, one might suppose that people would worry more about their security, and that politicians could more easily make the case for better armed forces. However, not many of the political leaders campaigning in this year's many European elections have demanded more defence spending—though by the summer of 2002 there were some signs that European defence budgets might rise. Jacques Chirac had promised a substantial rise in defence spending during his election campaign, and seemed likely to deliver. Chancellor-candidate Edmund Stoiber in Germany made the same promise. Meanwhile, Britain's three-year comprehensive spending review increased the defence budget in real terms. But relatively minor adjustments in Britain, France and Germany count for very little compared with the enormous growth in the US defence budget, which is rising from $280 billion in 1999 to something close to $400 billion by 2003.

The inability of Europeans to sort out the Greece–Turkey problem in the ESDP or boost defence budgets has led to understandable frustrations in the United States. Seen from Washington, Europe does not seem to be 'serious' about defence. But on the capabilities front the story is not all gloomy.

The real problem in Europe has been more the mis-spending of defence budgets than their size. Too many European armies are still focused on the Cold War objective of territorial defence, rather than on what is now required, namely the ability to deploy soldiers rapidly and sustain them in a distant place. But military reform is proceeding in many EU countries. During 2002, France has completed the transition to an all-professional army that will be more mobile than any conscript force could be. Italy and Spain are following France in abandoning conscription. Germany—while exasperating its partners with the slow pace of military reform—is restructuring its armed forces to cut the numbers of conscripts and increase the numbers available for service outside the NATO area. There are now over 8,000 German soldiers peacekeeping in various parts of the world; there were none ten years ago.

In the short run the EU governments are not going to redesign their ESDP. In the long run, however, they may reassess their military ambitions. They understand that the wider the gap between US and European capabilities, the less the Americans will listen to European views on military matters. The US is starting to put pressure on some European governments to develop the capabilities required for high-intensity warfare.

In the spring of this year, President Bush's National Security Council started to work on the idea that Europe should build its own 'strike force'—a standing force that would be available to the EU or NATO and able to fight beside US troops in a place such as Afghanistan. Such a force would consist of aircraft and ships and perhaps—though more controversially—of elite troops. NATO would act as a kind of 'portal' through which American commanders could call upon packages of European capability. The idea is that these commanders would be more willing to call upon European assistance if it were packaged by NATO. Such an initiative would require higher European defence budgets. But it is conceivable that, in the long run, the EU may be able to deploy not only the peacekeeping capability of the headline goal, but also some sort of strike force.

Police and judicial cooperation

The biggest impact of 11 September on the European Union has been in the field of police and judicial cooperation. The EU's justice and interior ministers have approved a raft of anti-terrorist measures which would otherwise have taken many years to pass. Arguably, only one of the measures agreed in the autumn of 2001—on the reinforcement of airport security—was a direct response to 11 September; the others were already in the pipeline. But the al-Qaeda attacks revived the EU's efforts to press ahead with the ambitious agenda for justice and home affairs cooperation that had been set at Tampere in Finland in October 1999.

In December 2001 the EU agreed on a common definition of acts of terrorism. Most member states did not have a specific law outlawing terrorism, which meant that they could not easily prosecute people for incitement to terrorist violence, raising funds for terrorists or membership of a terrorist group. In several EU countries terrorists could not be caught and prosecuted until they had committed murder or damaged property. The common definition—once transposed into national law by member states—will make it easier for governments to deal with terrorists. In April 2002 justice ministers agreed on a common range of penalties for terrorist and criminal offences, so that no one country is seen as a 'soft touch'.

At the Laeken summit in December 2001, EU governments were able to agree—once Italy's Silvio Berlusconi had dropped his objections—to a common arrest warrant. This is an enormous philosophical leap for the EU: it requires the member states to recognise each others' judicial systems. This principle had been agreed, in theory, at the Tampere European Council. In practice, however, the mutual suspicion of national authorities ensured that little progress was made.

The warrant will apply to serious organised crimes as well as to terrorist offences and will replace extradition procedures between member states. These procedures have shown themselves ill-suited to dealing with terrorists over the years. For example, French and Belgian courts refused to surrender Basque suspects to Spain, while France was unable to extradite Rachid Ramda, wanted for bombing the Paris metro, from Britain.

When the new system is up and running the judicial authorities in any EU country will have to surrender a suspect to another EU jurisdiction on the basis of a single warrant. Judges in the state surrendering the suspect will be able to question the procedure used by the requesting judge, but not the substance of the charge in the warrant. Since the EU warrants will apply not only to terrorist offences but also to most serious crimes, many criminals who have fled to another EU country to escape prosecution will have to leave Europe or hide.

Not only judicial, but also police cooperation has received a boost since 11 September. Europol, the European police office, has to rely on national police forces for both information and arresting suspects. However, since 11 September the EU has endowed Europol with enhanced powers, notably the right to demand information instantly from national forces, and to coordinate arrests by them. A special anti-terrorist team has been created within Europol, to encourage exchanges of information among the various national authorities. The European Council has also given Europol a specific mandate to work with its US counterparts on counterterrorism. Europol is supposed to become the central body for exchanges of information across the Atlantic. However, cooperation with the United States has run into difficulties. Some American agencies have not been impressed by Europol and prefer to work bilaterally with the EU member states.

Existing arrangements for extradition between the EU and the United States vary greatly among the member states. Some arrangements work smoothly and some do not. Furthermore, while most EU countries have bilateral agreements with the United States that cover cooperation against crime, including exchanges of information, some, including Germany, Denmark, Finland and Portugal, do not.

So, in April 2002, EU justice ministers gave the go-ahead for the negotiation of a new agreement with the United States to cover extradition and other sorts of judicial cooperation. It is unlikely that there will be an agreement soon, for the EU is demanding that those extradited to the United States do not face trial by special tribunals, life imprisonment or the death penalty. The Europeans will be uncompromising on the death penalty: the European Convention of Human Rights prevents extradition to countries which may apply it. The United States will be unwilling to offer blanket guarantees, but is probably willing to be flexible on a case-by-case basis.

The impact of 11 September on the EU's developing policies on asylum, immigration and visas has been less striking than on police and judicial cooperation. Nevertheless, heightened worries about terrorism have contributed to renewed efforts to develop common policies for the EU's external borders. Jack Straw, the British Foreign Secretary, called for the introduction of qualified majority voting on asylum and immigration policy in February 2002 in a speech in The Hague. In the spring and summer of 2002, the growing salience of immigration as a political issue in many countries has reinforced pressure on the EU to 'do something' about it.

The Seville summit of June 2002 approved further work on proposals by the Commission and some member states for the EU to create a common European border guard. The logic is evident: many of the EU's illegal immigrants come in through its southern underbelly, notably via Greece, Italy or Spain, while others come in through the central European states that are due to join the Union. The countries of northern and western Europe have an interest in preventing the entry of illegal immigrants, and therefore in helping the southern (and future eastern) member states with money, expertise and personnel to police their borders.

The minimalist option for European cooperation would involve joint training, the sharing of equipment and comparisons of best practice. Some of the Commission's more ambitious plans could lead to the establishment of fully integrated border-guard units, and perhaps naval patrols. Those serving in these units would have the power to check papers and arrest suspects. Fears of illegal immigration and drug trafficking are the main drivers of this initiative. But it is also true that anxiety over terrorism has created a political climate in which politicians are more willing to argue for tougher policing of the EU's external frontiers.

European integration in these areas leads to plenty of potential problems. Can the EU really become a single judicial space if the courts in some countries are extraordinarily inefficient or corrupt? And what safeguards need to be put in place at EU level to protect the civil liberties of individuals named in arrest warrants or watched by Europol? The debate over such questions is beginning, and rightly so. But there is no doubt that closer cooperation among police forces, judiciaries and security services is making Europe more effective at combating terrorism—and in the long run, a more useful partner of the United States. There have been a few well-publicised cases of magistrates in Belgium and Germany refusing to give the United States information on terrorist suspects, because of the legal difficulty of sharing information gained from those in custody. But cooperation between European and American police forces has generally worked well since 11 September.

Since that date transatlantic intelligence cooperation has been for the most part harmonious. The CIA is pleased with the information it has received from European agencies. It reckons that transatlantic cooperation has never been better, and says that no European intelligence service has held back information that it needed.

However, in the autumn of 2001 there was grumbling among the European agencies that the intelligence flow was one-way, and that they were receiving little in return for their help. By the spring of 2002 the tension seemed to have eased, with the Americans becoming more willing to share. The greatest exchanges of intelligence between the United States and EU countries have been with the 'big five'—Britain, France, Germany, Italy and Spain.

Problems ahead: Israel, Palestine and Iraq

The terrorist attacks of 11 September brought Americans and Europeans closer together. Most Europeans felt that they too were threatened. The help offered by European governments was appreciated in the United States. President Bush's clear and decisive lead on the need to fight the Taleban and al-Qaeda won much respect in Europe, even on the left of the political spectrum. In the spring of 2002, however, the Israel–Palestine conflict and the issue of Iraq began to weaken that spirit of transatlantic solidarity. In both cases, the Bush administration produced rhetoric and policies which many Europeans could not easily support. And then in June President Bush called for the Palestinians to get rid of Yasser Arafat, while in July the row over the International Criminal Court divided Europeans and Americans still further. The general consensus among commentators was that transatlantic relations had reached a new low.

As the year proceeded, the outlook in the Middle East looked increasingly bleak. The European governments agreed on the need to condemn Palestinian terrorism and Israeli aggression, and to support a secure existence for Israel and a Palestinian state. They have used their best endeavours to assist George Tenet's plan for a ceasefire, George Mitchell's proposals for confidence-building measures and Crown Prince Abdullah's suggestion that Israel withdraw to 1967 frontiers in return for the normalisation of relations with the Arab world. The Europeans knew that their own influence on events in the region was limited, and therefore urged the Bush administration to deepen its involvement.

There have been differences of emphasis among the EU governments. France, Belgium and the southern EU countries have been readier to condemn the Israelis, while Britain and Germany have been more reluctant to do so. But the presence of Javier Solana as the EU spokesman has helped the Europeans to paper over these cracks. He has worked tirelessly as an honest broker, winning the confidence of most parties in the region, including the Sharon government. Solana was the first Western politician to fly to Riyadh, in February, when Crown Prince Abdullah unveiled his initiative. And in April US Secretary of State Colin Powell insisted that Solana be part of the 'quartet'—alongside himself, UN Secretary-General Kofi Annan and Russian foreign minister Igor Ivanov—that coordinates international efforts to help the peace process.

Despite the best efforts of such politicians, at the time of writing the situation in the Middle East remains dire. This creates great dangers for European foreign policy, in particular because public opinion on the two sides of the Atlantic has a very different view of events. Most transatlantic disputes in recent years—whether on missile defence, ESDP or steel tariffs—have in essence been arguments among elites. Public opinion was not very interested in these matters and therefore did not have a great influence on politicians. But the Middle East is different. Public opinion cares strongly, both in the United States and in the EU. Many Americans equate the Palestinian suicide bombers with al-Qaeda terrorists. They regard Israel's invasion of Palestinian towns as justified. But whereas President Bush described Ariel Sharon as 'a man of peace', many Europeans regard him as more responsible than Yasser Arafat for the escalation in violence. They think the Israeli army has killed too many non-combatants and that it may have breached the laws of war.

Many American and European politicians, including Powell and Solana, have worked hard to avoid a public falling-out over the Middle East. However, public opinion is hampering their efforts. In April, during the Israeli occupation of the West Bank, the European Parliament passed a (non-binding) resolution in favour of economic sanctions against Israel. Romano Prodi, the Commission President, also called for such sanctions to be considered. Some European ministers have denounced Israel in extreme terms, later saying in private that they had to do so to placate domestic public opinion.

Similarly, in April Europeans were startled to see the effect of public opinion on US policy. President Bush demanded that Israel withdraw its forces from the West Bank 'without delay'. But a few days later, after pro-Israeli lobbies had mobilised on Capitol Hill, the President changed his mind. Europeans then watched in bemusement as Paul Wolfowitz, the right-wing pro-Israeli Deputy Defense Secretary, told a pro-Israeli rally in Washington that Palestinians had rights, only to be loudly booed for saying so.

Why are public opinions so divergent? This writer listened to a group of senior Republicans and Democrats, who hold or have held office at the highest level, who sat at the same table at a dinner in Washington in April. 'Europeans just believe in appeasement: throughout their history they have wanted to meet violence with concessions,' was one opinion. Another was that Europeans have an instinctive tendency to be antisemitic. According to a third view, because there are millions of Muslims in European countries, Europeans have a natural bias to the Palestinian cause. A fourth suggestion was that European television stations had failed to show the bloody scenes left by Palestinian suicide bombings.

It is possible that there is some truth in some of those points, though certainly not the last. However, a similar group of Europeans would come up with different answers to the question. They would argue that the long experience of terrorism in places such as Northern Ireland, Corsica and the Basque country has taught Europeans that military action alone cannot stop it; and that force, if disproportionate, can swell the numbers of terrorists and the international support they receive. Europeans point out that few American newspapers carried prominent photos of the destruction caused by the Israeli invasions of the West Bank, notably in the Jenin refugee camp. Finally,

Europeans observe that their pro-Israeli lobbies are less well organised and powerful than those in the United States.

The good news is that most European and American politicians agree on the rough outlines of the deal that is needed in the Middle East: land for peace. While working for a settlement, therefore, they should close their ears to those tribunes of the people who demand that one side or other be blamed. On this occasion, the less public opinion influences foreign policy the better. Otherwise there is the risk of a serious transatlantic rift over Israel and Palestine. And if that came about, the result could be a fracturing of European unity: some EU governments would want to shift the European line to prevent too great a divergence from the United States. By the summer the dangers of such a transatlantic rift seemed to be rising. Most Europeans reckoned that President Bush's big speech on the Middle East in June made a political settlement decreasingly likely, because he seemed to have abandoned any pretence of even-handedness between the two sides.

Iraq is just as likely to cause fissures among the allies. This year, it has become clear that Bush is determined to get rid of Saddam Hussein. The administration has sought to develop a 'doctrine of pre-emption', according to which an attack on a sovereign state may be justified if it is developing weapons of mass destruction (WMD) and intends to use them.

One faction within the administration, including Colin Powell, wishes to focus on the return of United Nations inspectors, and give Saddam the opportunity to let them go any place, any time, without hindrance; the assumption is that he will refuse, thereby legitimising military action. The second group, which includes leading officials in the Pentagon, believe that the UN is a distraction and a waste of time, that Saddam will humiliate the inspectors as he did before, and that the United States should just get on with removing him.

Most European governments, and citizens, were happy to support the United States in its fight against the Taleban and al-Qaeda. They understood that they too are threatened by Osama bin Laden and his network. But very few Europeans regard Iraq as a threat. True, Saddam is trying to develop nuclear arms and already has chemical and biological weapons. But he is a long way from having an atom bomb, and he has not used chemical or biological weapons since the 1980s. There is no evidence that he has worked with international terrorist networks. Deterrence seems to prevent him from attacking neighbours or using his biological and chemical weapons. As one British official puts it: 'Pre-emptive military action to stop Iraq getting nuclear arms is easy to justify, but Iraq—unlike Iran—is a very long way from having them, and there is not much point in taking pre-emptive action against biological and chemical weapons since Iraq already has the expertise.' Europeans worry about what comes after Saddam, as well as the impact of a war on Palestine, Saudi Arabia, Jordan, Egypt and the Kurdish problem.

However, Americans have become less tolerant of WMD since 11 September. They see that al-Qaeda and Iraq have a common interest in wanting to hurt the United States as much as possible. Despite the lack of evidence that Saddam has collaborated with al-Qaeda, they worry that he may hand his WMD to terrorists. Many Americans think Europeans naïve to believe they are safe from Saddam and his weapons. And they think that so long as Saddam is deposed swiftly, European and Arab allies will soon adjust to the change.

Iraq always has been, and perhaps always will be, the Achilles heel of EU foreign policy. On almost every issue of importance—such as the Balkans, Russia, China, Iran and even Israel–Palestine—the Europeans have developed either a common policy or at least a fairly common perspective. But not on Iraq. Britain has stuck doggedly to the US line, for example in maintaining the no-fly zones over southern and northern Iraq. France has often been critical of America's hard line on Iraq, sometimes teaming up with Russia and China in the UN Security Council. Other EU countries have fallen somewhere between the British and French positions. It was notable that, at a Brookings Institution–Centre for European Reform seminar in Washington in April 2002, the 'political directors' (top policy officials) of the British, French, German and Italian governments put forward very different views on Iraq, without any pretence of a common position.

In recent years, Britain and France have made a real and partially successful effort to bring their positions closer together. In May 2002 France—like Russia—signed up to the British and American plan for 'smart' sanctions against Iraq. The UN Security Council's new sanctions regime is designed to prevent Saddam from building up his weaponry, but not to hurt the Iraqi people. Nevertheless, if the issue of waging war on Iraq comes to the fore, Britain and France are likely to have very different views. Tony Blair has made it clear that he will want British forces to fight alongside those of the United States in any effort to rid the world of Saddam. France and many other Europeans may well want to stay out of such a conflict. Such a rift during a US-led war against Iraq would be disastrous for the credibility of the CFSP. It would also seriously weaken Blair's stature among European governments.

Of course, much will depend on how the United States goes about tackling Iraq. If the moderates in the administration get their way, it is possible that the US could build a broad coalition against Iraq. Suppose that the US works hard to get UN inspectors back into Iraq. Suppose that France, Russia and other key countries agree to a UN inspection regime which allows the inspectors complete access, at any time, to any place they want. Suppose that Bush makes a serious diplomatic effort with the Europeans, the Russians and the moderate Arab governments, to garner their support. Suppose, too, that Bush tries hard to re-energise the Middle East peace process, and that he forces Ariel Sharon to move towards a political settlement.

Assuming that Saddam rejected the inspection regime, or played games with the inspectors, it is plausible to imagine that the EU would take a common position in support of US military action. It is quite conceivable that France and perhaps some other EU countries could join the British in contributing forces to the US-led action. In these circumstances, Blair could avoid serious embarrassment among his European partners, and he could probably ride out political opposition at home. So long as the conclusion of the military operation was the departure of Saddam, and the loss of life had not been too great, European public opinion would probably welcome the outcome.

However, that relatively optimistic scenario requires a huge number of conditions to be met. If the United States decides to sort out Saddam on its own, most European politicians—and much of European public opinion— will oppose the United States. Thus transatlantic differences over Iraq, as over the Israel–Palestine conflict, threaten gravely to weaken the coalition against terrorism.

Finally, a stronger Europe?

By the summer of 2002, the two sides of the Atlantic appeared to be drifting further apart. This was partly due to economic disputes such as those over steel tariffs and farm subsidies, and partly due to the differing views on global governance—typified by American opposition to the International Criminal Court—that had plagued transatlantic relations before 11 September.

Nevertheless, some of the drift derived from the varying responses of Americans and Europeans to the threat of terrorism and the situation in the Middle East, and from their respective views of the others' response. Europeans see Americans as too keen to solve problems by force alone, reluctant to work with allies and international bodies, and unwilling to dwell upon the causes of terrorism. Americans see Europeans as naïve in their attitude towards 'rogue' regimes such as Iran and Iraq, unwilling to spend money on improving their outdated military capabilities and incapable of acting decisively.

Many European leaders are learning to acknowledge the strength of those American criticisms. They are starting to realise that, rather than carp about US unilateralism, they should do something about making the EU a stronger and more effective international actor. Then the Europeans would have a better chance of influencing the Americans. It remains the case that, so far, the Europeans have not increased defence budgets significantly. But they are starting to think harder about how they can enhance their military perform-ance. Furthermore, substantive discussions are under way on how to make EU foreign policy more effective. The Europeans have taken significant steps to strengthen their cooperation in the field of justice and home affairs. One consequence of 11 September has been a greater awareness of Europe's weaknesses, and a growing desire to address them. Europe remains primarily a soft power, but its edges are starting to harden.

Russian–Western Relations after 11 September: Selective Cooperation versus Partnership (a Russian View)

NADIA ALEXANDROVA ARBATOVA

THE terrorist attacks on 11 September against the United States will become a turning point, not only in the evolution of US domestic and foreign policy, but also in post-bipolar international relations at large. They confronted individual members of the international community with a new challenge and reality—the threat of terrorism. Prime Minister Tony Blair said in his speech to the Labour party conference at Brighton on 2 October 2001, 'The kaleidoscope has been shaken, the pieces are in flux and soon they will settle again. Before they do, let us re-order this world around us.' Yet it remains uncertain whether the post-11 September perceptions of politicians are in line with this task.

At the start of the anti-Taleban operation cautious optimism was widespread. Some analysts were identifying positive results of the crisis: the emergence of the broad international anti-terrorist coalition; Putin's foreign policy choice in favour of the West; the shift in the United States from unilateralism to multilateralism; the enhancement of EU cooperation on external and internal security; and NATO's performance as an increasingly political organisation, enabling Russia to develop friendly relations with it.[1] However, just two months after 'Black September' the weakness of the coalition was becoming increasingly evident, as were the confusion and inconsistency of the United States and other major players in adopting a new security strategy, let alone in implementing it.[2] Moreover, looking back one can say that 11 September has been a catalyst for the trends which emerged after the end of bipolarity: US arbitrariness and unilateralism in international affairs; Europe's dichotomy, embodied in the deep internal contradiction between the goals of European integration and those of Euro-Atlantic partnership; and NATO's gradual marginalisation in European security. As for Russian–Western relations, it is true that the Kremlin's decision to side with the United States and its allies in the fight against terrorism can be assessed as 'a moment of truth' in Russia's foreign policy evolution. President Putin faced a clear choice: either side with the United States and its allies, or hold aloof and confirm Western concerns about the incompatibility of Russian and European values. Moscow's decision to join the 'anti-terrorist coalition' raised a lot of expectations and hopes about a breakthrough in Russian–Western relations comparable to that of the early 1990s. But it is not yet clear what will come out of Russia's choice and

 Published by Blackwell Publishing, 108 Cowley Road, Oxford OX4 1JF, UK and 350 Main Street, Malden, MA 02148, USA

contribution to the anti-terrorist coalition—whether much closer relations with the West, paving a road to real partnership, or even greater differences, which would strengthen terrorism and increase the gap between Russia and the United States and NATO.

Europe or Asia?

In order to understand the Russian leadership's stake in the 'anti-terrorist coalition', it is necessary to return to the origins of the Putin phenomenon. After the collapse of the USSR, Russia's relations with Europe and the United States quickly passed through several stages: a romantic period in the early 1990s, characterised by a conspicuously pro-American foreign policy on Russia's part; a stage of mutual disappointment in the mid-1990s; and then a stage of mutual mistrust in the late 1990s, which resulted in 'Russian Gaullism', a more self-assertive, anti-American and pro-European foreign policy. The Kosovo crisis in spring 1999 formed a clear watershed in Russian–Western cooperation. Under the Putin presidency, relations confidently entered a pragmatic–minimalist phase, with Russian leaders and those of leading Western countries continuing to negotiate with each other, voicing all kinds of good wishes and important initiatives without any strategic goals.

Vladimir Putin was welcomed as 'a strong hand' by the majority of Russians, impoverished by the shock therapy model and Russia's foreign policy failures in its aim of becoming an equal partner of the West. He was required to do away with the legacy of the corrupt Yeltsin regime and to rebuild Russia's prestige in international relations. President Putin inherited from the Yeltsin period three major problems: first, a growing gap between the respective security perceptions in Russia and in the West in the wake of the Cold War; second, a complex interaction between the trends in Russia's domestic evolution and the tendencies within the international economic order, which could have a negative impact on relations among Russia, Europe and America; third, a very complex interplay of Russian and Western interests in the space of the Former Soviet Union (FSU) which, if not reduced to a common denominator, threatened to damage Russian relations with Europe and the United States.[3]

Although President Putin proclaimed himself a devoted partisan of Russian–Western cooperation, having supported ratification of the START II Treaty, the post-Kosovo dialogue between Russia and NATO, and strategic partnership with the EU, his foreign policy was one of *tous azimuths*. He left the doors to the west open; but he also opened many doors in the south and in the east, thus wittingly or unwittingly sending the West a message that Russia had an alternative. And if the West's inclusive strategy for Russia remains on paper only, the development of international relations will continue to be determined by the balance of forces and Russia will search for its own allies, including a closer association with China and cooperation with what the

United States calls 'rogue states'. This policy has raised doubts in the West about the compatibility of Russian and Western values.

Russia's 'Europe–Asia dilemma' should be seen not in terms of geography but rather as a choice of models for Russia's post-communist systemic transformation—its new economic and political system, geopolitical habitat, ideology and national identity, political allies and economic partners abroad. It is not so much a Europe–Asia dilemma as rather a North–South dilemma.

Russia's controversial and tragic history has provided a fertile soil for myths, psychological complexes, and ideological and political aberrations about the 'specificity' of Russia, its unique way of development and unparalleled value system, and its particular 'mission' in the world, all of which have been the subject of infinite debate in Russia and abroad. Political discussions on Russia's vocation have always become much sharper and laden with significant political implications when Russian–Western relations were deteriorating. Thus Putin's diplomacy in the period prior to 11 September was an intensive one, which was being pursued vigorously in all areas; but it was not clear what the foreign policy priorities of the Russian Federation were, in terms of either regions or problems.

The answer to these questions given by the Russian leadership on the morrow of 11 September was clear and unequivocal: Russia is together with the civilised world against terrorism. Moreover, for the first time since the Second World War, Russia, Europe and the United States have a common enemy. If this approach were generally shared, Europe's security landscape could be drastically changed, along with post-bipolar international relations in the Euro-Atlantic space.

The Russian political elite on 11 September

From the very first reaction to the attacks in America there was a broad political consensus in Russia that moral and political support should be given to the United States, but also that Russia should not intervene in Afghanistan on the ground. As for the question of military cooperation with the United States and its allies, the core of the political elite was against any Russian military involvement in the anti-terrorist coalition, for two reasons. First, the opponents of military cooperation between Russia and the United States argued that during the past decade Russia had been repeatedly humiliated by Washington and NATO. Now, they said, when they need Russia, they call us. But what will happen tomorrow, when they achieve their goal? Their second argument, no less important, was that Russia was more vulnerable than any other country because it had 20 million Muslims inside Russia and 35 million Muslims in its immediate neighbourhood. Russian military cooperation with the United States might result in destabilisation of the post-Soviet Muslim space, presenting Russia with a serious problem which it would then have to sort out on its own.

There were in addition marginal groups with highly idiosyncratic positions on the anti-terrorist coalition. Some human rights defenders, traditionally pro-Western, were against Russian involvement out of fear that it would untie the hands of Russian federal troops in Chechnya. A small number of former KGB people were in favour of Russian military cooperation with the United States, but accompanied by the introduction of a very tough political regime in Russia so that any opposition could be silenced. Of course, both these groups were peripheral and had no real say or influence—but their presence is an indication of the complexity of the political picture in Russia.

The democratic part of the political elite, which was in the minority, favoured Russian military cooperation with the United States, but only under certain conditions: namely, equal rights with the United States's allies in the military planning of anti-terrorist operations, and tangible guarantees, as under NATO's Article 5, that Russia would not be left alone. Unexpectedly, President Putin sided with this group of Russian democrats. What was the reason for his decision? Some Russian analysts said that he had no choice but to side with the United States as he had proclaimed himself a partisan of Russian–Western cooperation. Besides, the Taleban presented a real threat to Russia's national interests in the post-Soviet Muslim space, and that is why Russia was interested in joining the coalition. While it was the case that the Taleban was challenging Russia's interests not only in Central Asia but in the North Caucasus as well, Moscow could have taken a different line, offering the United States its benign neutrality, like China or India. In fact President Putin went much further, repeatedly hinting that he was willing to give broader support, besides sharing intelligence information, providing an air corridor for humanitarian cargoes, participating in rescue operations and supplying arms to the Northern Alliance.[4]

Putin's decision may be explained by two factors. First, Russia's participation in the anti-terrorist coalition provided him with a golden opportunity to improve the terms of Russia's relations with the West, not on the basis of unilateral concessions, as in the Yeltsin years, but on an equal footing, and to reclaim Russia's international prestige. This would be a very important achievement for Vladimir Putin personally, since he was called to perform this mission. Second, he hoped that the formation of the broad anti-terrorist coalition would change the West's position on the problem of Chechnya, the most sensitive problem for the Putin presidency.

During his trips to Germany and Brussels in early October 2001, Putin made several important statements, trying to achieve a real breakthrough in Russian–Western relations. He said that Russia was rooted in European values, that under certain conditions Russia could go further in anti-terrorist cooperation, and finally, that Russia would not be against NATO's expansion to the east if Russia were part of this process. 'Of course, we would reconsider our position with regard to such expansion if we were involved in such process,' he said in Brussels.[5] Put simply, he was ready to embark on the relationship of an ally with the United States and NATO. Unfortunately, neither Washington nor Brussels turned out to be ready for such a radical change. They were fearful that this new alliance partnership would confront them with additional problems and require rethinking of previous positions on NATO's enlargement, the question of the Anti-Ballistic Missile (ABM) Treaty and other strategic agreements.

Nor had Putin's anti-terrorist cooperation been approved by the majority of the Russian political elite, which was keeping a close watch on Russian–American relations and NATO's policy *vis-à-vis* Russia. Except for the communists' overheated rhetoric, there was no open political opposition to Putin, but dissatisfaction grew, as became apparent in the reaction to the President's annual message to the Federal Assembly in April 2002.

Those who belong to the Russian political class were dissatisfied by the fact that Putin did not give any clear instructions but proposed 'to think together'; that the head of the state regards himself as a liberal manager, but not as the elected political leader of the country, and that the society which is ready for serious reforms does not understand what sacrifices it should make.[6]

None of these critical comments was really fundamental, but they reflected the growing gap between President Putin and the Russian political elite. In the absence of any visible diplomatic success for the course taken by Putin, the political pendulum in Russia will swing in the opposite direction, leaving the President no choice but to reverse his foreign policy. Putin kept his freedom of manoeuvre by avoiding foreign policy issues almost entirely in his presidential message, so as not to anticipate the results of his three May summits with the US President, NATO and the EU. These, however, did not produce any surprises. The Russia–US and Russia–NATO summits were of mainly symbolic importance, re-establishing the situation which had existed in Russian–Western relations before the Madrid decisions and the Kosovo crisis. Undoubtedly this is important; but many of the questions raised by the Russian political elite remain unanswered. As for the Russia–EU summit, it has borne no fruit at all—no compromise was found on the problem of Kaliningrad.

To a great extent, this immobility can be explained by the domestic situation in Russia, specifically by the existence of the anti-Western opposition, which is keeping a close watch on Putin. Both the *rapprochement* between Russia and the United States and NATO, and the discord between Russia and the EU—Putin's flexibility in the first case and his toughness in the second—have been presented as diplomatic victories for the Kremlin. Indeed, Moscow's position on Kaliningrad at the Russia–EU May summit was just one element in the compensation offered to anti-democratic forces in Russia for the Kremlin's concessions to the United States and NATO: others were the regime's much tougher stance on various domestic issues, such as the law on the alternative civil service, which was changed under pressure from the military, the amnesty given to Colonel Budanov, who had killed a Chechen girl, and, indirectly, new attacks on the independent mass media.

Russia in the anti-terrorist coalition

Generally speaking, a broad international anti-terrorist coalition can be based only on a common legal approach towards the problem of terrorism as well as a common definition of terrorism. If this had been achieved, then we really could speak of revolutionary changes in post-bipolar international relations, and point to a model of international anti-terrorist intervention applicable to all areas where such problems exist (the Middle East conflict included).

Several considerations seem to be of the utmost importance. First, notwithstanding the geopolitical interests of individual members of the international community, militant separatists who use terrorist means to achieve political goals would be condemned by definition—be they KLA and Chechen extremists or IRA and Kurdish secessionists. Any double-standard approach towards secessionist movements is an obstacle to any agreed anti-terrorist action. A review of recent international experience shows that this approach has been widespread. The United States has been backing Ankara against Kurds in Turkey, while it has been tacitly supporting Kurds in Iraq against the odious regime of Saddam. The same can be said about Russia, which was supporting Abkhazian separatism (ironically, together with Chechen warlords in the early 1990s) in Georgia while waging its anti-terrorist war in Chechnya. Undoubtedly, a common definition of terrorism is one of the most confusing issues. Many variations have been introduced by journalists and political scientists, such as 'state terrorism', 'political terrorism', 'ethno-religious terrorism' and so on.

Second, a consistent anti-terrorist strategy requires the cooperation of all interested states, however distasteful they may be to the United States or other countries. Even in the case of an anti-Taleban operation (which was unique because the Taleban was assessed as a threat by many countries), the US leadership was not ready to involve directly those countries that had traditionally had troubled relations with Washington—Iran, India, China.

Third, anti-terrorist actions should be targeted against all countries that are hosting and supporting terrorism. This is an easy task if those countries are opponents of the United States; it is much more difficult if they are American allies, such as Turkey and Saudi Arabia, which are loyal to Washington but challenge Moscow's interests by supporting terrorists in Chechnya and the North Caucasus. So the key question is whether the United States, in its role after 11 September as the leader of 'the anti-terrorist coalition', is willing to reconsider its geopolitical interests for the sake of common values, namely the fight against terrorism. Undoubtedly, what came out of the 11 September crisis cannot be assessed as a real anti-terrorist coalition, but rather as an anti-Taleban coalition, which is still fragile. The new threat is being addressed within the framework of old priorities, with only minimal or superficial adjustments.

There are reasons for serious concern about the future of the anti-Taleban coalition. First, the Taleban was defeated but not eliminated. There is still a possibility that the remnants of the Taleban will continue a creeping guerrilla warfare and involve the United States and its allies in new clashes. Will the United States and its allies be ready to take high risks on the ground? What will happen if they suffer losses every day? How will Russia respond to this challenge after the tragic experience of Afghanistan in the 1980s and two devastating Chechen wars? Second, the new leadership of Afghanistan may fail to sustain the viable political coalition which is already being put at risk as a result of ethnic frictions, the competition for power and distribution of foreign financial aid. Third, mismanagement and deterioration of the situation in post-conflict Afghanistan may destabilise Pakistan, giving Islamic extremists an opportunity to get access to nuclear weapons and ballistic missiles, and exacerbating the risk of a large-scale conflict between India and Pakistan. Such developments would split the coalition and force its individual members to take sides. President Putin has already taken a real political risk in opening the door of Central Asia to the United States. The Americans have entered Georgia, having deployed their military units there to fight terrorism. In the absence of real cooperation between Moscow and Washington, there is a risk of new rivalry in the post-Soviet space between Russia and the United States.[7] If nothing serious comes out of NATO's 'Council at 20', the US anti-terrorist strategy will be judged by the majority of the Russian political elite as no more than American geopolitical and geoeconomic expansion.

The most serious threat to the coalition would be a US decision to take hostile action against the so-called 'rogue states' regardless of their direct involvement in the terrorist attacks of 11 September. This would be taken as new evidence that the United States is still prone to act unilaterally, neglecting the views of its allies. If the United States decided to act against all its political opponents, and in particular Iraq, this could split the anti-Taleban coalition and polarise the Muslim world. It would also have a negative impact on the European allies and particularly on Russian political elite and public opinion, which is very sensitive to the double-standard approach.

US multilateralism after 11 September?

After 11 September the United States realised that it could not cope with the threat of terrorism on its own. The military and economic weight of the United States had not prevented terrorist attacks, and there were hopes that the country would have to abandon its unilateral stance in international affairs. Initially these hopes seemed to be borne out. Washington had to involve not only some of its traditional allies but also Russia as a key country in the anti-Taleban coalition, particularly in the post-Soviet Muslim space. Russia's positive reaction to the American deployment of fighter aircraft and combat helicopters in Uzbekistan was crucial to air support of the Northern Alliance, to the cooperation of Uzbeks and Tajiks, and consequently to the breakthrough in the anti-terrorist military operation by the middle of November. In addition, and in contrast to the Kosovo crisis, the United

States was able to secure UN Security Council authorisation for its military operation as a result of Russian support.

However, at the same time, the way the United States was implementing its anti-terrorist strategy and conducting the military operation raised many concerns and doubts, not only in Russia but in Europe as well, about whether there really had been a shift in the United States away from unilateralism. The UK, France, Germany and Italy offered logistical support and combat troops, but the United States initially was reluctant to take up their offers, knowing that this would mean consulting with them on the campaign strategy. The Bush administration changed this stance in early November 2001;[8] but even then, US–European cooperation was uneven in some aspects. The military campaign as a whole was driven by sophisticated US firepower that in practice excluded cooperation with Europeans, who were not equipped to fight so far from their home bases. Partly as a consequence of this shrinkage of their contribution, the NATO allies were apparently left largely in the dark about the US planning of the war and its aftermath.

As for Russia, in spite of its willingness to participate as a real partner and the high domestic risk taken by President Putin in embarking on this partnership, the United States did not make a serious effort to involve Russia on a full-time basis. The partnership was limited by very selective cooperation. Moreover, the retreat of the Taleban revived the old euphoria, arrogance and temptation to prove that nothing has changed for the United States in its indisputable international predominance. Russia's support was taken for granted, and there was no reciprocation in any of the three areas of concern which existed before 11 September: the growing security gap between Russia and NATO/the United States; economic challenges; and rivalry in the FSU space. No concessions were made on NATO's enlargement to the Baltic states or on the issue of the ABM Treaty. Instead, Russia has been promised by NATO a new body for cooperation with no guarantees that it will not be just a new Permanent Joint Council (PJC). As for the ABM problem, the Bush administration half-heartedly agreed to negotiate further reductions of strategic forces, but Washington does not appear to be interested in radical cuts of nuclear arms.

Nor have concessions been made on debt restructuring. Russia devotes 30 per cent of its federal budget expenditure to debt payment, while suffering a shortage of financial resources for economic reforms, including developing a military structure that will not be at odds with American interests. No real military interaction (in the form of joint training or monitoring) has been promoted with Russia in the Central Asian republics of Uzbekistan and Tajikistan since the end of military operations in Afghanistan, to say nothing of the US military deployments in Georgia after the clash between Russian peacekeepers and the Georgian military in the area of Georgian–Abkhazian conflict (the Kodory Gorge valley). However uneven Russian policy in Georgia has been, the cavalier attitude of Washington towards Russia's vulnerabilities in the Transcaucasus region is interpreted by the majority of the Russian political elite as a US attempt to exploit the post-11 September situation to promote American geopolitical dominance in the Commonwealth of Independent States (CIS). Moreover, the provision of American military help to Georgia, a country whose policy has acquired a certain anti-Russian bias (not, unfortunately, without reason), might send the wrong signal to Chechen warlords and other extremist forces in the North Caucasus.

The evolution of US foreign policy after 11 September, then, has not assuaged Russia's concerns, nor helped President Putin achieve his immediate goals of reinstating Russian cooperation with the United States and NATO on an equal footing and changing the Western position on Chechnya. A fully fledged partnership was replaced with selective cooperation. The Chechnya problem was simply avoided by Washington during the first stage of the anti-Taleban military operation, only resurfacing in Russian–American relations with the end of the operation. Undoubtedly, the US position on Chechnya should have been different. It is telling that the very beginning of the anti-terrorist cooperation resulted in efforts by Moscow to reinforce political means of resolving the problem of Chechnya.

The agreements reached between Russia and the United States at the May 2002 summit in Moscow, which have been assessed by the Russian political elite as 'better than nothing', contain many uncertainties and a great deal of vague wording. They have been built around the US position and only symbolically reflect Russia's interests. One of the US arguments in favour of its withdrawal from the ABM Treaty was that nuclear deterrence had lost its meaning with the end of bipolarity; but the US–Russia warhead levels of 2,200–1,700 adopted in the new agreement are the best evidence of the fact that nuclear deterrence is still in place. 'Black September' did not change this reality, but only expanded the area in which Russian and American interests coincide and where new threats require close cooperation among the United States, Russia and their allies. If the ABM Treaty had been modified but not destroyed, it could have had a positive effect not only on the Russia–US nuclear relationship but on Russian–Western security cooperation as well. Instead, there is a risk that US withdrawal from ABM will undermine non-proliferation of WMD and their means of delivery, create new difficulties and frictions between Russia and the United States, and increase anti-Western opposition in Russia. Russia's inability to exert a positive influence on the nuclear policy of the United States can be explained by its intellectual weakness as well as by the inefficiency of the decision-making mechanism. If Russia had accepted amendments to the ABM Treaty and had not weakened its position by unilateral reductions and restructuring of its strategic nuclear forces, it could have maintained more fruitful strategic dialogue with the United States.

It would be an exaggeration to say that US behaviour has been aimed at challenging Russia's interests (although some in the Russian political elite take this view). The US leadership simply does not care about Russia's concerns and the personal stakes of President Putin. One Russian politician said that the United States is like a huge elephant going its own way, stepping on the paws and tails of other smaller or weaker animals. This suggests that the policy of the United States after 11 September has nothing to do with multilateralism as a new system of global governance in which national sovereignty is shared and managed by international organisations and treaties. This is not an appealing model for many American policy-makers.

Russia and the European Union

The events of 11 September were a catalyst for a trend which had been developing in Europe after the end of bipolarity. Europe's dichotomy, embodied in the EU–NATO 'cohabitation', had been supportable in Cold War times because of Europe's dependence on the United States in the security field. However, European integration and the Euro-Atlantic partnership (in its traditional form) became contradictory after the collapse of communism, which removed the very threat of global conflict. Trends such as growing insecurity in Europe, and US unilateralism and its very selective responses to Europe's security needs, cannot but exacerbate this divergence.

Russia's relations with the EU and NATO can be seen as just another example of Europe's dichotomy. Unlike NATO's enlargement, the EU enlargement and European integration are being assessed by Moscow as an objective trend in Europe's evolution after the end of bipolarity. Apart from the economic fundamentals of EU–Russia cooperation, there are no sharp conflicts of security interests between Russia and EU. On the contrary, Russia and Europe share common security and foreign policy interests related to the challenges of the post-bipolar world, including the growing US unilateralism in world affairs. The first real political problem emerged only with EU enlargement to the Baltic states, which raises the question of free access and transit to Kaliningrad—a Russian exclave which will become a Russian enclave in the expanded EU. At the same time, relations between Russia and the EU have traditionally been dependent not only on their internal developments but on the broader international context of the triangle EU–US/NATO–Russia.

Troubled relations between Russia and the United States/NATO after the Kosovo crisis, combined with US suspicions about the real goals of the European Security and Defence Policy (ESDP), created a very bad climate for cooperation between Russia and the EU. Washington worried that the purpose of ESDP was to undermine NATO and to marginalise the United States in European security. In such a situation, the more Atlanticist governments in Europe were fearful that too close a relationship with Russia would be assessed by the United States as a move to decouple the Euro-Atlantic alliance.

The US/NATO–Russia *rapprochement* after 11 September (however fragile and imperfect) created a more favourable international context for the EU–Russia relationship—all the more so as it was the Bush administration itself which was changing its security priorities, shifting the emphasis to the fight with terrorism on a global level. One consequence of this was to encourage the Europeans to take on a larger share of the burden of policing the Balkans.

The future of EU–Russia relations depends not only on the process of Russia's systemic transformation but also on how the European Union itself evolves. The events of 11 September showed the importance and predominance of politics and security over other EU external activities which, in the long run, may have a positive effect on European security and defence policy. At the same time the immediate impact of 11 September on the ESDP has been more controversial. Some of these challenges have been already described by leading European analysts.[9]

The growing insecurity of citizens gives nation-states greater legitimacy and autonomy, and puts the national interest at the forefront of every government's priorities. These sentiments often bring to power more nationalist and less pro-European governments, a trend which can create obstacles to the deepening and widening of European integration. Moreover, the fight against terrorism requires reinforcement of the machinery of state and tougher control over borders (particularly in the expanded EU), money laundering and illegal immigrants (the last of these issues directly affects the EU–Russia negotiations on Kaliningrad). The rationale of the ESDP was to give Europe the means to cope with challenges of the kind posed by the Balkans, while the struggle against terrorism, as was shown in Afghanistan, involves a different sort of conflict. So the crux of the problem is how to strike the right balance between usual and exceptional circumstances, provisional measures and strategic imperatives for the ESDP. There exist other challenges to European integration involving relations between the EU's large and small countries, for example the so-called 'Turkish veto' which has been blocking a series of arrangements on links between NATO and the EU, and many other factors.

Regardless of all these problems and uncertainties, it is clear that ESDP as well as cooperation with Russia will be badly needed, because European security is becoming more and more a European cause. At the same time, a clear vision of what kind of strategic relations between the EU and Moscow may be envisaged is still lacking both in Europe and in Russia. The strategies adopted by the EU and Russia towards each other in 1999 did not have any real strategic goals, since they were aimed merely at preserving the achievements of the previous years in the wake of the Kosovo crisis. The main legal document regulating the EU–Russia relationship is still the Partnership and Cooperation Agreement, which needs to be updated or built on by new agreements. 'The EU could, for instance, take a politically effective step by offering Russia a substantial association relationship.'[10] An association relationship seems to be completely consonant with both European and Russian interests. On the one hand, it is not a key to full membership, so it would not look too alarming for the EU; on the other hand, apart from clear goals (which are essential for building everyday policies), it would provide the EU with important leverage to influence democratic reforms in Russia.

It is encouraging that the importance of Russia's engagement is being recognised not only but Russian democrats but by European scholars as well. Charles Grant has proposed that

The best way for the EU to anchor Russia in a westward-leaning direction would be to offer the prospect of a joint EU–Russia political structure. Instead of the existing EU–Russia summits, a special council of EU and Russian ministers could meet regularly to discuss issues of common concern—such as the Balkans, organised crime, the environment or Prodi's proposal of a common economic space. Decisions of the council would require the consent of both partners but then be binding.[11]

Since American attention to the Balkans will certainly decline, west Europeans will attach increased importance to a cooperative relationship with Russia, which will among other things influence problem-solving in the Balkans.[12] How will this goal be achieved, if the EU becomes fully responsible for the Balkans? For the successful development of cooperation, it would be expedient to think about its legal framework ahead of time and to refer to the existing experience. In the planning stages of the International Force (IFOR), NATO had to come up quickly with some memoranda of understanding that would provide the legal basis for the participation of non-NATO troops in the operation.

Regardless of all the reasons for EU–Russia cooperation after 11 September, the May 2002 summit was a failure; as noted above, no compromise was found on the question of Kaliningrad, which has become the main point of discord in Russian–European relations. The arguments put forward by Russia and the EU are sound—both are concerned about their security. The EU fears illegal immigration not only from Russia but from Russia's near abroad, since its southern borders are transparent. Russia worries about its territorial integrity. The anti-Western party in Russia regards EU enlargement, coupled with NATO's expansion to the Baltic area, as a strategy of Russia's hostile encirclement. A solution can be reached only on the basis of compromise and mutual concessions—although the State Duma asked President Putin to take the most uncompromising position on the problem of Kaliningrad. Ironically, if the same approach is taken by the EU out of considerations of internal security, EU–Russia cooperation on Europe's external security will be curtailed.

Russia and NATO

The widespread perception that NATO is taking on a 'more political' role after 11 September is not shared by the majority of the Russian political elite. Visiting Brussels in October 2001, President Putin said: 'They keep saying NATO is becoming more political than military. We are looking at this and watching this process.'[13] Generally speaking, there is a big difference between a more political role and a less military role as a result of an inability to perform certain missions. It is like saying of an artist who cannot draw a human hand that he can become an abstractionist. The attacks of 11 September revealed NATO's irrelevance, since the Article 5 pledge was a purely symbolic gesture and the United States conducted a military operation largely alone, with support from the British. As with the EU, 11 September was the catalyst for a trend which had been initiated by the end of bipolarity—NATO's deep identity crisis. In its traditional shape, NATO became inadequate in the face of post-bipolar reality. Not only the so-called communist bloc but all the institutions created in the context of Cold War confrontation have been affected by the end of bipolarity. With the demise of the USSR, NATO's traditional goals—to keep the USSR out of Europe, the Germans down and the United States in—became irrelevant, and could not provide a glue for the Euro-Atlantic partnership. The Soviet threat does not exist any more. As for post-Soviet Russia, however imperfect it may be, it cannot play the same unifying role for Euro-Atlantic solidarity. Russia's military weight has diminished dramatically and, for all the concern about its unpredictability, it cannot be assessed as a direct threat to the West. This is all the more so since, after 11 September, Russia sided with the United States and its allies against the threat of terrorism.

As for the German factor, this goal lost its importance a long time ago. Germany has been a democratic state for many decades and is one of the main driving forces of European integration; even if there are some concerns about the economic and political ambitions of Germany, they lie outside of NATO's framework.

The third traditional goal of NATO—to keep the Americans in—is still regarded as the most important. However, the main reason for this was the threat from the east and Europe's dependence on the United States in countering this threat. After 11 September the United States is putting the emphasis on the fight against terrorism on the global level, which means that the American presence in Europe will continue to shrink, and the United States will use its NATO allies only selectively.

NATO's role in managing the Balkans crises is always given as a successful example of the alliance's new missions. But the fact that the mandate of the NATO-led peacekeeping forces in Bosnia was expanded three times tells its own story. The same can be said about Kosovo and Macedonia: uneven peace in Kosovo resulted in destabilisation of Macedonia. The post-11 September changes in the transatlantic relationship will accelerate the gradual disengagement of the United States from the direct management of the postwar Balkans and create new constraints on the allocation of resources to projects to foster Balkan stability.[14]

NATO's enlargement can be interpreted as another attempt of the alliance to find a new mission without making radical changes to its Cold War origins. Russia was offered the Founding Act and PJC, which were supposed to appease it and reconcile it with a new reality. This did not pass the first serious test—the Kosovo crisis. The ultimate irony was that this military campaign, as the first act of the enlarged NATO, could not but reinforce the concerns of Russia's public opinion and political elite.

The eastward enlargement of NATO can be seen as the embodiment of fundamental security differences between Russia and the leading Western countries in the Euro-Atlantic space, as well as a final victory of traditional approaches to European security, in spite of all the warm words about the indivisibility of European security after the end of bipolarity. It can also be seen as an expression of the West's disbelief in Russia's democratic future, although publicly NATO's leadership has never recognised the anti-Russian bias of this process. But the negative reaction after 11 September of the new central and east European members of NATO (in particular the Czech Republic) to Russia's admittance to the decision-making process in NATO has become the best evidence of the anti-Russian bias of NATO's enlargement.[15]

NATO is now paradoxical in three respects. First, on the one hand NATO's military power is quite sufficient to induce fears in the states which are not part of the alliance. Cooperation with Russia after 11 September did not remove these fears, because Russia is still where it was before those events. On the other hand, NATO's military power is not sufficient for performing new missions. It is very difficult for the military to take high risks on the ground when there is no direct threat to members' countries and homes. Besides, military power is not sufficient for the implementation of post-conflict strategies.

Second, on the one hand the United States does not want its leadership in NATO to be questioned, but on the other hand it is shifting the emphasis to new missions, in the first place to the fight with terrorism on a global level, thereby reducing its commitments to Europe.

Third, on the one hand NATO does not want to involve Russia in the Euro-Atlantic space of cooperation as a fully fledged partner, but on the other hand it will not survive in its traditional shape. If NATO's leadership does not rethink its strategy it will be gradually marginalised in Europe. Recent events have only confirmed this trend.

Undoubtedly, these paradoxes revolve around two fundamental and interrelated questions for Europe: the question of Russia's place in the post-bipolar Europe and that of the US presence in Europe. Only Russia's inclusion into the Euro-Atlantic space of cooperation could give new life to NATO and retain the American presence in Europe. If NATO took this path, it would be transformed into a new all-European security institution, which, in contrast to OSCE, would have the military potential to perform the post-bipolar missions—preventing ethno-religious conflicts, conducting humanitarian and rescue operations, peace enforcement and peacemaking.

President Putin made an attempt in Brussels in early October 2001 radically to change the nature of NATO–Russia relations. It was not reciprocated by NATO's leadership. Several weeks later George Robertson, NATO Secretary-General, published an article in the main Russian opinion newspaper,

Nezavisimaya gazeta, in which he expressed gratitude for Russia's contribution to the anti-terrorist coalition but repeated the argument almost literally borrowed from Russian 'Euro-Asianists', opponents to Russia's European vocation: 'Russia has a special role in the world. History, politics and geography locate Russia on the cross-roads of different, strategically important regions which have not yet achieved stability and prosperity.'[16]

This was interpreted by the Russian political elite as NATO's answer to Russia's overture. Later, Lord Robertson tried to correct his position; but his message had already reached the Kremlin. Shortly after the publication of the article, President Putin said in one of his TV interviews that Russia would not be queuing up before NATO, begging to be admitted. He said also that Russia was ready to cooperate with NATO where NATO was willing to cooperate with Russia. Thus he accepted, albeit half-heartedly, the emerging model of selective cooperation between Russia and NATO.

Unlike NATO's leadership, some of its individual members took Russia's position seriously, having tried to use the windows of opportunity after 11 September to include Russia in the Euro-Atlantic partnership. In mid-November 2001 Tony Blair wrote to NATO governments proposing that a new 'Russia–North Atlantic Council' should replace the Permanent Joint Council. This new body should consist of the ambassadors of the NATO governments and their Russian counterpart, who would meet every two weeks.[17] Blair's idea was transformed into NATO's 'Council at 20', but it is not clear yet what will come out of this idea. Russia's concern is that it may become just a new version of the PJC, which did not give Russia any real opportunity to participate in the preparation of decisions. On many occasions Russia was merely informed about the decisions made, without being consulted or asked to approve them.[18] So, much will depend on NATO's readiness to give Russia not just a symbolic but a real say in any new body. The agenda of the new body, moreover, looks too vague; it would have been better to limit it by restricting its remit to the most important issues, like the fight against terrorism and joint peacekeeping. Under present plans, any single NATO member would be able to remove any subject from the table of the new body, thus vetoing further discussions with Russia. If a compromise is not found, this would curtail cooperation between Russia and the United States/NATO in the most important area—the fight against terrorism.

However, it should be recognised that there is a certain contradiction in Russia's official position on the NATO–Russia Council. Moscow is interested in the emergence of a new body where it will have equal rights with NATO countries, but at the same time it insists on preserving the discredited PJC in parallel with the Council at 20. This can be explained by several factors, from Moscow's disbelief in the efficiency of the new body to the bureaucratic interests of the Russian foreign ministry in having as many structures for cooperation as possible, but it cannot be justified.

Some analysts think that a new window of opportunity can be opened by radical changes in the decision-making process within the guiding bodies of the alliance in order to preserve NATO's functional capabilities. Reform of NATO is being backed by Secretary-General George Robertson, who proposes cutting 400 structural divisions (and committees and commissions) and introducing majority-vote decision-making on matters other than weapons and defence. In his view, the consensus principle will impede effective work and prompt decision-making if NATO has twenty-six member states.[19] There is a chance that the reformed NATO will be better adjusted to working with Russia as a partner and will remove concerns of some NATO states about giving Russia a veto over alliance decisions.

Domestic and foreign policy challenges

In parallel with assessing the current trends and options in Russia's relations with the United States, NATO and the EU, one cannot ignore the way Russia itself will be evolving. In all countries foreign and domestic policies go hand in hand. In Russia this interdependence is especially acute. The very beginning of the 'anti-terrorist' cooperation immediately had a strong positive impact on Russia's domestic situation. It changed the balance of forces in Putin's entourage in favour of liberals. The spy scandal around Captain Alexander Nikitin, accused of having given classified information to Greenpeace, was ended with his acquittal shortly after Putin's decision to join the coalition. Moscow had to start political negotiations on Chechnya, and on 18 November 2001 representatives of President Putin and the Chechen President Aslan Maskhadov had a meeting at Moscow's international airport. The roots of these positive changes are understandable—being 'on board' means behaving according to the commonly recognised rules, while being kept at 'arm's-length' allows one to play according to one's own rules and interests. When it became clear that the anticipated breakthrough in Russian–Western relations was not in fact happening, some of these positive trends were reversed or frozen: no progress towards a political solution of the Chechen problem, new attacks on independent mass media (the TV-6 case), new spy scares, and growing anti-Westernism among the Russian political elite. All these processes are evolving in parallel with the Kremlin's endeavours to continue the anti-terrorist cooperation and to develop Russia's relations with the EU and NATO.

To a large extent this situation can be explained by the fact that Vladimir Putin has not created a solid political foundation for his foreign policy course. Moreover, he has launched most of these trends himself, having emerged with a strategy guided by three incompatible goals: a 'strong state' based on 'controlled democracy'; liberal economic reforms; and good relations with the West. The restoration of 'vertical power' (the Soviet-like federal centre) by the means of 'controlled democracy' (political squeeze on any opposition) for the sake of economic reforms is not a viable strategy in Russia. True, in Chile, South Korea and Taiwan economic reforms have been ushered in by authoritarian regimes with a strong element of state support and planning. But

Russia is too big a country to stop the authoritarian trend at the right point and at the right moment. This approach, too, is incompatible with good relations with the West, since 'controlled democracy' cannot exist without an external enemy. From this point of view, 11 September has been 'a defining moment' not only for Russia's foreign policy but for Putin's previous controversial policies based on bureaucratic consensus. It is very telling that Putin's foreign policy since 11 September has been supported by Russian democrats, who are the most consistent opponents of the 'controlled democracy' concept, and has not been backed by supporters of the strong state and controlled democracy. The need to correct Putin's strategy is obvious; the key question is: which of three elements will be changed?

Ironically, Putin's 'strong hand' strategy was accepted not only by Russians but by the West itself. Both Europe and the United States were tired of the roller-coaster of Russia's evolution under Yeltsin and viewed Putin as a leader capable of ensuring Russia's domestic and external stability (even if this was achieved by limiting democracy to some extent). Having preferred stability to democracy, the West unwillingly gave a green light to the trends which are now being perceived as obstacles to Russia's integration into the Euro-Atlantic space of cooperation after 11 September.

The primary responsibility for Russia's future rests with Russians, and it is for Russia to decide which was the aberration in its history—either the seventy years of communist rule or the one decade of its independence (however controversial it was). The leading countries of the West can support democracy in Russia, not so much by financial aid or deep involvement in Russia's domestic affairs, but more by creating a benign international environment for its democratic evolution. The post-11 September cooperation, if it could be transformed into a partnership, would offer this chance. But democratisation still remains the major precondition for Russia's integration into the Euro-Atlantic arena of cooperation. If there had been no retreat in the process of Russia's democratic evolution during recent years, the division between Russia and the West would have been erased for ever, and Moscow would have had more chances to implement a much more reasonable policy in the field of security than that imposed by the United States.

Notes

1 See Charles Grant, 'Introduction: A Coalition for Global Security', in *Europe after September 11th*, London, Centre for European Reform, 2001, pp. 1–2.
2 Alexei G. Arbatov, 'The War against Terrorism and the Transformation of the World Order', paper prepared for CEPS/IISS European Security Forum, 5 Nov. 2001, p. 1.
3 Alexei G. Arbatov, Karl Kaiser and Robert Legvold, eds, *Russia and the West: The 21st Century Security Environment*, New York, M. E. Sharpe/East–West Institute, 1999, p. 239.
4 Arbatov, 'The War against Terrorism', p. 3.

5 Gareth Jones, 'Putin Softens on NATO', *Moscow Times*, 4 Oct. 2001, p. 1.
6 Lidia Andrusenko, 'Political Elite is Disappointed by Putin's Message', *Nezavisimaya gazeta*, 24 April 2002, p. 2.
7 Armen Khanbabyan and Mikhail Khodarenok, 'At Geopolitical Fork', *Nezavisimaya gazeta*, 15 April 2002, pp. 1–4 (in Russian).
8 Steven Everts, 'A New Phase in US–European Relations', in *Europe after Sept. 11th*, p. 19.
9 Charles Grant, ' A Stronger European Foreign and Defence Policy', in *Europe after Sept. 11th*, pp. 36–41; Nicole Gnesotto, 'Terrorism and European Integration', in *Newsletter*, Institute of Security Studies, Western European Union, no. 35, Oct. 2001, p. 1.
10 Hans-Hermann Hoffmann and Christian Meier, 'Conceptual, Internal, and International Aspects of Russia's Economic Security', in Arbatov et al., eds, *Russia and the West*, p. 91.
11 Charles Grant, 'A More Political NATO, a More European Russia', in *Europe after Sept. 11th*, p. 61.
12 Marta Dassu and Nicholas Whyte, 'America's Balkan Disengagement?' in *Survival*, vol. 43, no. 4, Winter 2001, p. 124.
13 Jones, 'Putin Softens on NATO', p. 1.
14 Dassu and Whyte, 'America's Balkan Disengagement?', p. 123.
15 See Nadia Arbatova, 'NATO's Enlargement: How to Bypass Russia?' in *Nuclear Control*, Moscow, PIR-Centre (Centre for Political Studies in Russia), Dec. 2001 (in Russian).
16 George Robertson, 'After Sept. 11th: What Russia and NATO Should Expect', *Independent Military Review*, 2 Oct.–1 Nov. 2001, p. 1 (in Russian).
17 Grant, 'A More Political NATO, a More European Russia', p. 54.
18 Vadim Solvyov, 'Summit Elbows out other Summits', *Independent Military Review*, 19–25 April 2002, p. 1 (in Russian).
19 Sergei Tolsov, 'Ukraine and NATO: Prospects and Problems', at www.strana.ru, 27 April 2002.

Index

Abdullah, Crown Prince of Jordan 149
Achille Lauro 52
Afghanistan 3, 22, 44, 49
  bin Laden in 31
  peacekeeping operations 121, 143–4
  political coalition 160
  resistance to Soviet occupation 16, 53
  Taleban regime 2–3, 45
Aksoy v. *Turkey* 95
al Hijra Construction and Development
    Company 61
al-Itihaad 32
al-Qaeda 2, 12, 22, 27, 42, 100
  financing of 61–2, 68, 69
  11 September attack 25, 45, 54
  in Somalia 31–2
  and suicide terrorism 17
  supporters of 25, 26, 35–6
  see also bin Laden, Osama
al Shamal Islamic Bank (Khartoum) 61–2
Algeria 35
alternative remittance systems 61, 62
anarchists 11–12, 14–15
Angola 33
Annan, Kofi 149
anthrax 7–8, 41–2
Anti-Ballistic Missile Treaty 161, 162
anti-globalisation movement 51, 110
Anti-Terrorism, Crime and Security Act
    2001 (ATCSA) 74–5, 80, 85
  detention provisions 87–92, 94, 98, 99,
    100
  and human rights 86–7, 94–9
  judicial review 92–3
anti-terrorist norms 46, 50
Arab terrorism 51–3
Arafat, Yasser 50, 52, 150
assassinations 15
Assassins 14
asylum policies 147–8
asymmetric warfare 18–20, 23, 107
Aum Shinrikyo 1, 7, 13, 18, 20, 21

Balkans
  EU forces in 144, 165

NATO and 166
  see also Bosnia; Kosovo; Macedonia
Baltic states, NATO and 127, 128
banking systems
  correspondent 60–1
  vulnerabilities of 57–8, 60–2
Belgium 140–1
Benjamin, D. 25
Berlin, bombing of disco in 16, 52
bin Laden, Osama 2, 10, 11, 31, 45
  attack on World Trade Center 12, 13, 17
  financial knowledge 61, 62
  and Somalia 32
biological/chemical terrorism 20, 21, 41
Blair, Tony 138, 154
  on Iraq 140, 152
  and NATO 129, 168
  support for USA 113, 131, 139–40
  tests for humanitarian intervention 43,
    49
Bodansky, Y. 62
Bolkestein (EU Commissioner) 73
Bombay, car bombings 20
Bosnia 31, 122
Bradbury, M. 37
Brannigan and McBride v. *UK* 95
breeding grounds for terrorism 31–3,
    35–6
Bulgaria 128, 130
Burke, Edmund 14
Bush, George W. 58, 127
  and Iran 137
  and Iraq 54, 140, 152
  and the Middle East 151
  war on terrorism 40, 41, 47, 51, 123, 131,
    149

capital punishment 110
cell organisation 11, 15, 49
Central Asia 53, 106, 129, 130, 157, 160,
    161
charitable foundations 36–7
  fundraising by 60, 62, 69
Chechnya 16, 31, 157, 159, 162, 169
China 109

Chirac, Jacques 138, 140, 145
civil liberties 95, 132, 148
  and Anti-Terrorism, Crime and
    Security Act 87, 88, 89, 90–1, 99
civilians see non-combatant immunity
common arrest warrant 146–7
counterterrorism 19, 25, 27, 37, 132
  legislation 9–10, 80–5
  see also finance warfare
Criminal Justice Acts (UK) 65–6

Defence Capabilities Initiative 1999 124
defence expenditure 124, 145
Deobandi madrasas 29
deportation 86, 89, 90, 92
detention 5, 87–92, 94, 98, 99, 100
diasporas 37
direct action 88, 91
Direct Action (France) 15
disasters, intervention in 43
donations to terrorist groups 68–9, 71
drug trafficking, and funding of
    terrorism 65, 67

East Africa, bombing of American
    embassies 20, 32
economic targeting 57
education 28–30
  politicisation through 27
Egypt 35
enforcement terrorism 15
ETA 16
Ethiopia 28
ethnoseparatism 16
Euro-Atlantic Partnership Council 125,
    127
European Commission 139, 140
European Convention on Human Rights
    85, 86, 95, 147
  derogation from 86–7, 93, 95, 96, 97–9
European Security and Defence Policy
    (ESDP) 126, 127, 135–6, 142–3, 145,
    164
  global operations 132–3
  Greece–Turkey dispute 144
  USA and 163
European Union 135, 164
  anti-money-laundering 73–4, 137–8
  challenges to integration 138, 164

Common Foreign and Security Policy
    136, 140, 141
  defence budgets 124, 145
  enlargement 127, 129, 132, 135, 141, 163
  freezing funds 59–60, 138
  and Iraq 151–3
  and Middle East conflict 149–50
  military capabilities 124, 126, 136,
    142–6
  police and judicial cooperation 146–9
  response to 11 September 135, 136, 137,
    141
  rotating presidency 140–1
  and Russia 163–5
  security policies 125–7, 146–50, 153,
    164
  soft power of 136–8, 141
  and USA 105–6, 108, 110–11, 112–16,
    131, 133, 141, 142, 153
Europol 147
extradition 147

'failed states' 30
  as breeding grounds for terrorists 31–3
  economic activity 33–4
fanaticism 7
FBI, definition of terrorism 9
fear, exploitation of 8, 15, 23
finance warfare 57, 58–60
  anti-money-laundering 62–7, 68
  global cooperation 71–4, 76–7
  legislation 74–6
Financial Action Task Force on Money
    Laundering (FATF) 63–4, 70–1, 72–3,
    137
Financial Services Authority 75, 76
Financial Services and Markets Act 2000
    75–6
financing of terrorism 28, 67–71
  legitimate sources 68, 69, 71, 73
Finland, NATO and 128
FLQ 16
foreign aid 28, 37, 48, 137
France
  French Revolution 14
  military reform 145
  policy on Iraq 152
  and US hegemony 112, 113
freedom fighters 10, 15, 46

freezing of assets 59–60, 137–8

Georgia 159, 161
Germany
  liberal hegemony 107
  military reform 145
Gilpin, R. 107
Grant, C. 165
Greece–Turkey dispute 144
guerrilla tactics 41, 53–4
Gulf War 18

hacking 10
halawas 61, 62, 73, 74, 76
Hamas 16, 53, 138
Hassan, N. 27
hegemony 106–7, 117
  liberal 107–9, 118
  of USA 109–12, 118
Hizbollah 16, 53, 77, 138
Human Rights Act 84, 85, 86, 99
humanitarian intervention 43–4, 48, 49
  tests for 43, 48, 49–50
humiliation 28, 37
Hussein, Saddam 53, 54, 152–3

ideological terrorism 15
Ikenberry, J. 108
immigration policies 147–8
India 50, 106
information warfare 19
intelligence cooperation 60, 148–9
International Convention for the
  Suppression of the Financing of
  Terrorism 70, 72, 74–5, 137
International Criminal Court 144
International Security Assistance Force 3,
  121, 143–4
IRA 12, 47, 49, 80–1
Iran, EU agreement with 137
Iranian Revolution 16
Iraq 41, 42, 54, 106, 159
  USA and European disputes over
  139–40, 151–3
Ireland 15, 95
Islam 34, 37, 106
  militancy of 53–4
Islamic states, as breeding grounds for
  terrorists 35–6

Israel 16, 31, 47, 52, 53
  conflict with Palestinians 106, 149–51
Ivanov, Igor 149

Jacobins 14
Jenkins, B. 11
judicial cooperation 146–9
Justice 96

Kansteiner, Walter 32
Kashmir 31, 50
Kennedy, P. 131
Kindleberger, C. 107
Kissinger, Henry 113
Keohane, R. 109
Kosovo 31, 142, 143
  NATO and 166–7
  US operations in 119–20
Kosovo Liberation Army 27, 50
Krueger, A. B. 26, 28
Ku Klux Klan 14

Laqueur, W. 35
Lawless v. *Ireland* 95
leaderless resistance 17
Lebanon 16, 51, 52, 54
legislation, counterterrorist 74–6, 80–5,
  95
liberation movements 13, 15, 159
Libya 36, 52
  aid to Somalia 36
  USA and 16
Lundestad, G. 111

Maastricht Treaty 125
Macedonia 121, 136, 144, 166
McKinley, William 15
McVeigh, Timothy 17
Maleckova, J. 26, 28
marginalisation 37, 47, 48
markets 77–8, 110
Maskhadov, Aslan 169
mass casualty terrorism 1, 17, 20, 21, 22,
  23
Mead, W. R. 111
Menkhaus, K. 32
Middle East 25–6, 50, 51–3, 112–13
  see also Israel; Palestinians
military reform 145

money laundering 63, 71, 75, 138
  procedures against 62–7, 68, 69, 70, 71, 72, 73–4
Money Laundering Regulations 1993 66, 76
money transfers 61–2
motivation for terrorism 25
  religious 7, 20, 21, 34
multilateralism 44, 106, 111, 115, 116
Munich Olympic Games massacre 51
Musharraf, General 50

Napoleon I 106
Narodnaya Volya (People's Will) 15
NATO 119, 144, 146, 166
  in Balkans 122, 166–7
  enlargement of 127–30, 166–7
  and EU 125–7
  future of 121–2, 23–4, 167
  response to 11 September 119, 120–1, 131, 142, 166
  Russia and 129–30, 154, 158, 166–9
  USA and 116, 117, 119, 120, 123, 125, 131, 132–3, 167
'New Age of Terrorism' 7, 11
non-compliant countries and territories (NCCT) 64
non-combatant immunity 13, 48–9, 55, 150
North Caucasus 157, 159, 162
Northern Ireland, counterterrorist legislation 80–2, 84, 95
Northern Ireland (Emergency Provisions) Act 1973 81, 82
Northern Ireland (Temporary Provisions) Act 1998 81
November 17 (Greece) 15
Nye, J. 109

Oklahoma bombing 17, 20

Padilla, Jose 2
Pakistan 50, 106
  al-Qaeda in 2
  Islamic schools 29
Palestine Liberation Organisation (PLO) 16, 51–2
Palestinians 26–7, 50, 51, 140, 149–51
  suicide terrorism 2, 27–8

Pan Am Flight 103 16, 52
Partnership and Cooperation Agreement (EU–Russia) 164
Partnership for Peace 125, 127, 129
peacekeeping forces 136, 143–4
Petersberg tasks 126, 143, 144
police, cooperation in EU 146–9
poverty, as cause of terrorism 26–30
Powell, Colin 149, 150, 151
power, soft 118, 136–7, 141
Prevention of Terrorism (Temporary Provisions) Acts 74, 80, 81, 82
Princip, Gavrilo 15
Prodi, Romano 140, 150
proscribed organisations 100
publicity 11, 12
Putin, Vladimir 5, 160
  economic policy 169–70
  foreign policy 154, 155, 158
  and NATO 129, 130, 131, 157–8, 165, 167–8

Qadhafi, Col Muammar 52
Qatar 36
Qur'anic schools 29

Reagan, Ronald 52
Red Army Faction (Germany) 15
Red Brigade (Italy) 15
Reid, Richard 2, 17
religious fundamentalism 34
resistance to oppression 50
'revolution in military affairs' (RMA) 19, 20
Ridge, Tom 41
Robertson, George, Lord 124, 127, 128, 136, 167–8, 169
Robespierre, Maximilien 14
Robinson, J. 61
rogue states 18, 21
Romania, NATO and 127, 128
Rumsfeld, Donald 41, 119, 123
Russia 5–6
  in anti-terrorist coalition 159–60
  controlled democracy 159–60
  and EU 163–5
  Europe or Asia dilemma 155–6
  May 2002 summit 158, 162, 165
  and NATO 129–30, 154, 158, 166–9

relations with USA 129, 156–7, 161–3
response to 11 September 154, 156
and Western cooperation 155–6, 157, 170

Saudi Arabia 35, 36
attack on US military facilities 20
Schröder, Gerhard 137, 138, 139
Secretary of State for the Home Department
v. Rehman 97
11 September 1, 7, 12, 41
Sharia law 34
Sharon, Ariel 150
Shiite terrorism 16
Shining Path (Peru) 67
Shultz, George 52
Sicarii 14
Sierra Leone 33
Simon, S. 25
single-issue groups, possibility of
violence from 82–3
sleepers 38
Slovakia, NATO and 127, 128
Solano, Javier 136, 138, 141, 149
Somalia 28, 31–3, 34–5, 54
al-Qaeda in 31–2, 33, 34
funds from Islamic charities 36–7
Qur'anic schools in 29
Sharia law in 34
Somalia Aid Coordination Body 37
South Moluccans 16
special forces 142, 143
Special Immigration Appeals
Commission 91, 92–4, 96–7, 98, 99
Sri Lanka 16
state collapse, and terrorism 30–5
state of public emergency 96, 97, 98
state sponsorship 1, 2, 18, 21, 68, 71, 73
state violence 9, 11, 15
Stern, J. 27, 28, 29
Stoiber, Edmund 145
strategic terrorism 12, 22–3, 47
Straw, Jack 148
Sudan 31, 52
suicide terrorism 2, 16–17, 23, 27–8, 53
Sun Tzu 8
Syria 52

Taleban 157, 159–60
education of members 30

Tamil Tigers (Liberation Tigers of Tamil
Eelam) 16, 17
technology 7, 8, 54
terrorism 8, 16–17, 18–21
antecedents 14–16
causes 25, 26, 30, 35–6, 132
characteristics 10–14
defining 8–10, 13, 46–51, 87–8, 146, 159
postmodern 21–3
Terrorism Act 2000 9–10, 74, 80, 82–5, 87,
100
no provision for review 83–4
Terrorism Prevention Act 1996 (USA) 65
Thugs 14
Tokyo, subway nerve-gas attack 1, 7, 13
Toynbee, A. 107
trade 137
Tunisia 2
Turkey 144, 159

United Arab Emirates 36
United Kingdom 3, 12
anti-money-laundering measures 65–6
counterterrorism legislation 9–10, 74–6,
80–5; *see also* Anti-Terrorism, Crime
and Security Act
liberal hegemony 107
policy on Iraq 152
support for USA 112, 113, 139–40
United Nations 69–70, 121, 151, 152
United States of America 35, 53–4, 147,
159–60
anti-money-laundering measures 64–5
attacks on interests of 13, 20, 22, 54
defence budget 124
economic dominance 107–9, 111,
113–14, 131
and European military capability 142,
144, 145–6, 153, 163
foreign policy 105, 106, 109, 111–12,
115–16, 117–18
freezing funds 59–60, 74
and Iraq 151–3
and Middle East 149, 150–1
military dominance 109–10, 111, 113,
114–15, 131
and NATO 116, 117, 119, 120, 123, 125,
131, 132–3, 167
and Russia 129, 156–7, 161–3

United States of America (*cont.*):
  unilateralism 111, 114, 120, 131, 136,
    160, 161
  war in Afghanistan 3
USA Patriot Act 2001 74
USS *Cole*, attack on 20

victim status 48, 50
Vietnam 54, 109
vulnerability 2, 7, 12, 19, 48

Wadi al Aqiq 61
war 44–6

  rules of 13
  on terrorism 40–2, 45, 47–8, 51–5, 106,
    116, 119–20, 131–2
  weapons of mass destruction 1, 8, 18, 19,
    20, 21, 23, 41, 120
  Iraq and 151–2
Weathermen (USA) 15
Weinberger, Caspar 52
White, C. 94
Wolfowitz, Paul 32, 119, 150

Yemen 16, 36
Young Bosnians 15